# WHO
# MADE
# GOD?

## SEARCHING FOR
## A THEORY OF EVERYTHING

Edgar Andrews

**EP BOOKS**

1st Floor Venture House, 6 Silver Court, Watchmead,
Welwyn Garden City, UK, AL7 1TS

e-mail: sales@epbooks.org
web: http://www.epbooks.org

EP BOOKS are distributed in the USA by:
JPL Fulfillment
3741 Linden Avenue Southeast,
Grand Rapids, MI 49548.
E-mail: sales@jplfulfillment.com
Tel: 877.683.6935

First published 2009
First impression September 2009
Second impression November 2009
Third impression February 2010
Fourth impression July 2010
First paperback edition 2012
Reprinted October 2012
Reprinted May 2013
Third edition 2016

**British Library Cataloguing in Publication Data available**
ISBN 978–1–78397–123–7

Thoughtful, readable, witty, wise. I discovered things I didn't know!

**Fay Weldon, novelist, broadcaster and playwright**

As a distinguished scientist, Professor Edgar Andrews is well qualified to counter the current outpouring of attempts to airbrush God out of existence — and in this book he does so with intelligent and infectious enthusiasm. Richard Dawkins' *The God delusion* is an obvious target and he expertly dismantles its atheistic claims, reducing them to rubble with a lightness of touch I had never before come across in a book of this kind. Readers, with or without scientific backgrounds, are likely to find themselves turning the pages with smiles on their faces. I know of nothing quite like it.

**John Blanchard, author, lecturer and conference speaker**

With vigorous panache and deft argument, Dr Andrews tackles one of the key issues of our times — does God exist and why should we believe that he does? In a masterly combination of science and theology, he reveals the absurdity of the so-called 'new atheism' and presents a solid case for Christian theism. Highly recommended.

**Michael Haykin, Professor of Church History, The Southern Baptist Theological Seminary, Louisville, Kentucky, and Research Professor, Queen's University, Belfast, N. Ireland**

Edgar Andrews is thought-provoking, witty, extremely readable, and ultimately devastating in his critique of evolutionary atheism. He demonstrates that a right understanding of the scientific enterprise poses no threat to biblical Christianity — indeed, that the kind of world we live in is precisely what the biblical account of God and creation would lead us to expect. Richard Dawkins has more than met his match!

**Robert Strivens, Principal , London Theological Seminary**

Starting with the hypothesis of God, Professor Andrews sets out to demonstrate that the existence of the God of the Bible makes better sense of what we can actually learn from science than does atheism. On his way to this conclusion he also points out the scientific and logical inadequacies of evolutionism. He succeeds in doing so with a deceptively light touch — but there is nothing lightweight about either his analysis or the rigour with which he pursues his case. This is apologetics at its best: immensely instructive for the Christian and utterly devastating for the atheist.

**Daniel Webber, Director, European Missionary Fellowship**

The American public is far more religious and Christianized than in the UK. However, Dawkins and friends have made some real inroads to the public here and even among some Christians. Also Ben Stein's recent film *Expelled* did very well at the box office in the USA and brought much attention to the atheistic agenda, especially in our academic and scientific communities. As a result this issue is gathering steam here.

I recommend this book. I like the style; it is more approachable than a straight rebuttal. I think, for example, of Dawkins' own writing style, which is more conversational than academic, and people are reading his books. My thoughts are that both Christians and unbelievers are dealing with the same issues. You will never convince those truly entrenched in atheism but there are many on the fence that could use a good rebuttal of this type.

**Gary Gilley, pastor and author, USA**

In our increasingly multi-disciplinary world, we need those rare scholars who are able to combine the expertise of two different fields of study. Edgar Andrews possesses this unique ability, bringing together scientific and theological expertise to present a work that is both engaging and palatable — a synthesis that makes this book a very important and unique contribution to the larger arena of faith and science. This is not simply another book on Intelligent Design, nor is it a defence of Theistic Evolution. *Who made God?* masterfully weaves a mature Christian theology with recent scientific findings to produce a nuanced and compelling argument that maintains the integrity of both science and theology. Coupled with a witty and playful writing style, this makes the book a 'must' read for those who question the intersection of science and Christianity.

**David H. Kim, Redeemer Presbyterian Church, New York (Rev. Kim has a degree in molecular biology from the University of Pennsylvania and spent two years in human molecular genetics working with the human genome project)**

The question which forms the title of this book is one I am asked frequently, an issue people struggle with. Thankfully, Professor Andrews has now written a very thorough but incredibly readable book dealing with this important subject. Drawing from an amazing breadth of learning, Professor Andrews writes in an easy conversational style, dealing comprehensively with the question. Beneficial for the ordinary person in the street, this book should be in the hands of all who truly want answers.

**Philip Swinn, Vicar of St John's (Church of England) , Hatfield, UK**

If you have been looking for a thoughtful, cogent and accessible counterpoint to the recent flurry of publications by the so-called New Atheists, you need look no further than Edgar Andrews' *Who made God?* Rather than offering an *ad hoc* response to the assertions made by Richard Dawkins and the like, Dr Andrews instead asks us to consider a different way into the conversation — to approach belief in the biblical God as a thesis in and of itself, one that is worthy of our thoughtful consideration. He asks us to apply the methodology of hypothesis to the question of God to see how it fits — and it, in fact, proves to fit remarkably well. With great clarity and rousing humour, Dr Andrews applies the thesis of God to questions like the problem of time, the nature of humanity and the question of morality, and demonstrates how belief in God is characterized by a simple elegance and a far-reaching explanatory power.

**Rev. Abraham Cho, Fellowship Group Director**
**Redeemer Presbyterian Church, New York**

Though a layman, I have read a fair amount in apologetics and this is one of the most vivid and helpful works in that field that I've ever encountered — disarming, teeming with verve and humour, conversational, yet deadly serious, disciplined and coming from a scientifically and legally trained mind.

**Scott Kauffmann, Executive Director, Redeemer Labs, New York**

This is a book that needs to be brought to the attention of our sceptical age whose world view is one of 'atheism by default'. Professor Andrews gets down under atheism's radar and exposes its claims with humour, science and devastating logic. More than this, he fills the void that is left with attractive and intelligent theistic realities.

**Stephen Bignall, pastor and lecturer, UK**

Being a busy mother of four children and not a great reader, especially on the subject of science and how creation fits in, I was pleasantly surprised that I could easily follow *Who made God?* And what I have read has given me some very helpful explanations to answer the questions of my non-Christian friends over coffee.

**Tanya Bancroft , mother and housewife**

# Contents

# Preface to the third edition

Welcome to the third edition and ninth printing of *Who made God? Searching for a theory of everything.* First published in September 2009, it has since been extensively reviewed by both friend and foe and translated into Dutch, Estonian and Korean. It should come as no surprise, therefore, that some of the material covered in the book has become the subject of further debate during the five intervening years, notably as a result of the publication of two best-selling books by atheists—*The Grand Design* by Stephen Hawking and Leonard Mlodinow (Bantam Press, 2010) and *A Universe from Nothing* by Lawrence Krauss (Atria Books, 2013). There has also been a courteous exchange of views with Victor Stenger, whose book *God, the failed hypothesis* (Prometheus Books, 2007) I subjected to a detailed critique in *Who made God?* but who has since died. All three books have as their avowed purpose to dispose of the 'cosmological argument' for the existence of God and to demonstrate how science alone can (allegedly) explain the origin of the universe without needing to appeal to a supernatural creator. Hawking and his co-author put it thus;

> "Because there is a law like gravity, the universe can and will create itself from nothing ... Spontaneous creation is the reason there is something rather than nothing, why the universe exists, why we exist.

It is not necessary to invoke God to light the blue touch paper and set the universe going" (p.180).

Interestingly, all the key arguments advanced in the Hawking and Krauss books for a God-less origin of the universe were anticipated and answered in *Who made God?* at least in outline. This doesn't mean, of course, that I wrote my prior publication using a magic crystal ball but rather demonstrates that the ideas offered in these two books were not, in fact, new. Nevertheless, such is the popularity of anti-God utterances by prominent scientists that these books have sold in their millions and continue to attract an enormous following in spite of their speculative nature and self-evident logical deficiencies.

Rather than amend the text of *Who made God?* in this new edition, I have chosen to add an appendix to cover the issues raised by Hawking and Mlodinow and by Krauss. This appendix consists largely of a review of *The Grand Design* because *A Universe from Nothing* adds very little in terms of ideas to the former work. I do however include a short note on Krauss' book to cover speculations he makes that go beyond those of Hawking and his co-author, while also adding some further thoughts of my own. The appendix thus expands upon issues already addressed in the original text of *Who made God?* such as the origin of the laws of nature, the multiverse, and the meaning of 'nothing' in the expression *creatio ex nihilo* ('creation out of nothing'). I also provide a link to the full conversation with Victor Stenger.

**Edgar Andrews**
Welwyn Garden City, February 2015

# To get you started ...

During my frequent travels in the USA from 1970 to 2000, one small thing always amused me. As I settled in my seat for yet another intercity flight (let's say to Houston) the pilot would welcome us on board and add, 'If Houston is not in your travel plans for today, this would probably be a good time to deplane.' Very occasionally, a red-faced passenger would do so. By analogy, if you bought this book expecting a boisterous put-down for God, then now would be a good time to ask for your money back.

After all, 'If God made everything, who made God?' is the sceptic's favourite question, asked repeatedly by such as Richard Dawkins and his fellow 'new atheists'. They wield it like a sword—drawn from the twin scabbards of science and philosophy and calculated to decapitate any theists foolish enough to stick their heads above the parapet. In reality, however, the sword is all haft and no blade. Not only can theists safely raise their heads but they can take a good look round at the barren 'landscape' of reductionism. What they will see is a cabal of academic atheists diligently reinventing the Vienna Circle—the air full not of flashing swords but of grinding axes. (The Vienna Circle was the 1920s philosophical school that invented logical positivism, a failed philosophy if ever there was one.)

However, my purpose in this book is not just to refute the assertions of atheists or respond to their writings. It is altogether more positive than that. As I explain in chapter three, the scientist's dream is to develop a 'theory of everything'—a scientific theory that will encompass all the workings of the physical universe in a single self-consistent formulation.

Fair enough, but there is more to the universe than matter, energy, space and time. Most of us believe in the real existence of non-material entities such as friendship, love, beauty, poetry, truth, faith, justice and so on—the things that actually make human life worth living. A true 'theory of everything', therefore, must embrace both the material and non-material aspects of the universe, and my contention is that we already possess such a theory, namely, the hypothesis of God.

In these pages—which are designed to be read and enjoyed by expert and layman alike—I shall review not only the findings of modern physics (my own discipline) but also deep questions of origins. Among other things, we'll consider the origins of the universe; of time; of law in all its aspects; of life; of the human mind; and of morality. In doing so, we'll be able to compare and contrast the predictions of the hypothesis of God with those of atheistic naturalism, concluding that the former is superior in every way.

In this context, astrophysicist Robert Jastrow writes: 'At this moment it seems as though science will never be able to raise the curtain on the mystery of creation. For the scientist who has lived by his faith in the power of reason, the story ends like a bad dream. He has scaled the mountain of ignorance; he is about to conquer the highest peak; as he pulls himself over the final rock, he is greeted by a band of theologians who have been sitting there for centuries.'[1]

This book sets out to explore how the biblical hypothesis of God provides a comprehensible, intellectually consistent and spiritually satisfying view of being that encompasses man's experience of life, the universe and everything. We can only make a small beginning here but what we find must surely trump the barren nihilistic landscape of atheism.

## Acknowledgements

My warmest thanks are due to the many friends and colleagues who have spent time reading the manuscript as it developed and offered helpful comments and encouragement—and in some cases technical appraisal.

In the first category I would particularly like to mention (alphabetically) John Blanchard, Bob Dickie, Philip Duce, Hilary Fox, Gary Gilley, Scott Kauffmann, Rachel Russell, Robert Strivens and Fay Weldon. On the technical front I am specially indebted to Nancy Darrall (biology) and Professor Andy McIntosh (thermodynamics).

**Edgar Andrews**
Welwyn Garden City, England, 2009

# CHAPTER ONE ...

... in which we set out to answer the unanswerable question, 'If God made everything, who made God?' We'll discover that it is unanswerable only in the same sense as the question, 'How long is a piece of string?'—which remains a nonsense question until we define which piece of string we are talking about. In the same way, to answer the challenge 'Who made God?' we must define what we mean by 'God'.

In particular, we'll examine three contentions beloved of atheists. Firstly, the claim that 'we made God' (that God is an invention of the human mind); secondly, the idea that God is so complex that he is too improbable to exist; and thirdly, the suggestion that God has to have a cause because everything else does.

## New words?

*Ontology*: The study of existence or 'being'.

*Entropy*: The quantity in thermodynamics that measures randomness.

*Savant*: A wise person; a thinker.

*Stasis*: A condition where no changes occur.

*Tautology*: A statement that seems to impart new information but actually repeats what is already known. For example: 'This cat was extraordinarily feline', meaning, 'this cat was unusually cat-like'.

*Thermodynamics*: The study of heat and energy (especially their flow and transfer).

# 1. Sooty and the universe

Myself when young did eagerly frequent
Doctor and saint, and heard great argument
About it and about: but evermore
Came out by the same door as in I went.

Edward Fitzgerald
Rubáiyat of Omar Khayyám of Naishápúr

In an interview with John Naish for *The Times* newspaper,[1] the novelist and science-fiction writer Iain Banks declared himself as follows: 'I'm an evangelical atheist; religions are cultural artefacts. We make God, not the other way round ... Religion is one way to explain the universe, but eventually science comes along and explains it ...' He continued: 'I can remember walking down the street in May 1963 ... trying to work out how the world had been formed. I thought that Sooty must have magicked it with his wand. Then I wondered what Sooty could have been standing on in this unformed Universe in order to create it. And who made Sooty? That's when atheism came thundering through me.'

Sooty, you may remember, was a glove-puppet on children's TV who (according to the *Guinness Book of Records*) starred in the longest-running children's programme in the UK, starting in the 1950s. By species a bear, Sooty played the xylophone and kept a wand with which he performed magic—accompanied by the catchphrase 'Izzy wizzy, let's get busy!' Quite versatile for a bear.

No doubt the young Iain Banks didn't give the matter the full consideration it deserved, but his whimsical observation sums up the opinions of a surprisingly large number of people in our twenty-first-century Western world. And, of course, 'Who made Sooty?' readily translates into adult-speak as 'Who made God?' It's an FAQ—a frequently asked question—commonly posed by those who would banish the very ideas of God and 'creation'. It is a question that Richard Dawkins asks repeatedly, in various ways, in his best-selling book *The God delusion.*[2] The logic behind the question runs something like this.

If God exists, then presumably he created everything (why else would we need him?). But if God exists, who made *him*? And since no one can answer that question, it does nothing to solve the riddle of the universe to say, 'God made it.' We simply push the mystery one step further back and that is a pointless exercise. No one can doubt that atheists regard the 'unanswerable question'—'Who made God?'—as a formidable weapon in their war against faith, if not the ultimate weapon of ontological mass destruction. But, of course, there is more to the unanswerable question than meets the eye. It crops up in a surprising variety of philosophical contexts—like Sooty, it is truly versatile.

When I first began visiting the USA regularly on business, I was struck by the huge versatility of one little word—check. Not only could you write a check to pay a bill and check that your airline hadn't gone bankrupt overnight, but you could request your check at the end of a restaurant meal, check the boxes on your laundry list (or any other form for that matter), check your luggage at the airline desk, check in or check out of a hotel, check out a new product, check your hasty words when you got mad with some officious bureaucrat, and so on. Then, of course, the word lends itself beautifully to portmanteau usage, as in checklist, raincheck and checkup (I never did encounter checkdown but I'm still optimistic). Why, with a few more words like 'check' we could halve the weight of our dictionaries!

The 'unanswerable' question 'Who made God?' gets around in much the same way, turning up in a variety of different contexts that will repay closer examination. Let's look briefly at three of them—the 'we made God' hypothesis, the 'improbability of God' calculation, and the 'unanswerable question' dilemma.

## Did man make God?

As we saw earlier, there is one answer to the question that atheists are happy to accept—the answer '*We* made God.' As Banks might say, religion has it back to front—we are not God's creation; he is ours. God is a mental construction that mankind once needed to 'explain' its existence but which is no longer required because science explains everything instead. As this book develops, we shall see that attempts to make science explain everything are doomed to failure, but for the moment we'll concentrate on the 'we made God' hypothesis.

Perversely, theologians inadvertently prop up this hypothesis by one of their own time-honoured arguments. I refer to the so-called 'ontological argument' for the objective existence of God. Savants of all stripes are given to making wise-sounding pronouncements that we accept as true even though we don't really understand them (or is that *because* we don't really understand them?). A good example is the famous aphorism propounded by René Descartes (1596–1650)—*Cogito ergo sum* ('I think, therefore I am'). Obvious? Not really. Philosophers have been quarrelling over the validity of the statement ever since it was made.

The 'ontological argument' for the existence of God falls into the same category. Ontology (from the Greek verb 'to be') is the science or study of being or of the essence of things. The ontological argument for the existence of God states that the existence of the *idea* of God necessarily implies the objective existence of God.[3] *The Stanford Encyclopaedia of Philosophy*[4] puts it thus: 'Ontological arguments are arguments, for the conclusion that God exists, from premises which are supposed to derive from some source other than observation of the world—e.g., from reason alone. In other words, ontological arguments are arguments from nothing but analytic, a priori and necessary premises to the conclusion that God exists.'

Sooty would approve. I may cherish the idea that I am a gifted concert pianist. After all, I have played the piano since I was five years old. It's a noble dream but sadly it's still only a dream. It's 'all in the mind'—there is no corresponding objective reality. The same applies to believing in Santa Claus or fairies.

Perhaps I am too simplistic, but it seems to me that the ontological argument leads nowhere. It states that the *idea* of God exists in people's minds. No problem with that. The difficulty arises when we draw the conclusion that this idea *must* correspond to some objective reality outside of ourselves. Why should it? Why should the idea of God in our minds necessarily imply that God exists as an external and independent reality?

To be fair, many do see merit in the ontological argument and it has been profoundly debated by philosophers from St Anselm of Canterbury in the eleventh century, to Descartes and Leibniz, to recent philosophers like Kurt Gödel, Charles Hartshorne, Norman Malcolm and Alvin Plantinga.[5] And although I see little merit in ontology as an absolute proof of God's existence, it can be effective when used less ambitiously to refute the claim that 'We made God,' as we shall see shortly.

But for the moment let me point out three small problems with the 'We made God' hypothesis. First, it falls into the very same trap that the atheist cunningly sets when he asks, 'If God made everything, who made God?' Because when he confidently declares that we made God it must then be asked, 'If we made God, who made us?' Since the answer 'God made us' is obviously excluded *ab initio*, the question 'Who made us?' is no more answerable than 'Who made God?' Just to reply, 'Evolution made us' simply will not do. As Scott Adams has observed, 'Evolution isn't a cause of anything; it's an observation, a way of putting things in categories. Evolution says nothing about causes.'[6] Or to put it more simply, if evolution made us, who made evolution?

The atheist will no doubt reply that evolution is simply the way nature works; it is just part of the 'everything' that theists wrongly attribute to God. But the logic of this contention leads us in an unexpected direction—and I've written a diminutive one-act play to prove it.

[On stage, three people: 'theist', 'first atheist' and 'second atheist' engaged in an argument. Enter left 'enquirer' wearing a duffle coat and a puzzled expression.]

*Enquirer*: Excuse me interrupting, but can you tell me who made everything?

*Theist*: Yes; God made everything.

*First atheist*: Oh? So who made God?

*Second atheist*: We made God.

*Theist*: Then who made us?

*First atheist*: Evolution made us.

*Theist*: Who made evolution?

*Second atheist*: It's part of everything; 'everything' made evolution.

*Enquirer*: Excuse me interrupting ... but who made everything? Oh, never mind.

[Enquirer exits left (the way he came in) wearing an even more puzzled expression.]

When the M25 ring-road motorway around London was finally completed in 1986, a number of motorists I knew drove around the whole 117-mile circuit just for the fun of it. Since they finished up exactly where they started, you may feel it was a pointless exercise. But a philosophical argument that ends up where it started is even more pointless—and such, as our little drama indicates, is the claim that 'We made God.'

The second problem with this contention is that it is devoid of any evidential basis, as we shall see in due course. It is not, in fact, an explanation at all. It doesn't explain religious concepts, religious experience or the almost universal religious instinct of mankind, ancient or modern. Rather, it is a smokescreen concealing ignorance, a speculative shrug of the shoulders concerning the substantial phenomenon of religious belief. Like many atheistic arguments, it is at heart a tautology. Beginning with the hidden premise that God does not exist objectively, it looks for (and finds) an alternative explanation of religious faith and experience entirely within ourselves. It then reasons as follows: since God definitely exists in the minds of those who believe, and since God does not exist otherwise, then God must exist *only* in the minds of those who believe. Bingo! We made God.

Thirdly, whenever A makes B (and whatever A and B might represent) it is reasonable to assume that A (the creator) is greater than B (the creation). Beethoven was greater than any of his compositions and Rembrandt, Turner or Picasso greater than any of their pictures. When my wife makes a cake, however well it turns out, it is soon gone—a thing of transience and insignificance in comparison with the one who made it. But if man fashions a *transcendent* and all-powerful God out of his own imagination, the creation is greater than the creator—which, while not proving the existence of God, takes a lot of explaining. I accept that my reasoning here is ontological in character but it remains valid, I think, as a refutation of the 'We made God' hypothesis. After all, Richard Dawkins argues strenuously that a God who made the hugely complex universe must be even more complex than his creation (see below). I assume I'm allowed to say the same thing when it's a case of man allegedly creating God.

## The problem of probability

'Who made God?' crops up less obviously in a probability argument presented by Richard Dawkins in *The God delusion*.[7] And here we must begin with a lengthy note of caution. Probability arguments are often used in debates relating to God, science, creation and evolution, but they are almost always used naively. Probability theory is a branch of mathematics, concerned initially with discrete numbers (like the probability of getting heads or tails when you toss a coin) but extending also to continuous 'distribution functions' (like a curve showing people's probable incomes plotted against their age). Either way, it's all mathematics. The theory can, of course, be *applied* to the real world as in the examples given, but there is nothing of the real world built into the theory itself. For example, its coin-tossing calculations take no account of the possibility that the coin might land on its edge and get stuck in that position—something that could happen quite often if you're tossing the coin on a soft sandy beach.

A famous example is Sir Fred Hoyle's calculation of the probability of spontaneously forming a protein molecule from its amino-acid constituents, which he likened to the probability that a whirlwind in a junk yard would assemble a Boeing 747. Good fun, of course, especially for creationists, but it's just number-juggling and takes no account of physical and chemical realities (such as the presence or absence of water, catalysts and competing chemical reactions). In the absence of a realistic chemical scenario, there is no way of knowing whether such abstract calculations have any meaning.

Equally, however, the claim that anything (like the origin of life or a particular genetic mutation) must happen by chance if you wait long enough is also fallacious. Again, this claim is based on the idea that no mathematically possible event has zero probability. But what is *mathematically* possible may be *physically* impossible. Consider the claim that 100 monkeys banging the keys of 100 typewriters (with no lunch breaks) will eventually produce the works of Shakespeare. Not true *unless everything the monkeys type is immediately put into quarantine so that it cannot be altered or revised.* This is a completely unrealistic scenario for real-world processes like chemical reactions or genetic mutations, where the whole system undergoing change remains available for further amendment. The well-established theory of chemical rate processes tells us that all real-world processes are reversible—they can go backwards as well as forwards, and the net result is the balance between forward steps and backward steps. For a process to go forward on average requires a payback of free energy. If there is no such payback, each forward step will sooner or later be cancelled out by a backward step and the system will remain in stasis. Applying this to the monkeys (this time *without* allowing the output generated to be quarantined) we see that progress towards a Shakespeare folio would actually go backwards, not forwards. This follows because the likelihood of the next keystroke being an error is much greater than the likelihood of it being correct (there being twenty-six letters in the alphabet, one would be correct but twenty-five would be mistakes). So if you started the monkeys with a typescript lacking just a single sonnet but otherwise complete and correct, it wouldn't be long before *The Merchant of Venice* was in total disarray—let alone *Much ado about nothing.*

This monkey business confuses us because any scenario which contains the hidden assumption that all text generated is immediately quarantined, will have a physically unrealistic outcome. Consider another example, which I'll call 'instant Shakespeare'. Suppose we had one monkey for every single alphabetical character in Shakespeare's works, and each monkey had its own typewriter with just twenty-seven keys (the alphabet plus a space). We line the typewriters up in a fixed order, instruct each monkey to strike one key only, and examine the result. If it isn't the works of Shakespeare we replace the monkeys by a completely new team and start all over again. Sooner or later, a team of monkeys *will* produce the desired result because the mathematical probability of this happening is not zero. It might take a little longer than eternity to generate our instant Shakespeare but that's a detail. The point is that for one team of monkeys the works would be produced at a stroke, avoiding the reversibility hazards of a step-by-step process. However, we have it on the authority of Richard Dawkins himself that in the real world complex products (like life, monkeys or Shakespeare's works) *cannot* be achieved in a single jump but must develop progressively by the accumulation of many small steps. He even wrote a book called *Climbing mount improbable*[8] to prove it—confirming my assertion that mathematical probability arguments must pass the test of physical reality or be rejected.

In order to apply mathematical probability theory to the real world, therefore, requires us to build the real world into the scenario. In physics and chemistry the result is something called 'statistical mechanics', which is one approach to the science of thermodynamics. The mathematical theory of probability can only be applied correctly to the real world through the filter of thermodynamics.

## The probability of God

In the science of thermodynamics the statistical probability that a given system (or arrangement) will arise spontaneously in nature is related mathematically to the degree of order or complexity of the system. Systems with low complexity (high entropy or randomness) are likely to arise spontaneously, while systems with high order or complexity (low entropy or randomness) are unlikely to do so.

Oh, sorry for the techno-talk; let's put it this way. If you see a pile of bricks by the roadside, they could have fallen off the back of a lorry (low complexity, high probability of happening spontaneously). But if you see a neat bungalow built of bricks it is most unlikely to have arisen by accident (high complexity, low probability of happening by chance).

Don't know any thermodynamics? So, let's learn some. Take a china soup bowl and drop it on a stone floor (preferably without the soup). Very likely it will become less ordered (or less organized)—instead of one piece of china having a nice symmetrical shape, there will be many pieces of different shapes and sizes. Now collect these pieces together and drop them on the same floor. Did they reassemble themselves into the 'ordered' form of an unbroken bowl? No? Oh well, that's thermodynamics for you. Disordered states of matter arise spontaneously; ordered states do not.[9]

Of course, you can sit down with a tube of superglue and painstakingly stick the bits together to reassemble a single bowl. You won't make a perfect job of it, of course, but you will—after expending much effort and some skill—make the pieces more 'ordered' by joining them together in a unique relationship (any other relationship would let the soup leak out). But the increased order of the repaired bowl has only been achieved at the cost of directed energy input and intelligent effort. It could never have happened on its own.

Consider another example. If I let a small child get her sticky fingers on my computer keyboard, this page would continue as a random jumble of characters—one meaningless sequence out of an almost infinite range of equally possible sequences. If, on the other hand, I retake control and continue to develop my argument in carefully chosen words, there are only a limited number of symbol sequences that could serve this purpose. The sticky finger jumble is a high-probability arrangement because there are so many different ways to achieve it, but it has low complexity because it is random and meaningless. By contrast, my reasoned argument requires a low-probability arrangement of symbols, because there are only a limited number of ways of expressing what I want to say. But because what I say is (hopefully) meaningful, my page is a system of high complexity (high information content) and has a negligible probability of occurring accidentally or spontaneously.

Now, we know that the physical world represents a highly improbable arrangement of matter and energy—an *extremely* improbable arrangement as it turns out. The study of physics has shown that the laws and fundamental constants of nature give every appearance of being fine-tuned to permit the existence of intelligent life on earth[10] (this is known as the anthropic principle).

The argument for the improbability of God, as advanced by Dawkins[11] and others, seems to boil down to the following reasoning: (1) By common consent, the world is a highly improbable and complex system; (2) if God created the world he must be more complex than the world he created; therefore (3) God is less probable than the world; indeed, he is fantastically improbable; so (4) God probably doesn't exist. Although produced with a flourish, the argument holds no more water than a sieve. Firstly we have to accept the dubious assumption that the science of thermodynamics (or statistical mechanics)—which was developed to describe the behaviour of matter and energy—applies to theology and God. You might just as well apply it to love, music or politics, but I promise you it won't work.

Secondly, there is excessive sleight of hand in the use of the word 'improbable'. In thermodynamics it refers to the number of different ways a system can be arranged or ordered. The repaired soup bowl is highly improbable (thermodynamically speaking) because it is uniquely formed—there is only one way to arrange the pieces to rebuild that particular shape. By contrast, the broken bowl can consist of many different arrangements of shards. It could break into just two pieces or ten or a hundred. An almost infinite variety of shapes and sizes could result from the fracture. There are thus a huge number of possible arrangements for a broken bowl—and that means that (thermodynamically speaking) the broken bowl is highly probable. But because the repaired bowl is 'improbable' and the broken bowl 'probable' it doesn't mean that all soup bowls are broken. However, let's skip over these logical death-leaps in Dawkins' reasoning and suppose that in some way the argument does have relevance to God. What does it actually prove?

Having agreed, presumably, that the world does exist *in spite of* its extreme complexity and organization (high improbability), the argument goes on to say that God is unlikely to exist because he is ... well, er, highly improbable. OK, so God is arguably *more* complex and thus *less* probable than the physical universe. But by what logic must we accept that one highly improbable entity exists (the universe) while another highly improbable entity (God) does not exist—simply because he is too complex or organized to do so? In my neck of the woods they call that special pleading (when they are feeling polite).

## The unanswerable question

The third context in which 'Who made God?' appears is the most obvious one. The question is deemed unanswerable because the only possible reply from those who believe in the objective reality of God is 'No one made God.' And if no one made God, then he can't be there, can he? After all, for every effect there must be a cause, and an effect that has no cause must be imaginary.

Once again, in their enthusiasm to prove their point, the proponents of this argument get their shoes on the wrong feet, entangling physics with metaphysics. Cause and effect do indeed reign supreme in the physical realm and the natural world—both science and normal life would be impossible unless they did. But why should they operate in the same manner in a spiritual realm (if such exists)? We have a choice. Firstly, we can assert *a priori* that there is no such thing as a spiritual realm—that nothing exists that is not physical and open to scientific investigation. On this basis we can proceed to claim, with some logical justification, that every possible effect must have a cause, because that is how the physical world works. But what we *cannot* do is use this claim to disprove the existence of God on the grounds that he doesn't have a cause. Why not? Because our argument would be completely circular. We begin by assuming that no spiritual realm exists (so goodbye, God) and conclude by 'proving' our initial assumption. Big deal.

So let's try to find a different route through the maze, this time without cheating. To avoid assuming at the outset what we want to prove, we must start by allowing that there might indeed be a spiritual realm. Because cause and effect is only proven for the physical world, we can no longer insist that cause and effect are relevant when it comes to the origin of a spiritual entity like God. Therefore God doesn't *have* to have a cause—he can be the ultimate uncaused cause, a being whom no one made.

Unanswerable questions are not necessarily clever questions. In their favour is the fact that they may be unanswerable because of their implicit logical force. They may be rhetorical questions—statements disguised as questions—which brook no contradiction because they embody self-evident truth. But as the song has it, 'It ain't necessarily so.' A question can also be unanswerable because it is a nonsense question, the fault lying in the guile or folly of the questioner rather than the dimwittedness of the respondent. The famous court-room question, 'Have you stopped beating your wife; answer yes or no?' comes to mind, even though it was probably never actually put. More familiarly, we may be asked, 'How long is a piece of string?' and be stumped for a response because there can be no logical answer to an illogical question.

Such questions can only be answered by refusing to give an answer—by challenging the very premise or logical legitimacy of the question. Twenty fascinating years acting as an expert witness in numerous court cases—in Britain's High Court and courts in the USA—taught me never to yield the initiative to the cross-examining barrister or attorney. Unanswerable questions would be slipped in among a string of fair ones, and a witness could easily be taken off his guard. 'How long is a piece of string?' is a nonsense question not because there is no such thing as a piece of string, nor because a given piece of string has an indeterminate length. It is a nonsense question because it fails to *define* which piece of string is being talked about. 'Who made God?' is 'unanswerable' for the same basic reason—the word 'God' is left undefined. What if we define 'God' as 'the uncreated creator of all things' (as indeed we shall later)? Then the nonsense of the question becomes immediately obvious—'Who created the uncreated one?' And if we define God as a lesser being who *was* created by some other entity—or as Richard Dawkins might insist has evolved from some simpler substance because he is too complex to just exist—we are forced to transfer the nonsense question to this higher entity or simpler substance. And that, of course, would take us back to where we started. So let's move on instead.

# CHAPTER TWO ...

... in which we challenge the common but mistaken idea that science explains (or some day will explain) everything, leaving no room for God to take responsibility for the universe and the way it works. To make the point, we sit down to a humorous 'breakfast' of yogurt, cereal and toast to illustrate the fact that science actually explains nothing, except in terms of its own bizarre concepts.

These include such non-intuitive ideas as the warping of space and time, and the wondrously strange world of quantum mechanics—where the same particle can be in two places at once, and one particle knows what another is doing even when miles away from it. Einstein wasn't at all happy about this state of affairs and believed that there must be some deeper and more intuitive underlying truth. In short, science can describe the fundamental structures of matter, energy, space and time but can hardly be said to *explain* them.

## New words?

*Phenomenology*: The way phenomena (things that are seen or observed) manifest themselves.

# 2. Yogurt, cereal and toast

Alice laughed. 'There's no use trying,' she said. 'One CAN'T believe impossible things.' 'I daresay you haven't had much practice,' said the Queen. 'When I was your age, I always did it for half-an-hour a day. Why, sometimes I've believed as many as six impossible things before breakfast.'

Lewis Carroll, *Alice through the looking glass*
ch. 5, 'Wool and water'

I begin this chapter with two apologies. First, I apologize for overworking the White Queen. The quote at the head of this chapter appears in almost every book of the present genre I've ever read, and is used with equal abandon by authors on both sides of the 'Who made God?' divide. My only excuse is that I need the quote more than most because this chapter is all about breakfast and impossible things.

My second apology is that, quite likely, you won't understand some of things you read in this chapter and the next, because we shall be getting into some pretty difficult stuff about what constitutes the universe (and we won't get much help from Sooty). However, for your encouragement, let me point out that you are actually not meant to understand it—if by understanding we mean grasping a matter in terms of self-evident or intuitive ideas. Indeed, the whole point of these two chapters is to demonstrate that, far from explaining everything, science actually 'explains' nothing. What science does is *describe* the world and its phenomenology in terms of its own specialized concepts and models—which provide immensely valuable insights but become increasingly non-intuitive as we dig ever deeper into the nature of physical reality. As Alice might say, the 'explanations' afforded by science grow 'curiouser and curiouser' as it opens up the world around us. So if you don't understand what follows in these two chapters you will, in a sense, have proved my point.

Lewis Carroll doesn't tell us what the White Queen had for breakfast but in this chapter I'm going to offer you a fun meal of eye-popping, mind-boggling physics. Lost your appetite? Don't worry, it's as simple as yogurt, cereal and toast.

But first let me elaborate on 'explanations'. When atheists appeal to science to support their atheism, they generally imply that science offers straightforward explanations of natural phenomena—explanations that are really obvious once you get the hang of them. Science is represented as common sense wrapped in mathematics. Remove the wrapper and you are left with self-evident truth—in distinct contrast to the fables promoted by the 'God squad' to justify their unbelievable beliefs. It is this kind of thinking that lies behind Iain Banks' opinion that 'Religion is one way to explain the universe, but eventually science comes along and explains it.'

But what exactly do people mean when they say 'science explains' something? Take the word 'explain'. It's a very convenient term and I shall continue to use it, but it nevertheless conceals a conceptual minefield. My edition of *The Shorter Oxford English Dictionary* lists no fewer than seven definitions of the word—to make smooth; to open out or spread out flat; to unfold, to make plain or intelligible; to interpret; to account for; to make oneself understood, to speak plainly;

to speak one's mind (against or upon). Yet none of these definitions gets to the heart of what we mean by a scientific explanation.

When we say 'science explains' something we usually mean that there exists a scientific *description* of the phenomenon in question. Thus the force of gravity—rather important since it keeps us from bumping around on the ceiling like helium balloons—can be expressed by a simple mathematical formula. The formula equates the gravitational force between two objects to the product of their masses multiplied by a universal constant (the 'gravitational constant') and divided by the square of the distance between them. But does the equation 'explain' why you don't bump your head on the ceiling? Not really. It tells us there is a force that keeps your feet on the ground, but you knew that already. It also quantifies that force, allowing us to calculate its strength in any particular case, which is extremely useful. But it doesn't tell us *why* there is such a force, why it follows an inverse square law, and why the 'gravitational constant' has the value that it does. The equation is a description of gravity rather than an explanation.

Well, what about Einstein? Didn't he 'explain' gravity in his magnificent theory of general relativity? Up to a point, yes. The theory attributes gravitational effects to the curvature produced by massive objects in space and time (called 'space-time' when taken together)— much as a bowling ball placed on a trampoline would distort the sheet and make a marble on the sheet run towards it. But for all its elegance, the theory remains a description of gravity rather than an 'explanation'—not least because it introduces the non-intuitive idea that space-time itself (not just things *in* space-time) can be curved.

A genuine explanation, I suggest, would consist of a train of reasoning that leads back *only* to premises that are intuitive or self-evident. But scientific 'explanations' definitely don't do that. What they do is simplify, unify and quantify our perception of the world around us; that is, they describe a wide range of different phenomena or experiences in terms of a small number of unifying concepts—and do so mathematically and quantitatively, allowing theory to be checked by experiment and put to practical use. So, a successful theory of gravitation will accurately describe such diverse effects as a planet's orbit around its star, the trajectory of an artillery shell, and why your soup bowl falls towards the floor when you let go of it.

It is not unreasonable to say that the sole purpose of scientific research is to discover principles or theories that unify human experience. This is extremely valuable because it not only helps to satisfy our curiosity about the world we live in but represents knowledge that can be applied for our benefit. (It can, of course, also be applied to do us harm; science has no built-in morality.) But although scientific theories advance our understanding of the way things work in our universe, they seldom, if ever, trace our experiences and observations back to *a priori* concepts that need no further explanation. Indeed, in their search for unification they often lead us into profound and inexplicable mysteries—conceptual quagmires like 'curved space-time' from which there is no escape. Since 'not a lot of people know this', let me make my point over a working breakfast of yogurt, cereal and toast.

## Yogurt

When I read physics at the University of London, England, during 1950–53 it was a heady time for the subject. Until fifty years earlier it had been widely believed that our physical understanding of the universe was just about complete—there were few riddles left for physics to explain. But then in 1900 the 'quantum theory' burst on the scene, driving a coach and horses through the snug smug world of classical physics and transforming our perception of nature. Nor is this ancient history—the originator of quantum theory, Max Planck, died in 1947, just three years before I went to university.

Quantum theory accounted for many things that classical physics couldn't, such as why hot objects don't radiate an infinite amount of energy; why atoms don't self-destruct by their negatively charged electrons collapsing into their positively charged nuclei; and why light from hot gases is not smeared across the whole rainbow spectrum but is emitted at specific wavelengths (so-called spectral lines, corresponding to distinct colours).

The basic discovery of quantum theory was that energy can only be transferred in discrete packets called 'quanta'. Take that pot of yogurt on your breakfast table. Suppose you visit your local supermarket to buy this item and find that its price ticket reads, 'Strawberry yogurt; 39.25p' (or cents if you prefer). No matter how much you may want it, you can't have it because you can't actually pay the stated price. Why not? Because there is no such thing as a quarter-penny coin. You don't feel inclined to pay 40p because that's too much, and the shop won't sell it for 39p because that's too little. At the root of the stand-off is the fact that our currency is 'quantized'—it is only available in one penny units ('quanta') with nothing in between. So no exchange of cash for goods is permitted unless it involves using whole pennies. It's just the same for energy on a microscopic scale; it can only be transferred (emitted or absorbed) in discrete units or quanta.

That's why gases like hydrogen emit and absorb light at specific wavelengths. The hydrogen atom can only emit light energy if its electron jumps from one discrete energy level to another, releasing a whole quantum of energy. Quantum theory predicts *exactly* what this amount of energy should be and thus the specific wavelength (colour) of the emitted light. This, incidentally, is how we know we live in an expanding universe. The spectral lines of a given gas all move to longer wavelengths if their source is moving away from us. This gives rise to the so-called 'red shift' observed in light from distant galaxies. Not only does the red shift show that the galaxy in question is moving away from us (if it were getting closer the shift would be towards the blue end of the spectrum) but the size of the red shift tells us how fast it is moving. Neat, how an understanding of the sub-microscopic world of quantum theory contributes directly to our knowledge of the large-scale universe! That's the kind of thing that makes physicists really happy.

Quantum theory (or quantum mechanics, as it is more properly called) is a highly successful theory, being borne out experimentally in many more ways than I have mentioned. It describes very accurately how nature works on the sub-microscopic scale of particle physics—involving atoms, protons, electrons, photons ('particles' or quanta of light) and lots of other tiny wingdings you don't really want to know about. But there is a heavy price-tag attached to this success, a price that Albert Einstein for one was reluctant to pay. The 'price' is that we have to take on board the wondrously weird world that comes packaged with quantum mechanics.

## Cereal

My favourite breakfast cereal consists of a light mixture of grains, raisins and sultanas. Without the last two ingredients it would be rather bland and tasteless; the fruit makes all the difference. But when you open a new packet you never know where the fruit will be. Sometimes it is nicely dispersed throughout the box but more usually it is all at the bottom or all at the top. If you knew in advance where it was you could turn the box appropriately and shake it to encourage the fruit to migrate upwards or downwards as required. Not knowing where it is frustrates all such measures. This is a bit like quantum mechanics (let's call it QM for short) because there also it's hard to know where things are until you 'open the packet' and take a look.

I'm sure Alice would insist that you can't be in two places at once, but then she hadn't studied QM. According to QM, a subatomic particle like an electron is not so much in two places at once as in *every* place at once (at least potentially)! Instead of thinking of the electron as a tiny billiard ball having a precise location in space, QM says we have to think of it as being associated with a 'wave function' or probability wave that spreads out over the whole of space and time. This wave tells us the likelihood or *probability* that the electron will be found in a particular place at a particular time.

In Baroness Orczy's *The Scarlet Pimpernel*, Sir Percy Blakeney declares:

They seek him here, they seek him there,
Those Frenchies seek him everywhere.
Is he in heaven? Is he in hell?
That demmed, elusive Pimpernel.

It's a bit like that with electrons—and with photons and protons, neutrons and muons, and even arguably with Schrödinger's cat (no time to explain; look it up with Google). We simply don't know where they are or what state they are in until we 'open the packet' and do an experiment to find out. However, there is an important difference between the Scarlet Pimpernel and our electron. Although the Pimpernel couldn't be found, he *was* somewhere definite all the time. But quantum theory demands that before we look for our electron it *really could be anywhere*. In fact, some go as far as to suggest that the electron doesn't actually exist until we pin it down by making a measurement.

Oh, and that's not all. Once we find our elusive electron (or other particle) the very act of locating it disturbs it so much that we have no idea what its other properties were before we found it. In other words, once you measure one property of a particle (like its position) you lose all information about some equally important property (like its speed). This is the so-called 'uncertainty principle' first propounded by Werner Heisenberg in 1926 and means that we can never know *everything* about even a single particle—let alone all the particles that make up our physical world. Thus the future course of events is unpredictable, not because of our ignorance but on account of the very way the universe is made.

## Toast

Ready for the toast? Good. While you are waiting for the toaster to pop, why not telephone your cousin George in Bloemfontein? He's having breakfast too (as long as you are in the UK). As you cradle the telephone between your cheek and shoulder, and try to butter your toast at the same time, the toast slips off the plate and falls to the floor (gravity isn't always good for you). Naturally, it falls buttered side

down. Your cry of dismay makes George jump and he also knocks his
buttered toast to the floor. But his toast, lucky fellow, lands buttered side
up. So you each start again with a fresh piece of toast, only to repeat
the original accident. This time, strangely, your toast lands buttered
side up while George's lands buttered side down. Intrigued by the
counter-coincidence, you agree to try it again, this time deliberately.
You each butter the toast and drop it on the floor—ten more times.
Spookily, whatever happens to your piece of toast, exactly the opposite
happens to George's. It's as if George's toast somehow knows what
your toast is going to do and deliberately does the opposite. Incredible?
Of course. But that's what sometimes happens in the weird world of
QM, not with toast but with particles like photons which are said to
be 'entangled'.

A typical experiment was conducted by French physicist Alain
Aspect and co-workers in the early 1980s. It went like this. A stream
of vaporized calcium atoms was created in the middle of a laboratory,
and two photon detectors were positioned thirteen metres apart at
opposite sides of the room. The calcium atoms were 'excited' (raised
to higher energy) by shining a laser beam on them, and when they
relaxed back to their normal state each atom emitted two photons (light
quanta)—which were shot out like bullets in exactly opposite directions.
Let's call the two photons a 'photon pair'. Of course, different atoms
shot out their photons 'every which way', but some of these photons
travelled in just the right direction to be caught by the detectors. One
photon of each pair was caught by the detector on the left and the
other by the detector on the right, the two photons arriving at their
respective detectors simultaneously. OK so far? Fine. Now let's look
at the detectors, which are rather clever.

Each detector records the arrival of a photon but it does much more
than that. It also measures the photon's 'spin'. A photon (along with
other particles) can be likened to a spinning top, so 'spin' is simply
one of its properties. The photon spins about an axis, just as the earth
spins on its axis. Also, just as the earth spins at a constant speed, so
the photon can only spin at one speed because (like so much else in

the QM world) its spin is quantized. Unlike the earth, however, the photon can spin in either direction, clockwise or anticlockwise. Also, the photon can spin about *any* axis it chooses. Fortunately, the earth can't do this because if it did the North Pole might suddenly turn up in Birmingham or Brisbane.

Now, when the two photons of a pair are detected and measured, their spins are always found to be opposite. If one lands buttered side up, as it were (clockwise spin), the other lands buttered side down (anticlockwise spin). Like the spooky toast, one photon seems to know what the other is doing thirteen metres away. OK? Take a sip of coffee.

At first sight there doesn't seem to be a problem. Surely the two photons simply take on opposite spins when they leave the parent calcium atom? But Aspect's experiment, and others like it, prove otherwise. By randomly 'turning' each detector to measure the photon's spin about different axes, and using some clever reasoning that we can't go into here, it proves that (1) a photon's spin is indeterminate until it is actually measured; and (2) as soon as it is measured (but not before) its twin photon arriving at the other detector thirteen metres away instantly 'knows' what spin it has and adopts the opposite spin.[1] No matter how far apart the detectors are placed, the result is the same. As far as we know, if the two detectors were respectively in London and Bloemfontein, one photon of a pair would always 'know' what happens to the other when it hits its detector.

Hovering on the interface between physics and philosophy, physicists are still arguing about the significance of all this. But standard QM actually explains it rather well—the photon in London has a wave function (or probability wave) that extends to Bloemfontein and vice versa, so the two photons never actually lose touch with each other. It's as if you and your cousin met up in Cairo and parted again, one heading for England and the other for South Africa, while staying in touch all the time by conversing on your mobile phones. The photons remain entangled, with their spins indeterminate, until the spin of one is measured. Only then does each photon decide what spin it has.

Why should we believe such unbelievable things? Because, whether we like it or not, that's the only way to 'explain' a lot of experimentally verified scientific observations.

Sorry if your coffee got cold.

## Einstein and QM

The philosophical impact of quantum theory was immense because it overthrew the long-cherished concept of determinism in nature. Determinism is the idea, first propounded by the French mathematician Pierre-Simon Laplace (1749–1827), that if you knew everything about every particle in the universe you could predict 'what happens next' and so determine the future course of all physical events.[2]

Albert Einstein agreed with Laplace; he didn't like the 'spooky' implications of QM one little bit. He could not deny that the theory was highly successful in describing and predicting what goes on in the sub-microscopic underworld—indeed, he himself made notable contributions to the development of the theory. But he always believed that QM was not, and could not be, the ultimate reality—because it relies on ideas like probability waves and indeterminacy that are seriously counter intuitive (they simply don't 'make sense').

Unhappy with the apparent randomness of nature it revealed, Einstein maintained that QM could only be a provisional and approximate description of the fabric of the universe. Maybe it's all we *can* know, he argued, but there must be an underlying reality in which particles *do* have well-defined positions and speeds and *do* follow deterministic laws. He believed that quantum mechanics 'would eventually go beyond a mathematical description of probabilities and find an explanation in the form of deeper causal mechanisms'.[3] This belief led him to propound his famous aphorism, 'God does not play dice with the universe.'

Einstein had his supporters, including many distinguished physicists who were themselves involved in developing QM, such as Max Planck,

Erwin Schrödinger, Louis de Broglie and, more recently, David Bohm. For example, de Broglie considered that: 'The idea of chance ... comes in at each stage in the progress of our knowledge, when we are not aware that we are on the brink of a deeper level of reality which still eludes us.'[4] But the consensus among physicists today is that the 'unbelievable' oddities of the quantum world are here to stay. Science's 'explanations' leave us staring into an incomprehensible abyss. As J. B. S. Haldane put it: 'The universe is not only queerer than we imagine, it is queerer than we can imagine.'[5]

# CHAPTER THREE ...

... in which the wonderful world of physics grows 'curiouser and curiouser' (to borrow Alice's charming phrase). When we ended the previous chapter we knew that the tiny particles that constitute matter and energy behave in very odd ways, but at least we knew what they were. But as the twentieth century unfolded, this simplicity was wrecked by the discovery of a veritable zoo of previously unknown particles. The horrible truth began to dawn. Physicists no longer knew what things were really made of.

Into this chaotic scene rode a white knight—string theory—which claims to explain everything we previously didn't understand. But just like quantum mechanics, string theory comes at a huge cost in comprehensibility, requiring space to have ten or more dimensions for starters.

Nevertheless, this could be the 'theory of everything' that everyone is looking for—or not, as the case may be. Some think the white knight is just an empty suit of armour, an impostor that can, in fact, explain nothing.

## New words?

The new words in this chapter are all explained in the text. However, we do meet for the first time the use of a mathematical 'shorthand' for very large or very small numbers.

The expression $10^5$ means one followed by five zeros, that is, 100,000. This saves a lot of space when we start talking about numbers like $10^{26}$, for example. Also, by putting a minus sign in front of the superscript, it helps us handle very tiny numbers. Thus $10^{-2}$ means 1/100 (one hundredth or 0.01) and $10^{-26}$ means a decimal point followed by 25 zeros and a 1.

# 3. Stringing it all together

'How often have I said to you that when you have eliminated the impossible, whatever remains, however improbable, must be the truth?'

Sir Arthur Conan Doyle's Sherlock Holmes
in *The sign of the four* (1889)

Since it's Saturday morning and I don't have to go to the office (or take the grandchildren to school), let's linger at the breakfast table for some light conversation.

'So you say that science doesn't actually *explain* anything—it only *describes* things (albeit, in a way that is stimulating and useful). And this is because scientific explanations can only "explain" things in terms of ... well, other things that we *can't* explain or even imagine. So it's out of the frying pan into the fire, eh? But aren't you bamboozling me by deliberately choosing crazy examples like quantum theory? Why don't you give me a scientific explanation of something really simple like, "Why does water run downhill?"'

'OK, I'll do that. Water runs downhill because the force of gravity pulls it towards the centre of the earth.'

'That's better. But you'll have to tell me what you mean by the force of gravity.'

'Happy to oblige. Any object that has mass (like water) is attracted to any other object that has mass (like the Earth) by a gravitational force that is proportional to their masses and inversely proportional to the distance between them squared.'

A slight shadow passes over the questioner's face. 'I know what distance is, of course, but what's mass?'

'Well, mass is the quantity of matter in a body.'

'You're not catching me out like that. Matter is made of particles, right? So we're back to all that quantum stuff. You'll have to do better than that.'

'OK. Let's go back to Isaac Newton (he of the falling apple). Mass is the property of a body that gives it inertia.'

'What's inertia?'

'Inertia is what keeps a body moving in a straight line at constant speed unless you apply a force to it.'

'Why should it do that?'

'Well, that's actually a tough question, but some physicists believe it might be due to "empty space" not being empty at all but filled with an "ocean" of Higgs bosons. Sorry, because that brings us back to quantum mechanics.'

'Higgs bosons? Pigs' trotters more likely! Forget mass. What makes one thing attract another? What is gravitation all about?'

'Well, the current scientific explanation is that any object that has mass distorts the fabric of space around it, making other objects want to move towards it. That's true of your coffee cup or even the spoon, but the curvature of space they produce is so tiny it can be ignored. However, the Earth is a different matter—its mass is big enough to cause some serious curvature of space, so that if you drop the spoon it will move towards the centre of the Earth. Oh, and the gravitational force is transmitted by as-yet-hypothetical particles called "gravitons", which, rather oddly, don't have any mass.'

The questioner is understandably frustrated. 'Now we're back to mass (or not, as the case may be), not to mention quantum mechanics, pigs' trotters (or whatever) and curved space! I asked you a simple question but all you do is lead me round in circles. Call yourself a scientist? You can't even explain why water runs downhill!'

'I rest my case. Let's go shopping; I need to get some string.'

'String? Whatever for?'

'You'll see.'

## Things aren't always what they seem
As a teenager I was, like Sooty, 'into' magic—or rather, conjuring, which is not quite the same. The difference is that while some people *believe* in magic, anyone watching a conjuror *knows* he's being fooled. I performed at fetes, concerts and parties, and have especially fond memories of the street parties held to celebrate the end of World War II. One conjuring trick I did involved the 'impossible' feat of restoring the integrity of a rope that had been cut in half. I would display a piece of rope about a metre long, loop it with my right hand into my left, and cut the loop with a pair of scissors. I then turned my left palm towards the audience to show them what appeared to be two separate and roughly equal lengths of rope hanging side by side, with four indubitable and clearly visible ends between them.

What the audience could not see, however, was that both the top ends actually belonged to one very short piece of rope looped into a much longer single piece—the intersection of the two loops being covered and hidden by my thumb. It was a simple matter then to palm and dispose of the short piece while displaying the remainder as the 'original' uncut rope—usually to a round of applause.

The moral, of course, is that things aren't always as they seem. Things we consider 'impossible' can and do happen—they only *appear* to be impossible because we lack the necessary insight to grasp their possibility. In the previous chapter I talked about some seemingly impossible things (like curved space and an electron being everywhere at the same time) that are nevertheless accepted by scientists as being 'strange but true'—things that are essential to make sense of their experiments and observations. But in making sense of some things they are forced to invoke other things that themselves don't make sense—concepts that run counter to all our intuitions and *a priori* ideas.

In this chapter we're going to see another example of this—'string theory'.[1] The latest version is actually called hyperstring theory, but I'll keep it simple and stick to 'string'. Like my rope trick, it's the short bits that make the magic. In fact the strings of string theory are so short that if you wanted to tie them in a bow around an atomic nucleus you would have to join billions of them end-to-end to do so. (For the technically minded we are talking about strings of the order of the Planck length, $10^{-33}$ cm; that's $10^{26}$ times smaller than a typical atom.) Kindly suspend your unbelief—it's not a conjuring trick, honestly. It is a scientific hypothesis and in chapter 4 it's going to help me introduce a major theme of this book, namely, what people sometimes call 'the hypothesis of God'.

## Cosmic rays

Let's go back a bit. Although the quantum theory sparked a revolution in physics (not to mention philosophy) it still left the structure of matter fairly simple. Everything was composed of atoms, and each atom was composed of a central nucleus (a bundle of positive protons and uncharged neutrons) surrounded by 'shells' of negatively charged electrons. That was it—the basic constitution of matter. Physicists, being simple souls, like that kind of simplicity.

However, there were clouds on this placid horizon. For starters, it was discovered that the whole Earth is bathed in high-energy radiation. At first this was blamed on natural radioactivity in the soil and rocks, but there seemed to be rather too much radiation for this to be the only cause. So in 1912, an intrepid scientist called Victor Hess took a balloon flight to 17,500 feet (without oxygen, which was rather risky) to measure how this mysterious radiation varied with altitude. Surprisingly, it increased, showing that much of it was not coming from radioactivity on Earth at all, but from outer space. This radiation was dubbed 'cosmic rays', though there are actually no 'rays'—just a continuous fusillade of individual particles.

When I was a student at University College, London, in the 1950s much of the physics research there was devoted to studying cosmic rays. Researchers examined the microscopic 'tracks' left by energetic cosmic ray particles in blocks of photographic emulsion. From these tracks they could work out the mass and electrical charge of each cosmic ray particle—which in turn told them what kind of particle had caused a particular track (a proton, for example). Other researchers used 'cloud chambers' in which the normally invisible particles were induced to leave tracks of tiny water droplets, much as aeroplanes leave vapour trails in the sky. To cut a long story short, the cosmic ray particles were eventually found to include not only things we knew about, like protons, neutrons and electrons, but also some strange new and short-lived particles called 'mesons' (because their masses are intermediate between those of protons and electrons).[2]

Well, of course, things could only get worse. Particle accelerators ('atom smashers') were invented in which beams of particles (like electrons and protons) could be made to travel faster and faster, raising their energy dramatically before allowing them to smash into a target or collide head-on with another beam travelling in the opposite direction.

The debris from these collisions consisted of yet other particles which could be detected just as cosmic rays had been.

Before long it became evident that there existed a veritable zoo of esoteric short-lived particles—mesons of various kinds together with 'anti-particles' like positrons ('electrons' with a positive charge) and neutrinos (particles with virtually zero mass that can pass clean through the earth from one side to the other without hitting anything— there's marksmanship for you). Then, much more recently, ultra-high energy 'atom smashers' showed that even protons and neutrons are not 'fundamental' at all but are themselves composed of 'quarks', which come in all shapes and sizes. There are up-quarks, down-quarks, top-quarks, bottom quarks, charm-quarks, strange-quarks—here a quark, there a quark. It's more like old MacDonald's farm than a zoo. All very exciting for physicists and veterinarians, no doubt, but all rather confusing for everyone else. But there was yet another problem disturbing the once-tidy world of nature—one that at first seemed to have no connection with the exuberant proliferation of fundamental particles.

## Getting it all together

Everyone likes music but most of us like a particular kind of music— any old music won't do. There's classical and jazz, metal and rock, opera and folk, rave and reggae, and so forth. They sure don't mix and match. They're all music (at least to their devotees) yet they have little in common. They simply go their separate ways, doing their separate things, attracting their separate fans and even generating their own separate 'cultures'. They are irreconcilable.

The problem for physics was similar. Like four diverse music styles, there were four irreconcilable kinds of force in nature: gravity; the electromagnetic force; the strong nuclear force (which holds atomic nuclei together); and the weak nuclear force (which pulls them apart, causing radioactive decay). For decades these four fundamental forces defied all attempts to bring them together in a single theory. This state of affairs drove physicists frantic because it was very untidy, and it is an article of faith for them that the universe must ultimately be a tidy, rational place. It was this belief in the rationality of nature that drove Albert Einstein to spend his latter years struggling to unify his general theory of relativity with quantum mechanics, sadly without success. At the time, Einstein was pretty much a lone ranger in his search for a theory that would encompass everything, but in recent decades many other physicists have been bitten by the same bug and become obsessed with the search to unify the four forces of nature with a single theory. And things are beginning to happen.

The once obstinate refusal of the four basic forces to get together is at last yielding to scientific onslaught, and some victories have been won. For example, the electromagnetic force and the weak force can now be viewed as different cases of a single 'electroweak' force. And string theory, although it is the new kid on the block and still not accepted by many in the research community, is getting a lot of physicists excited. Why? Because it might just offer the holy grail of 'a theory of everything'—uniting all the forces of nature, accounting for the existence of all those maverick particles and, in short, describing just how the physical universe really works.

## Front runner
Many consider the string theory to be the front runner in the Einstein stakes—the race to unify our scientific view of nature. The theory was born in the late 1960s and early 1970s to explain the behaviour of subatomic particles which experience the strong nuclear force. Yoichiro Nambu (followed by Lenny Susskind and Holger Nielson) realized in 1970 that these strong interactions could be described by a quantum-mechanical model in which particles were not just non-dimensional point objects but one-dimensional strings.

By the mid 1980s, such progress had been made that, according to the theory, all the fundamental particles that make up our universe—protons, neutrons, electrons, quarks, mesons, photons, neutrinos etc.; and even the hypothetical 'gravitons' that are supposed to carry the force of gravity—could be regarded as minute 'strings'. That is, instead of thinking of a proton (for example) as a dot it should be regarded as a short string which can vibrate like a violin string (or a guitar string, if that's your preferred scene).

Personally, I love violin music, especially Mozart's violin concertos. I once tried to learn to play the violin but could never produce more than a few basic sounds (OK, noises, if you insist) no matter how hard I tried. But a professional violinist can make the violin talk, generating an amazing range of sounds and tonal qualities. Everything depends, of course, on the way the strings are coaxed to vibrate in different modes by the musician's master touch.

Well, just as a violin string can vibrate in different ways to produce different musical sounds, so the minute strings of string theory can vibrate in different ways to produce—guess what? That's right; different fundamental particles. So one string vibrating in three different ways can 'be' three different fundamental particles (though not all at once). No wonder particles are so thick on the ground. On this assumption, the theory claims, we can explain all the fundamental particles of nature and the way they interact, using nothing more than, well, a piece of string. (I tactfully ignore the horrendous mathematics involved in reaching this conclusion.)

Because different vibrational modes correspond to different fundamental particles, the theory neatly explains why there are so many different kinds of particle, and why one kind can decay into one or more other kinds. To put it another way, a given string can turn up in a variety of different disguises, each one corresponding to a different fundamental particle. This, of course, represents a huge simplification of the whole business—the zoo actually only keeps one kind of animal but the creature is cunningly dressed up differently in each cage to make you think you've got biodiversity.

But there is even more icing on the cake (sorry, I'll sort those metaphors out some time). As early as the mid 1970s it was realized that string theory actually predicts the existence and properties of 'gravitons'—the as-yet undiscovered particles that transmit gravitational attraction from one object to another. With this discovery, the force of gravity came dramatically in from the cold. Instead of standing outside the whole framework of quantum mechanics and fundamental particles as it once did, gravity could now be treated by QM just like the other three basic forces of nature. Now that's neat—really neat. Have we at last found the 'theory of everything'?

## Crumpled dimensions and other small problems

Well, perhaps. But beware; the 'explanation' or simplification achieved by string theory comes at an incredible price in credibility—there is nothing here remotely resembling the self-evident end-point that would denote an honest-to-goodness explanation.

I already said that for all this to work, the strings themselves have to be so tiny as to be almost non-existent. You would need $10^{26}$ of them end to end to stretch from one side of an atom to the other—that's not 1,000,000 of them or even 1,000,000,000 of them, but 'one followed by 26 zeros' of them. That's an awful lot of strings though not, of course, all that much string. Needless to say, we have no hope of ever actually seeing such strings—we can only infer their existence from the success of the theory (or their non-existence if the theory fails).

Oh, and that's not all. For these strings to 'do their stuff' they must exist not in one dimension like any self-respecting thread, nor in the three dimensions of space, and not even in the four dimensions of space-time. They must wriggle around in ten, eleven or even twenty-six dimensions (take your pick) depending on the version of string theory you prefer. Now there's magic for you! Or perhaps it's just a conjuring trick? No, it's called physics and a great deal of serious and expensive research is being devoted to it at this very moment.

But if there are all these spare dimensions lying around, how come we never noticed? Why do we blithely assume that there are just three dimensions of space plus one 'dimension' of time? The reason given is that all these extra dimensions are crumpled up like balls of paper—rather like discarded pages in a would-be author's waste bin. Except that this waste bin would be smaller than an atom and the authors are probably 'Maxwell's Demons' (insider joke; look it up with Google). But physics *does* want you to take seriously the belief that unimaginably tiny strings vibrate in the crumpled folds of unimaginably tiny dimensions and thereby magic into existence the entire zoo of fundamental particles that go to make up energy, force-fields, atoms, molecules, objects and, yes, us.

Why on earth should intelligent and well-paid scientists devote their lives to studying unbelievable strings they will never see, playing cosmic music they will never hear, in mind-blowing multiple dimensions they can never enter? Well, as you may have guessed, there is a reason for it all. Incredible as the theory may seem, it could turn out to be the 'theory of everything' that Einstein so longed to see—describing the fabric of the universe and thence the workings of the whole physical cosmos, unifying the behaviour of subatomic particles and immense galaxies. To gain such a breathtaking perspective, brilliant scientists are willing to suspend judgement and believe 'impossible' things—both before and after breakfast. Although the jury is still out on the validity of string theory,[3] a lot of scientists are working on it—keeping their research students busy and their fingers crossed.

### Common sense

As we have seen, string theory is only one of many aspects of modern physics that are counter-intuitive—that seem impossible or unbelievable when approached using common sense. Why is this? Because common sense (which is not to be despised) relies only on the evidence provided by our common senses—sight, hearing, smell, touch and taste (plus, perhaps, a woman's intuition). However, these senses have their limitations. They cannot penetrate the infinitesimal world of quantum mechanics, nor can they observe the bizarre (counter-intuitive) behaviour in that world—it is truly a realm beyond our senses. Such 'unseen' things have to be inferred by scientists indirectly and set in order by generalizations that start life as hypotheses—mental constructs that help us to corral the strange beasts of this invisible world. In fact, whenever we need to investigate things that lie beyond the immediate reach of our senses, we have to begin with a hypothesis and see if it can lead us to conclusions that square with the reality we *can* experience directly. This applies to unseen things in both science and religion, and particularly so when science and faith impinge on one another—as in the question 'Who made God?' Clearly, we are going to need to use hypotheses if we are to pursue the question, so let's take a look at the subject.

# CHAPTER FOUR ...

... in which, beginning with earthquakes and Bob the postman, we start to lay foundations—otherwise known as 'hypotheses'. That's how science usually works, by using hypotheses as a basis for theory-building, first proposing a foundational idea and then testing whether its predictions make sense and correspond to reality. We'll call this 'the hypothetic method' and consider its merits and pitfalls, before introducing 'the hypothesis of God'.

This begins by proposing that God exists, and goes on to explore where this assumption leads us, as we try to get our minds around the 'whys and wherefores' of the cosmos, life and ourselves. We'll work the idea out in detail as the book progresses.

## New words?

*Syllogism*: An argument that draws a conclusion from two separate initial assertions (or premises) which contain a common term. For example: All *birds* have feathers; all ostriches are *birds*; therefore all ostriches have feathers. A false syllogism is one in which the conclusion is invalid because it is hidden somewhere in the premises.

*Teleological*: Relating to purpose or design; devised or ordained in advance for a purpose.

*Palaeontology*: The study of fossils.

*Magisterium*: Teaching authority.

# 4. Pouring concrete

We shape our buildings: thereafter they shape us.

Winston Churchill
*Time*, 12 September 1960

Earthquakes are not very common where I live and I'm not quite sure how I would fare if one struck. One thing is certain, however—my car would be safe. I have the only quake-proof garage in South Hertfordshire.

When we moved to our present house we had an extension built that incorporates a garage. The builders duly dug out the foundations or 'footings' to the prescribed depth of one-point-three metres and (again as prescribed) invited the local building inspector to take a look before they poured the concrete. The inspector was not a happy man. Muttering darkly about tree roots and past subsidence, he ordered the builders to keep digging to a depth of two metres. 'Two metres?' gasped the builder. 'It's only a one-storey flat-roof garage!' The inspector brooded for a while. 'Better make it three metres,' he pronounced, cheering up noticeably. So our foundations go down further than the building rises. As I said, quake-proof.

Whether such extreme precautions were necessary we shall never know (barring an earthquake). What we do know is that, whatever you build, foundations are important. Nothing new about this, of course. Two thousand years ago, Jesus Christ ended his famous 'Sermon on the Mount' with a cautionary tale about foundations. 'Therefore whoever hears these sayings of Mine, and does them, I will liken him to a wise man who built his house on the rock: and the rain descended, the floods came, and the winds blew and beat on that house; and it did not fall, for it was founded on the rock. But everyone who hears these sayings of Mine, and does not do them, will be like a foolish man who built his house on the sand: and the rain descended, the floods came, and the winds blew and beat on that house; and it fell. And great was its fall.'[1]

Perhaps the inspector had a point. An edifice (even a humble garage) is only as strong as its foundations. And that brings us back to hypotheses.

### Foundations

What is a hypothesis? It is a foundation, something solid to build upon. Unfortunately, as the saying goes, not many people know that. They think of a hypothesis as a flying kite—something flimsy and airborne, an idle notion that defies common sense and lacks evidential legs (kites have legs? No, I just enjoy mixing metaphors). They attach the dismissive prefix 'mere', allowing the idea in question to be dismissed as a 'mere hypothesis', something that can safely be ignored.

Yet in truth a 'hypothesis' is the exact opposite of all this! It derives from two Greek words meaning respectively 'beneath' (*hupo*) and 'placing' (*thesis*) and signifies something 'placed beneath' as a foundation. Far from being insubstantial, foundations have a way of outlasting the buildings they support. Ask my builder or any archaeologist. Much of what we know about ancient civilizations is revealed by the foundations of cities and dwellings—foundations that remain long after the grand edifices built upon them have crumbled into dust.

Understood in this way, hypotheses play a key role in our lives and have a special place in science, which is one reason I spent so much time on string theory. Unlike general relativity and quantum mechanics, string theory remains (at the time of writing) a hypothesis—a foundational idea that promises to powerfully unify our perception of the universe but still remains untested in many critical respects. But that's how all science begins. Scientific theories are seldom born ready-made.

## How hypotheses are born

Hypotheses are ideas or insights that not only spur us to investigate further but also provide the grounds for doing so. They begin life in our observations of the world around us. Our curiosity is aroused and we begin to note and even record certain experiences. We find ourselves asking questions like 'How did that get there?' or 'Why does this always happen?' And with such questions, of course, arises the need for answers or explanations. An hypothesis is our first attempt at rationalizing what we observe (whether we realize it or not, there is a scientist lurking within every one of us).

Quite often we come up with more than one hypothesis to explain an experience. For example, if no mail has been delivered at my home by 11.00 this morning it could be because (1) the postman overslept; (2) there wasn't any post for me so he didn't call; or (3) there is a postal workers' strike that no one told me about. Usually I would leave it at that and get on with my day. But if I were expecting a large cheque in the post, or writing a PhD thesis on the logistics of mail distribution, I might well be motivated to investigate further—to test the various hypotheses to find out what was really going on.

How do we carry out such tests? By doing 'experiments'—deliberate actions or observations aimed at verifying or refuting each hypothesis. In the 'missing mail' example I could ask my neighbours if they had received any mail. If they had, it would rule out hypotheses 1 and 3 and confirm hypothesis 2. As a second 'experiment' I could phone the local sorting office to ask if Bob, our local postman, had reported for work that day, which would confirm or refute hypothesis 1—and so on.

Such everyday experiences often pass unnoticed, but there is no essential difference when a scientific hypothesis is at stake, except that the whole thing tends to get more formal. A scientific hypothesis is only worthy of the name if it leads to testable predictions—effects which we can look for, often in specially designed experiments. A positive result will help to confirm the hypothesis while a negative result will tend to falsify it—though no single result may settle the matter once for all. And in some cases the 'experiment' has already been done, though it was not at the time recognized as relevant to the case in hand. That is, the hypothesis may predict something we already know but which was previously unexplained, wrongly explained, or simply overlooked. In this case the hypothesis is made more secure by its *consistency* with already known facts or observations. Here lies the good news for string theory—it is consistent in a rather elegant way with what is already known about fundamental particles. The bad news is that the theory has trouble rising above hypothetical status because it hasn't yet made any *unique* predictions (things that can't be explained by any other hypothesis or theory).

This, more or less, is how science normally proceeds. It involves a sequence, namely, observation, hypothesis, prediction, testing (by existing knowledge or new experiment)—the prediction(s) leading to verification, modification or falsification of the hypothesis. I will call this approach to advancing knowledge 'the hypothetic approach', using 'hypothetic' to mean 'pertaining to hypotheses' as distinct from 'hypothetical'. Of course, being a human activity, science can't be contained within an idealized framework, and there are occasions when it over-flies the hypothetic process on wings of sheer inspiration—or illuminates our perception of the world by flashes of insight that seem to come from nowhere. Nevertheless, without the hypothetic process science as we know it could hardly exist.

## Hypothetic hazards

Working with hypotheses is not without hazards. The most obvious of these arises if I become too eager to prove that my hypothesis is better than yours. Let's take a walk along the beach. Suppose I have conceived the hypothesis that most of the pebbles on this particular beach actually come from the erosion of rocks on the far side of the estuary. If I am right, the pebbles will be black rather than grey. I plan to pick up a random selection of pebbles and see what proportion of them are black. But in spite of a genuine desire to be unbiased, I am almost certain to favour black pebbles over grey ones—helping to 'prove' my hypothesis. In other words, we tend to select evidence that supports our hypotheses and ignore evidence that militates against it. This is why new clinical drugs are always tested in double-blind trials—in which neither the patient receiving the treatment nor the doctor administering it knows whether a given patient is receiving the actual drug or a look-alike placebo.

A second hypothetic hazard is more subtle. Since the hypothesis is a foundational assumption, there is a real danger of arguing in a circle and finishing up where we started. If, for example, I begin with the assumption (hypothesis) that 'a God exists who created all things', I cannot subsequently use the existence of the universe as an argument for the existence of God. In other words, reasoning that goes as follows is invalid:

1. A God exists who created the universe.

2. The universe exists.

3. Therefore it must have had a creator (a God who created the universe).

In a valid syllogism the statements (1) and (2) would lead to a conclusion (3) that is not contained in either (1) and (2), but in this example we simply end up by deducing what we assumed in the first place. Interestingly, if we abandon the hypothetic method and remove proposition (1) we also remove the fallacy and arrive at what is, in essence, the traditional 'cosmological argument' for the existence of God (which reasons from the existence of the cosmos to the need for a 'first cause'). However, as we shall see, there are distinct advantages in persevering with the hypothetic approach in spite of the potential pitfalls.

A further example of circular argument is the idea promoted by some atheists that 'science disproves the existence of God'. The assertion is based on the claim that science presents no evidence for the existence of supernatural forces or phenomena. It sounds plausible until you look a little more closely. The argument can be expressed as a syllogism as follows:

1. Science is the study of the physical universe.

2. Science produces no evidence for the existence of non-physical entities.

3. Therefore non-physical entities such as God do not exist.

Again the fallacy is clear. In point (1) 'science' is defined as the study of the physical or material world. This statement thereby excludes *by definition* any consideration by science of non-physical causes or events. The proposition then argues from the silence of science concerning non-material realities that such realities do not exist. By the same logic, if you define birds as 'feathered creatures that fly', there's no such thing as an ostrich. It's fairly obvious in this example whose head is in the sand. The correct conclusion, of course, is not that ostriches are mythical but that (on your restrictive definition of 'bird') they are not birds. In the same way, to define science as the study of the material universe simply prohibits science from making statements about a non-material entity like God. If the remit of science is deliberately restricted to the physical realm, the fact that science (so defined) tells us nothing about God has no bearing whatever on his existence or non-existence, as most scientists recognize.

A related but distinct hazard is the 'hidden hypothesis' whereby an otherwise invalid argument is bolstered by an unstated assumption. This device can turn a silly syllogism into powerful propaganda, as the following example suggests:

1. (Hidden hypothesis) Nothing has objective reality that cannot be experienced by our natural senses.

2. Science is the use of our natural senses to study objective reality.

3. Science produces no evidence for the existence of non-natural causes or entities.

4. Therefore non-natural entities (for example, God) have no objective reality.

The hidden hypothesis (1) is quietly absorbed into the definition of science given in (2) so that science is no longer just the study of the natural-physical-material universe (as in our earlier example) but becomes transmuted into the study of reality as opposed to non-reality. If we buy into this idea we inevitably conclude that science is the only means of acquiring genuine knowledge or establishing 'true' truth.

This idea—that the only meaningful (and non-tautological) statements are those capable of being verified by sense experience—is actually a venerable philosophical theory known as 'logical positivism'. It claims that what cannot be verified by science has no reality, and implies that in studying the material universe science actually encompasses all legitimate knowledge. Logical positivism was the philosophical flavour of the day in the 1920s and 1930s and was popularized by A. J. Ayer in his book *Language, truth and logic* (1936). But Alfred Ayer himself, writing fifty years later, declared: 'Logical positivism died a long time ago. I don't think much of *Language, truth and logic* is true ... it is full of mistakes.'[2] In spite of this, many philosophers recognize in the 'new atheism' of writers like Dawkins, Dennett, Harris, Stenger and

Wolpert a reincarnation of this discredited school of thought—and
do so with grave concern.

## The hypothesis of God

What, then, if we adopt the hypothetic approach (avoiding the hazards)
and apply the methodology of science to the idea of God? A shocking
proposal? Not at all. Theology once reigned as 'the queen of sciences'—
in an era when 'science' had its original meaning of 'knowledge' and
well before modern science saw the light of day. For theology to
employ hypotheses is less a matter of borrowing science's clothes
than of claiming them back. There is nothing to stop us advancing
'the hypothesis of God' in which we assume that God exists and see
where it leads—following the example of the string theorists and
science in general.

To adopt the hypothetic approach is, of course, to diverge from
historical theology. Traditionally, theologians down the centuries
have sought to prove the existence of God by a variety of arguments.
We briefly considered one of these—the ontological argument—in
chapter 1. But there are other such arguments which seek to reason
directly from human experience to the existence of God. One such
'proof' is the cosmological argument proposed by Thomas Aquinas
which says, basically, that since every effect has a cause, there must
exist behind the universe a first cause—because otherwise cause and
effect would have to go back in an infinite regression which, like the
tower of tortoises, is impossible.

Not heard about the tortoise (or turtle) tower? Then you haven't read
Stephen Hawking's book *A brief history of time*—a book reputed to be
the most started-but-not-finished book of modern times. In fact you
haven't even begun to read the book because the tortoises appear on
page one. Hawking retells the story of a little old lady who challenged
the speaker following a lecture on astronomy and the solar system.
'Your lecture is all wrong. The earth is really a flat plate supported on
the back of a giant tortoise,' she said. 'So what is the tortoise standing
on?', asked the lecturer with a superior smile. 'On the back of another

tortoise,' she replied. 'And what is *that* tortoise standing on?' pressed the lecturer. It was the lady's turn to be scornful: 'It's tortoises all the way down!' she declared triumphantly. Whether true or not, the story is either a libel on little old ladies or a tribute to their wisdom—since she might well have been deliberately allegorizing the cosmological proof and the fallacy of infinite regression!

Mind you, some atheists seem to be turtle-lovers too. Victor Stenger[3] (of whom more in chapter 5) argues that '[if] the universe had a cause, why could that cause itself not be natural?' He seems to think it could, but then he would be obliged to explain the natural cause of the cause, followed by the cause of the cause of the cause, and so on *ad infinitum*. It's not only little old ladies who think that such things constitute 'explanations'.

A third philosophical argument for the existence of God is the 'teleological' argument or the argument from design. The universe has every appearance of purposeful design and this becomes ever more evident as science progresses—revealing that the 'inner workings' of the cosmos are essentially rational. For example, who could have guessed before 1953 (when James Watson and Francis Crick discovered the structure of DNA) that the specification for life itself is 'written' on huge molecules using an elegant genetic language having an alphabet of just four 'letters'?

Yet another argument for the reality of God is the moral argument which traces the existence of human morality back to a transcendent moral source. However, although philosophical arguments like the cosmological, teleological and moral 'proofs' of God retain their power, they have certain drawbacks. One problem is that even if we find these arguments convincing we finish up with a strictly utilitarian God— one whose nature is limited to certain lowest-common-denominator attributes. He is the primal cause, the cosmic designer and the fount of morality, but perhaps that is all he is. By contrast, the 'God hypothesis' approach gives us much more freedom to explore the nature of God because we can make any assumptions we choose concerning the attributes of God and then see where these assumptions lead us.

A second advantage is that however simple is the hypothesis with which we begin, we can build upon it as we proceed—just as science develops a hypothesis step by step into a received and proven law of nature. With the philosophical approach, God is the end point of our deliberations. With the hypothetic approach he is the starting point.

## A nice knock-down argument

Almost everyone talks about the 'hypothesis of God', Christians and atheists alike, so they all must believe it worthy of consideration. One atheist has even written a book entitled *God, the failed hypothesis: How science shows that God does not exist.*[4] Now, he wouldn't have written a whole book about a meaningless concept, would he? The author must agree with me at least on one point—no hypothesis can be pronounced a failure unless it is first stated and then tested. So let's accept that to consider the hypothesis of God is, at very least, a rational avenue of approach.

The snag is, however, that almost everyone who uses the term means something different by it. That celebrated terminological authority, Humpty Dumpty, explains the problem with casual brilliance.

'I don't know what you mean by "glory",' Alice said.

Humpty Dumpty smiled contemptuously. 'Of course you don't—till I tell you. I meant, "there's a nice knock-down argument for you!"'

'But "glory" doesn't mean "a nice knock-down argument",' Alice objected.

'When I use a word,' Humpty Dumpty said in rather a scornful tone, 'it means just what I choose it to mean—neither more nor less.'[5]

So it is with the word 'hypothesis' as applied to God. It means just what people choose it to mean. For example, Richard Dawkins[6] insists that God must be treated as a scientific hypothesis. 'The presence or absence of a creative super-intelligence is unequivocally a scientific question, even if in practice—or not yet—a decided one ... Did [Christ] come alive again three days after being crucified? There is an answer to every such question, whether or not we can discover it in practice, and it is a strictly scientific answer.'[7] So, *exeunt left* historians and *exeunt right* theologians (sorry, lads, but that's what the stage director says).

On the other hand, for science writer and palaeontologist Stephen J. Gould, along with many other scientists, all questions of religion lie outside the competence of science: 'The net, or magisterium, of science covers the empirical realm: what is the universe made of (fact) and why does it work this way (theory)? The magisterium of religion extends over questions of ultimate meaning and moral value. These two magisteria do not overlap nor do they encompass all enquiry (consider for example the magisterium of art and the meaning of beauty).'[8] This idea that science and religion offer *complementary* (yet equally valid) descriptions of the universe and human experience is popular among Christians who find it a convenient way to sidestep the genuine conflicts that exist, for example, between a belief in creation and a belief in evolution (but more of that later).

For others, like the present author, however, the matter cannot be pigeon-holed in either of these opposing ways, or any other. The 'hypothesis of God' means that the assumption 'God exists' is a starting point for enquiry *of all kinds*—historical, theological, scientific, aesthetic and more. Any attempt to lock God up in a box, whatever its shape, will inevitably lead to contradictions and failed hypotheses. It's like replacing a house (three dimensional) by the architect's plans of the house (two dimensional) and then trying to open the front door and step inside. By removing any of the 'dimensions' of God—by including him entirely within the material world or diligently excluding him from it—we reduce the hypothesis of God to a caricature of God.

To return to our starting point, therefore, the hypothesis of God is a foundation on which to build—an assumption that leads to a whole host of conclusions that can be tested against human experience including (but by no means limited to) scientific observations.

It may come as a surprise to learn that the Bible begins in exactly this way. Its opening words are, 'In the beginning God created the heavens and the earth' (Genesis 1:1). The first four words constitute an assumption that someone called 'God' exists and is sufficiently real to have created the real universe (the Hebrew word 'created' implying 'creation out of nothing'—*creatio ex nihilo*). That's quite an assumption; it is in fact the hypothesis of God.

# CHAPTER FIVE ...

... in which we undertake a brief critique of Victor Stenger's book *God, the failed hypothesis: How science shows that God does not exist*. Having introduced the hypothesis of God, we take up the challenge of one particular atheist who pronounces this hypothesis a failure and claims that science proves it so.

We'll see that the claim is wholly without merit, being based on faulty reasoning and tendentious interpretations of science. Stenger's first mistake is to suppose that all hypotheses are scientific hypotheses, which brings him into conflict with friends and foe alike. He then constructs and dismantles a number of straw men (including belief in a flat Earth and assorted ancient cosmologies) before claiming that simplicity begets complexity—perhaps not realizing that Richard Dawkins claims the exact opposite.

Dr Stenger goes on to argue unconvincingly against the concept of 'irreducible complexity' and intelligent design, but we're able to put him right with the help of Sir Fred Hoyle's jumbo jet and a box of flat-pack furniture. Eventually he vanishes into the black hole of his own logic, but we shan't see that till chapter 10. Quite entertaining.

### New words?

*Stoat*: A British mammal related to the weasel but much larger.

# 5. Ferrets and fallacies

Darwin chased God out of the old haunts of biology, and he scurried for safety down the rabbit hole of physics. The laws and constants of the universe, we were told, are too good to be true: a setup, carefully tuned to allow the eventual evolution of life. It needed a good physicist to show us the fallacy ... but Victor Stenger drives a pack of energetic ferrets down the last major bolt-hole and God is running out of refuges in which to hide.

Richard Dawkins, in a back-cover commendation
of *God, the failed hypothesis* by Victor Stenger

In chapter 6 we shall get to grips with the serious business of 'defining God', but first let's take a leisurely diversion in search of ferrets and fallacies. The ferrets are the imaginative invention of Richard Dawkins in the above citation, but the fallacies come courtesy of Victor Stenger, author of *God; the failed hypothesis: How science shows that God does not exist.*[1]

Let me make something clear—I did not write my book in response to anyone else's book. While books-in-reply serve an important function, I have always felt that they put their authors on the back foot, so to speak. A robust thesis, no matter how outrageous, always seems to trump a thoughtful antithesis—perhaps because a positive assertion has greater 'sex-appeal' than a negative rebuttal. Nevertheless, lest I be accused of ignoring the case against my own thesis, I will make an exception and devote this chapter to Victor Stenger's strange assertion that science proves the non-existence of God. Even Richard Dawkins doesn't go that far—and feels compelled to muster all manner of moral, philosophical, historical and sociological arguments in his quest to prove that God is a 'delusion'. Why would he do that if he thought that science could do the demolition job all by itself?

## Climbing Everest in a T shirt

Before we look in detail at Dr Stenger's proposition, a few general observations might be in order. We already noted in the previous chapter that palaeontologist Stephen J. Gould, who was quite a 'heavyweight' in expounding science to the masses, dismisses out of hand the notion that science 'shows that God does not exist' or could ever do so—and Gould was an agnostic leaning towards atheism. I have the feeling that Dr Stenger might be like a man climbing Everest in a T shirt—brave but somewhat alone. Indeed, even the prestigious US National Academy of Sciences has gone on record with the following statement: 'Science is a way of knowing about the natural world. It is limited to explaining the natural world through natural causes. Science can say nothing about the supernatural. Whether God exists or not is a question about which science is neutral.'[2] Stenger obviously disagrees, but his disagreement here is with the scientific community at large rather than with those who believe in God.

Then again, if science proves the non-existence of God, how is it that most of the leading scientists of the past 200 years never noticed? These range from Bible-believing Christians—like Michael Faraday (1791–1867), James Clerk Maxwell (1831–1879) and Arno Penzias (b. 1933)—to countless scientists who have subscribed, or still subscribe, to some concept of transcendence. Among the latter was Albert Einstein (1879–1955) who, though he rejected the idea of a personal God and might best be described as a pantheist, nevertheless complained, 'In view of such harmony in the cosmos which I, with my limited human mind, am able to recognize, there are yet people who say there is no God. But what really makes me angry is that they quote me for the support of such views.'[3]

James Joule (1818–1889), who propounded the first law of thermodynamics (on the conservation of energy) and made important contributions to the kinetic theory of gases, had no doubt about this matter: 'It is evident that an acquaintance with natural laws means no less than an acquaintance with the mind of God therein expressed.'

Stephen Hawking (b. 1942), in the final chapter of *A brief history of time*, uses the word 'God' eight times in four pages of text. While he does not declare himself on the question of God's existence, he clearly admits the possibility and on each occasion uses the name of God in a serious manner.

Martin Rees (who became president of the Royal Society in 2005) declares, 'Let me say that I don't see any conflict between science and religion,' and adds, 'I go to church as many other scientists do. I share with most religious people a sense of mystery and wonder at the universe and I want to participate in religious ritual and practices because they're something that all humans can share.'[4] The point is not that Martin Rees goes to church, or even whether he believes in God, but that he sees no *conflict* between science and faith. Such a conflict must surely exist if science proves the non-existence of God. The fact is that Stenger makes little attempt to prove that God does not exist; his actual contention is that science cannot prove that God *does* exist—which is a completely different thing. There appears to be considerable confusion in his mind between these two claims.

### Ferret fallacy one—all hypotheses are scientific

Dr Stenger sets out the thesis of his book with what, at first sight, appears to be admirable clarity. He writes: 'My analysis will be based on the contention that God should be detectable by scientific means simply by virtue of the fact that he is supposed to play such a central role in the operation of the universe and the lives of humans. Existing scientific models contain no place where God is included as an ingredient in order to describe observations. Thus if God exists he must appear somewhere within the gaps or errors of scientific models.'[5]

And again: 'As far as we can tell from current scientific knowledge, the universe we observe with our senses and scientific instruments can be described in terms of matter and material processes alone.'[6]

And yet again: 'The thesis of this book is that the supernatural hypothesis of God is testable, verifiable and falsifiable by the established methods of science.'[7]

But the apparent clarity is illusory, for there are subtle shifts between these three statements. He implies in turn that God should be detectable: (1) by scientific 'models'; (2) by scientific measurements, that is, by 'our senses and scientific instruments'; and (3) by scientific 'methods'. These are three quite different claims—relating respectively to models, measurements and methods—and by moving rapidly between them as he develops his argument, Dr Stenger (perhaps unwittingly) bamboozles the unwary reader. In less respectable circles it's called the three-card-trick, or 'Find the lady'.

He would no doubt protest that he is simply embracing all aspects of science in his analysis, but that would only be true if models, measurements and methods *all* excluded consideration of God. We would then arrive at the same conclusion as the National Academy of Sciences—namely, that science has nothing to say about God. However, just as in the three-card-trick one card is special, so (in Stenger's argument) the *methods* of science differ from its models and measurements. The methods of science, he asserts, allow God into its hallowed halls while its models and measurements exclude him.

This lets him have it both ways; God ought to be detectable by science because of its methods, but goes missing by virtue of its models and measurements. Far from God voluntarily seeking refuge in the rabbit hole of science, it is Stenger (following Dawkins) who tries to stuff God down the hole of scientific methodology. He then seals all other exits and conducts a thorough search of the burrow, and when he finds the deity is not in residence, he declares him non-existent. If Dr Stenger took the trouble to look over his shoulder, however, he might see the landowner (aka God) standing there, a twelve-bore shotgun under his arm, observing the rabbit hunt with much amusement and a trace of impatience.

Let's return to Stenger's three statements. The first, far from being evidence for the non-existence of God, simply says that scientists today choose not to invoke God when they build scientific models of the material universe. That's hardly surprising, because God is not a material entity subject to model building. A mathematical model of the solar system doesn't invoke God, yet Johannes Kepler (1571–1630), when he discovered the mathematical laws of planetary motion, is said to have cried out, 'O God, I am thinking your thoughts after you!' There is no symbol representing God in Kepler's equations but that didn't stop him ascribing *the laws themselves* to the divine mind.[8] Come to think of it, Kepler's laws contain no symbols for 'love' or 'hate' either, but that doesn't mean that love and hate are non-existent.

Stenger's second statement relates not to scientific *models* but to scientific *measurements* or data. It says that our physical senses, even when aided by scientific instruments, are unable to detect God—with the implication that if God is undetectable he is therefore non-existent. But why should our *physical* senses be able to detect God if, as Jesus declared, 'God is Spirit, and those who worship Him must worship in spirit and truth'?[9] Our five physical senses, no matter how much enhanced by scientific instrumentation, remain *physical*—adapted to explore material and physical objects and processes, not spiritual ones. To dismiss the existence of spiritual entities because they don't show up on our radar screens is like denying the existence of beauty because nothing answering to that description emerges from the chemical analysis of a cut diamond. The apostle Paul declares that 'The fruit of the Spirit is love, joy, peace, longsuffering, kindness, goodness, faithfulness, gentleness, self-control.'[10] These are abstract concepts and subjective experiences. We can discern their *effects* on human behaviour but the spiritual concepts *themselves* are accessible neither to our senses nor our scientific instruments. But they are undeniably real.

In contention (3) Dr Stenger moves the goalposts once again. Whereas claim (1) was about scientific *models*, and claim (2) about scientific *measurements*, claim (3) is all about scientific *methods*. And by 'methods' he doesn't mean using microscopes, telescopes and atom splitters but rather the *methodology* we discussed in the previous chapter, entailing observation, hypothesis and testing—leading to verification or falsification.

The distinction between the measurements (or data) of science and the methodology of science is important. Stenger berates the American National Academy of Sciences (no less) for stating that 'Science is ... limited to explaining the natural world through natural causes. Science can say nothing about the supernatural.'[11] Clearly, the NAS is talking here about the findings or data of science—pointing out that they relate only to the natural world. Stenger disagrees, claiming in (2) that scientific data should reveal God if he exists. But then for the rest of the book he shifts his ground to claim (3), namely, that the *methodology* of science can be applied to God.

Now, as we saw in chapter 4 when considering my missing mail, this methodology is by no means limited to science but is integral to our rational thought processes. My three undelivered-mail hypotheses were not 'scientific' hypotheses and my conclusions would hardly be admissible as scientific data—if only because a glitch with one morning's post is not statistically significant. But neither of these facts invalidates the hypotheses or renders their conclusions untrue.

Stenger's first fallacy now lies open to our gaze. He begins (quite correctly) by saying that the existence of God can be addressed using the hypothetic approach. He next labels this approach 'scientific' because it is commonly used by science—conveniently forgetting that it is also a methodology applicable to life in general. Thus by claiming that *every* hypothesis is 'scientific', he can assert that the hypothesis of God must be a *scientific* hypothesis. Finally, he concludes that God doesn't exist because he cannot be found among the scientific data gathered by microscopes, telescopes or atom splitters.

Let's go over that again. Stenger's chain of reasoning is as follows:

1. The hypothetic approach is applicable to God.

2. The hypothetic approach is integral to science.

3. *Therefore all hypotheses are scientific hypotheses.*

4. *Therefore the hypothesis of God is a scientific hypothesis.*

5. *Therefore the hypothesis of God can be tested by scientific experiments.*

6. The data gathered by scientific experiments do not reveal the existence of God.

7. *Therefore God does not exist.*

The fallacious statements are italicized. Later, I shall also look more closely at statement 6 in relation to the laws of nature, but for the moment four fallacies in one argument are enough to keep us going.

When a Christian believer (who may also happen to be a scientist) experiences the love of God 'shed abroad in [his] heart',[12] he doesn't dash off a scientific paper about it and submit it to the *Journal of Applied Physics* or the *Proceedings of the Royal Society*. His experience simply doesn't constitute 'scientific' data. But his scientifically trained mind may well go through the process of hypothetic reasoning—and conclude that God is real.

## Ferret fallacy 2—my opponents are ignorant

When can the construction of a 'straw man' be called a fallacy? Answer: when the constructor thinks the straw man is real. Otherwise he is guilty of falsehood rather than fallacy. Dr Stenger is atheism's Don Quixote, enthusiastically (and perhaps innocently) tilting at windmills and riding down straw men. Here are a few examples:

> The fossil record, the existence of transitional species, and the actual observation of evolution in the laboratory falsify the hypothesis of a God who created separate 'kinds' or species of life-forms at one time in history and left them unchanged since.[13]

Leaving aside the contentious issues of transitional species and exactly what kind of 'evolution' is observable in the laboratory, Stenger's straw man here is the claim that Christians believe that the created 'kinds' in the book of Genesis: (a) were species as defined today; and (b) have remained unchanged ever since. Even among the most fervent creationists, I know of no one who holds either of these views. In my own 1978 book *From nothing to nature*[14] I suggest, for example, that all canine species (wolf, dog, fox and so on) have probably descended from a single biblical 'kind'. I also point out that, in tracing all races of man back to an original pair, the Bible itself shows that great changes and diversification can occur within species over time. What creationists deny is not the occurrence of mutations and natural selection, nor their ability to generate change, but the absolute power of such mindless, haphazard processes to manufacture the teeming life of planet earth starting from some primeval soup or elementary spark of life.

However, when it comes to creating straw men, it is difficult to beat Dr Stenger's panoramic statement on page 48, which reads as follows:

> Before the age of science, religious belief was based on faith, cultural tradition, and a confidence in the revealed truth in the scriptures and teachings of holy men and women specially selected by God. As science began to erode these beliefs by showing that many of the traditional teachings, such as that of a flat earth at rest at the centre of a firmament

of stars and planets, were simply wrong, people began to look to science itself for evidence of a supreme being that did not depend on any assumption about the literal truth of the Bible or divine revelation.

This synopsis of the history of Western thought is commendably brief. It is also completely wrong. Firstly, religious belief has not undergone a transformation since the 'age of science' dawned; it is still based on faith, tradition and revelation, all of which retain a vigorous validity to this day. Secondly, science has proved remarkably ineffective in eroding 'these beliefs' for reasons already cited from Stephen J. Gould and the US Academy of Sciences. On the contrary, they remain robust elements of human civilization (why else has Stenger felt the need to write his book?). Thirdly, the only 'traditional teachings' that had a 'flat earth at the centre of a firmament of stars and planets' were those of ancient China—Western and Middle Eastern cosmologies have never combined these elements.

Fourthly, did religionists really believe in a flat Earth before the advent of the scientific age? Not since Aristotle presented evidence for a spherical Earth in 330 BC,[15] observing that southbound travellers see southern stars rising higher above the horizon.[16] He also pointed out that the shadow of Earth on the Moon is always circular, and that only a spherical Earth could cast a circular shadow at all lunar phases. In 240 BC, Eratosthenes even calculated the Earth's spherical circumference.[17] In his treatise *The reckoning of time*, the venerable Bede (*c.* 672–735) explained the varying duration of daylight in terms of 'the roundness of the Earth', and continues, 'for not without reason is it called "the orb of the world" on the pages of Holy Scripture and of ordinary literature. It is, in fact, set like a sphere in the middle of the whole universe.'[18] And anything Bede wrote was required reading for the priests of his day.

It is true that mediaeval scholars allegedly reverted to flat-Earth beliefs, but Jeffrey Russell (professor of history at University of California, Santa Barbara) argues in his book *Inventing the flat Earth:*

*Columbus and modern historians*, that the flat-Earth theory is little
more than a fable used to denigrate pre-modern European civilization.

Geocentricity is a different matter. As the quote from Bede indicates,
Dr Stenger is correct to say that the ancients believed in an Earth-
centred universe. But here's the fact that fells his house of cards—this
geocentric system was the product not of religious faith but of Greek
science! Anaximander (sixth century BC) taught that the Earth was
a cylinder situated at the centre of the universe. The Pythagoreans
disputed the centrality of the Earth, holding that it was in motion
around an unseen fire, but Plato (fifth century BC) believed that the
Earth was a sphere, stationary at the centre of the universe and orbited
by the stars and planets. Greek astronomy eventually settled for the
geocentric 'Ptolemaic system'—proposed by Claudius Ptolemaeus
during the second century AD and accepted by all and sundry until the
'Copernican revolution' in the sixteenth century, when geocentricity
was finally put to rest. But then, the headline: 'Sixteenth-century
science disproves second-century science!' doesn't read as well as:
'Sixteenth-century science disproves religious belief!'

On page 175 Stenger makes the following extraordinary statement:
'Throughout the Bible, the universe is referred to as a "firmament" that
sits above a flat, immovable earth.' He even gives us Bible references
in an attempt to prove his point, claiming to have consulted 'both
the King James and Revised Standard versions'. Perhaps he should
also have consulted a Hebrew lexicon, because he builds his case on
a total misunderstanding of two Old Testament Hebrew words. The
first word he mangles is 'firmament', which is a general term meaning
'expanse' (Hebrew *raqia*). Genesis 1 does not use the word to mean
'universe' but simply 'sky'—the expanse where the birds fly (v. 20) and
which separates earthbound waters (the waters 'under' the firmament)
from the clouds (the waters 'above' the firmament; vv. 6–8). When
Genesis 1 describes the sun and moon as 'lights in the firmament of
the heavens' it is merely using phenomenological language—these
bodies are *visible* in the sky (the same applies to the three other Bible
verses that use 'firmament' to locate the stars).

Since 1957 Sir Patrick Moore has presented his long-running BBC series on popular astronomy entitled *The sky at night*. No one has ever protested that the programme should be called *The universe at night*—or that Moore is teaching that birds and stars inhabit the same cosmic space. Most people have the common sense to recognize that phenomenological language is appropriate in a popular science programme and that the visible universe is what we *see* when we look up into the sky.

The second word that Stenger didn't check out properly is 'circle'. He states: 'Isaiah 40:22 says Earth is a "circle". Note that a circle is flat' (p.189, note 2). In fact the verse in question doesn't say this at all—it says God 'sits above the circle of the earth', which means that the Earth *has* a 'circle' not *is* a 'circle'. Stenger reminds us that a circle is flat but omits to mention that it also has a hole in the middle (be careful where you step!). I suspect that Isaiah would have seen the absurdity of calling the Earth a circle when (if he really believed in a flat Earth) he could have called it a disc.

However, although this demonstrates Stenger's careless way with words, his real problem is that the Hebrew word *chug*—translated 'circle' or 'circuit' in our English Bibles—can mean variously 'circle, arch, vault or compass'. Like our own vague word 'round', it can be used to indicate both two and three dimensional objects. Almost certainly, Isaiah meant 'vault' and was referring not to the Earth at all but to the heavens. If Dr Stenger had had the patience to read the whole verse he would have learnt that the God who sits above the 'vault' of the earth (that is, who is higher than the heavens) also 'stretches out the heavens like a curtain and spreads them out like a tent to dwell in'. You're reading poetical phenomenology, Victor, not early Greek science!

Reading Stenger, anyone ignorant of the Bible would conclude that it teaches a 'flat earth at rest at the centre of a firmament of stars and planets', but nothing could be further from the truth. Stenger sires an orphan child (by Greek science out of Chinese mythology), rejects it, and leaves the baby on the Bible's doorstep. In fact the Bible is entirely innocent of such teachings—nowhere does it discuss the shape of the Earth or claim that it lies at the centre of the universe. It frequently *describes* the universe as observed from Earth (don't we all?) but it does so without a hint of geocentric dogmatism.

## Ferret fallacy 3—simplicity begets complexity

Dr Stenger's chapter titled 'The illusion of design' is positively Dickensian—I have in mind *The old curiosity shop*. He spends the first half of the chapter dismissing in turn Paley's watch, creationism, Intelligent Design, irreducible complexity, information arguments and even the legal definition of science. How can he cover so much ground in thirteen pages? By making assertions rather than advancing arguments. He simply declares that all his opponents (and most of his friends) are wrong, while sending the reader on a paper-chase to other literature to find the argumentation on which his claims are based. Of course, no one can cover every base in a single book, but remember that this particular book claims to *prove* the non-existence of God. We are entitled therefore to *proofs* not assertions.

The nearest Stenger gets to a reasoned argument in these pages relates to Michael Behe's 'irreducible complexity' argument, according to which complex functional biological systems cannot evolve by natural selection. Behe invites us to think of a traditional mousetrap. For the trap to function as such, it must contain an irreducible selection of components—a base, a spring, a 'hammer', a restraining arm and a release catch. If any of these components is missing, or even unmatched to the others, the mousetrap will not work. Many biological systems are the same—in order to 'work' and benefit their owner, they require the presence and interaction of several indispensable components. Can such a system be built up, bit by bit, under the influence of natural selection? No, says Behe, because natural selection cannot operate on a biological system that performs no survival-related function—since in such a case there is nothing to 'select'. A mousetrap that has a base, hammer and release mechanism, but has not yet acquired a spring, is non-functional and of no value to the grain-store owner.

I once watched a stoat hunt down and kill a rabbit—just the kind of 'selective pressure' that should (according to Darwinian principles) cause the emergence of a tribe of super-rabbits that could outrun stoats. No problem with that. But natural selection is never going to endow cabbages with a turn of speed sufficient to outrun their rabbit predators, because cabbages can't move in the first place.

Natural selection can only work by preserving or 'selecting' fortuitous improvements in some *functional* aspect of an organism. For example, if random mutations help some rabbits run faster than others, these rabbits acquire a better chance of survival and thus enhance their opportunity to reproduce. The rapid-rabbit gene can thus spread through the colony and become dominant. By contrast, however, a random mutation that provided a cabbage with a flight reflex would not be subject to natural selection because this new trait would have no functional value in a static vegetable. Only *functioning* systems (that is, systems that affect survival and/or reproduction) can be modified by natural selection.

Behe's point is that complex biological systems cannot evolve step-by-step as taught by neo-Darwinianism, because *until* they have become functioning systems they serve no purpose and natural selection cannot operate upon them. In asking how a irreducibly complex system could arise, we're not asking how rapid-rabbits might evolve from also-rans but how a cabbage might grow legs.

Stenger's rebuttal of Behe's 'irreducible complexity' argument boils down to asserting that the component parts of the biological systems with which Behe illustrates his case may already be waiting in the wings—but serving unrelated purposes (Francis Collins offers the same explanation in *The language of God*[19]). If all the parts are already present in the organism, all they have to do is get together to create a novel functioning entity. Hey presto! Irreducibly complex systems—such as the incredible multi-component, chemically-fuelled 'outboard motor' that drives a bacterial flagellum—can arise spontaneously.

But this is no rebuttal at all! Dr Stenger has obviously never bought a piece of flat-packed furniture. I can assure him from personal experience that having all the components together in one place and moving them around randomly is most *unlikely* to assemble anything that works. Each flat-pack component is already specifically adapted to fit the 'grand design', but it still takes tools, instructions and intelligence to assemble the bits into a functioning entity. And remember, natural selection cannot help because it only works on an already functioning system.

Or consider this. Astrophysicist Sir Fred Hoyle famously likened the chances of life arising spontaneously (from *existing* molecular precursors) to the probability that a whirlwind in a junk yard could assemble a Boeing 747 aircraft.[20] His reasoning was by no means foolproof but let me at least borrow the analogy. Even if *all* the component parts are present but are busy fulfilling different roles, the probability that an irreducibly complex biological system will spontaneously self-assemble is comparable to the chance of a whirlwind in a Boeing *components warehouse* creating a 747. All the necessary component parts are *there*, but it takes something more intelligent than a tornado to put them together. And if such an assembly process didn't involve teleology (that is, purpose), why should it occur at all?

Dr Stenger asserts that the self-assembly of complex biological systems is common—and then ruins his case by citing as his *only* evidence the repetitive patterns often found in nature or generated by computers. It depends, of course, what you mean by 'complex' but I suspect that most people would agree that a repetitive pattern is something simple, not complex—because such patterns can be generated by applying simple rules. I can instruct my computer to repeat endlessly the first three letters of the alphabet, and it will happily generate on the screen a nice repetitive pattern—abcabcabcabc... Only the simplest instructions are required. But if I ask the computer to finish this chapter for me while I go for lunch, the task will be altogether too complex for it to handle. The essence of complexity doesn't lie in repetitive patterns but in the way a system *departs* from such patterns. Take another example. A simple electrical sine-wave is a repetitive up-and-down pattern that can be transmitted as a radio wave. But if I want that radio signal to act as a carrier for complex information—a song, for example—I must modulate or distort the sine-wave in a complex non-repetitive manner. That is, information can only be sent using the sine-wave by superimposing on its simplicity a complex series of dips and blips that encode the sound of music.

One final thought. Doesn't Dr Stenger's idea that simplicity begets complexity totally contradict Richard Dawkins' argument that God, having created an exceedingly complex universe, must be even more complex and thus highly improbable (see chapter 1)? According to Stenger's principle, a simple (and thus highly *probable*) God could create a complex world. But then, consistency never was atheism's strong point.

## Ferret fallacies galore

Although we are barely half way through Stenger's presentation, we need to leave it there for the present—otherwise this chapter would turn into the 'book in reply' that I said I wasn't writing. Many of Victor Stenger's remaining fallacies will be picked up anyway in subsequent chapters as we deal with the implications of belief in God.

# CHAPTER SIX ...

... in which, having left our atheists looking for God down a rabbit hole, we now get on with the serious business of defining what we mean by 'God'. We'll consider some common misconceptions about God—like the 'God of the gaps'; the complementary God; the 'don't blame me' God (who takes responsibility for nothing); the absent-landlord God; and the lowest-common-denominator God.

Having clarified who God isn't, we are free to ask who he is. Advancing the 'hypothesis' of God allows me to define God any way I like without pre-empting discussion about his nature. So I can (and do) define God as 'the God of the Bible'—without fear of being accused of assuming what I want to prove. Any proof will come as, in the remainder of this book, we compare what my hypothesis predicts with reality.

We'll discover that my definition necessarily introduces the concepts of eternity, creation and revelation. As the book unfolds, we shall then test the explanatory power of the hypothesis by checking out its implications and seeing how well they agree with the evidence from science, the humanities and personal experience.

## New words?

*Epistemological*: Relating to knowledge or thought.

*Predicated*: Affirmed on the basis of some stated grounds.

*Hubristic*: Contemptuous; having overweening pride.

# 6. Defining God

The first person he met was Rabbit. 'Hallo, Rabbit,' he said, 'is that you?' 'Let's pretend it isn't,' said Rabbit, 'and see what happens.'
A. A. Milne, *Winnie the Pooh*[I]
chapter 8 ... in which Christopher Robin
leads an 'expotition' to the North Pole

In chapter 5 we left our atheists looking down a rabbit hole in search of God, perhaps not realizing that all you are likely to find down a rabbit hole is a rabbit. Or more likely (rabbits being rather good at multiplication) not just one rabbit but all Rabbit's friends and relations—a veritable pantheon of *Oryctolagus cuniculus*. As Rabbit himself admits (*loc. cit.*), 'I didn't ask them ... They just came. They always do.'

So also, if we insist on looking for God in all the wrong places we are likely to find not one but a multitude of candidates for that name; we don't have to ask them, they just appear—they always do. And this, of course, creates a problem. In chapter 1 we saw that questions like 'How long is a piece of string?' are nonsense questions unless you define what you are talking about—for example, by changing the question to, 'How long is *this* piece of string?' Similarly, 'Who made

God?' remains nonsensical until we give a definitive answer to another question, namely, 'Who *is* God?' Only when this particular identity crisis has been resolved can we formulate a sensible hypothesis of God and expect to make progress. So in this chapter I am going to define what I mean by God. Remember that by employing the hypothetic approach I do not have to be right in adopting one definition rather than another. The validity of my concept of God will depend not on my initial assumptions but on how well my hypothesis fits human experience. So please don't accuse me of circular reasoning or of pre-empting the debate when I adopt a definition of God that conforms to my Christian beliefs.

But before I offer my own definition of God, I need to consider at least some of the many and varied caricatures of God that are on offer today. This is necessary if only because the confusion on the subject is almost total, even among many who profess to be theists. I don't intend to review the beliefs of the world's religions—you'll need to consult a good book on comparative religion if you want that. Rather, I shall review those definitions of God that are most germane to our enquiry, while at the same time illustrating some of the pitfalls that await the unwary in a religious supermarket near you!

### The God of the gaps

Let's take a ride on London's subway system. As our train pulls alongside the platform, a sonorous but disembodied voice intones, 'Mind the gap'. For some reason that I have not bothered to research too deeply, London's underground trains don't always fit the platforms—often leaving a gap into which an unwary passenger might fall with dire consequences (it has been known to happen). Health and safety regulations require that we be warned about this possibility. I'm sure that's sensible, although as the warning reverberates around the station you do sometimes get the feeling that 'big brother is watching you'.

But there are other gaps—involving epistemological platforms and trains of thought—against which theists like myself are continually warned by our philosophical big brothers. Whenever we suggest that

God might just possibly be responsible for something, we are sternly admonished to beware 'the God of the gaps'. In fact, we are accused of appealing to this strange deity any time we dare to attribute to God *anything* that happens or exists in the real physical world. The argument goes like this.

During the aeons before science (let's call this period BS) human beings were incredibly primitive and ignorant. They understood very little about the world in which they lived and certainly could give no logical explanations for the phenomena they observed or the experiences they underwent. However (giving credit where credit is due) they found a simple and ingenious solution—they invented one or more invisible deities and blamed him (or them) for anything they couldn't understand. Thus 'God' comfortably filled the gaps in their knowledge—though this was not too obvious at first because, of course, they were so stupid that their 'knowledge' consisted entirely of gaps.

With the dawn of modern science (*anno scientiae* or AS) from the seventeenth century onwards, all this began to change. The stars and planets ceased to be chess pieces manipulated by a capricious deity and were found to obey simple mathematical laws. All kinds of other natural phenomena were similarly explained as they yielded to scientific enquiry. The final mystery—that of life itself and the nature of man—eventually evaporated like mist before the rising sun of Darwinian evolution. One by one, the gaps in human knowledge that once could only be filled by invoking God have been filled instead by science, and God has been declared redundant. This, at least, is the narrative we are urged to accept as universal truth today. Predicated as it is upon man's universal ignorance prior to AS, this scenario puts me in mind of Mark Twain's wry comment about his dad: 'When I was a boy of 14, my father was so ignorant I could hardly stand to have the old man around. But when I got to be 21, I was astonished at how much he had learned in seven years.'[2]

However, evidently, science hasn't yet finished the gap-elimination job. Even the most hubristic atheism accepts that some gaps still remain in our knowledge, into which religious souls will go on squeezing God. Little things, like what caused the universe; how life arose; what evolutionist Theodosius Dobzhansky called 'the biological uniqueness of man'; and the whole question of human morality and the meaning of life. But of course, these are mere details and materialistic science will eventually come up with answers to all these questions leaving no gaps for God to fill. Like Lewis Carroll's Cheshire cat, he will vanish away, leaving only the smile (or frown?) behind.

But God is not a God of the gaps, nor has he ever been. This view of the deity is a parody on religion that has never been embraced by thinking man. As we saw in the previous chapter, when Johannes Kepler discovered the mathematical laws of planetary motion he didn't say, 'Well, that's one less thing to explain by appeal to God.' Instead, he claimed that the very laws he had discovered were the 'thoughts' of a transcendent Deity—a conclusion that stood in the best traditions of a Judaeo-Christian belief system that had already existed for four millennia. As St Paul declares: 'God, who made the world and everything in it, since He is Lord of heaven and earth, does not dwell in temples made with hands. Nor is He worshipped with men's hands, as though He needed anything, since He gives to all life, breath, and all things ... for in Him we live and move and have our being.'[3] God certainly doesn't dwell in temples made of gaps.

### The complementary God

Not, notice, the *complimentary* God as in free tickets or favourable book reviews, but *complementary* with an 'e' as in complementary colours. Many people believe in this false god. Drs Stenger and Dawkins don't and, oddly, neither do I. The 'complementarians' argue that science and religion are two totally distinct and self-contained realms or 'magisteriums' that must not be allowed to overlap. They provide separate and complementary descriptions of reality that are equally true but cannot interact.

The idea can be illustrated by a painting—let's say Frans Hals' 'The laughing cavalier' in the Wallace Collection in London. A scientific description of the painting could be given by specifying in scientific terms the chemical composition, colour, transparency, reflectivity and texture of every point on the surface (and through the depth) of the paint layers—together with similar data relating to the canvas. Such a *scientific* description would be complete, leaving nothing unspecified and, in theory at least, enabling an exact clone of the painting to be produced even by someone who had never seen the original. On the other hand, an equally self-contained *aesthetic* account could be given which would describe the painting in terms of its subject matter, pictorial composition, artistic technique, brush strokes, perceived colours, aesthetic impact, and the purpose and 'message' of the artist (what exactly is the cavalier laughing about?).

Both kinds of description are complete. Either, in principle, could be used to reproduce the painting in every detail so that neither description 'needs' or relies upon the other. Yet both descriptions are valid and 'true'. In the same way, argue the complementarians, the world around us (and even our experience of it) can be described either scientifically or theologically. Both descriptions are valid and 'true'—they are parallel universes that simply do not interact in any way.

This is essentially the position adopted by Stephen J. Gould and by the US National Academy of Sciences whom I cited with approval in chapters 4 and 5 because they agree that science, being the study of the material world, cannot pontificate about the existence or nature of God. So why should I now oppose their views? Because they *also* believe that religion and God can tell us nothing about the nature of science—and with that I disagree profoundly. They are right to limit science to the physical and material realm but wrong to exclude God from that realm.

Less obviously, complementarity is also the position adopted by Christian authors like Francis Collins (in *The language of God*) and Kenneth R. Miller (in his *Only a Theory: Evolution and the Battle for America's Soul*). These writers embrace Darwinian evolution as the only 'true' explanation of life on earth and reject any suggestion of 'intelligent design' or of 'special' (that is, miraculous) creation by God. Working within a broadly Christian paradigm, they accept that God did create everything but argue that in doing so he used only natural (scientific) processes, including Darwinian evolution, to accomplish his ends. Pure complementarity is actually inconsistent with theism because it imprisons its 'God' within the natural laws that he has ordained. It is the logical bedfellow of deism not theism.

Although complementarity has been around for a long time, Francis Collins' book *The language of God*[4] is an outstanding example of the genre. Hailed (and advertised) as presenting 'evidence for belief', and highly praised by such worthies as Desmond Tutu and Alister McGrath, the book is little more than an exposition of standard neo-Darwinian evolutionary theory—upon which the author superimposes his personal faith that God has created (and presumably still creates) simply by letting evolution run its course. Even the title of the book is misleading. 'The language of God' is, of course, the genetic code, the 'language' in which the information that constitutes life is 'written' or encoded on molecules of DNA. Francis Collins knows a thing or two about this, having led the US government's human genome project which defined for the first time the complete genetic information for a human being.

Not unreasonably, the reader looks expectantly, chapter after chapter, for Collins to justify his claim that the genetic code is indeed a language devised by God. But disappointment awaits. Collins says absolutely nothing about the origin of the genetic code except to warn us on pages 92–93 that while 'no serious scientist would currently claim that a naturalistic explanation for the origin of life is at hand ... that is true today, and it may not be true tomorrow'. Even this admission of temporary ignorance is airbrushed out on page 200 where he states: 'While the *precise* mechanism of the origin of life on earth remains unknown, once life arose the process of evolution and natural selection permitted the development of biological diversity and complexity over very long periods of time. Once evolution got under way, no special supernatural intervention was required' (emphasis added).

*Precise* mechanism? We haven't the foggiest idea of *any* naturalistic mechanism for the origin of the 'language of God'.

Oddly he continues: 'But humans are also unique in ways that defy evolutionary explanation and point to our spiritual nature ...' Inconsistent? Yes, but that's complementarity for you. As Dr McCoy might say, 'It is God, Jim, but not as we know him.'

## The hand-wringing God

Religious leaders often promote this third false God, especially when called upon to comment on natural disasters in which innocent people perish. Having expressed sympathy for the victims, their next priority is to exonerate God from all involvement. 'Don't blame God,' they admonish us, 'He had nothing to do with it and is just as upset about it as we are.' Even in some conservative Christian circles there is a growing affection for the idea of the 'openness of God'—the view that God has no more prior warning of such events than we do and can do nothing to stop them. The only difference between God and man is that God reacts better to these things than we do (after all, he's had more experience). Clearly, the hand-wringing God is, like ourselves, a victim of circumstance and needs our protection from calumny on such occasions.

Somehow, that doesn't sound like the God described by Isaiah—you know, the one who 'declar[es] the end from the beginning, and from ancient times things that are not yet done, saying, "My counsel shall stand, and I will do all My pleasure"'.[5] Nor is he the Lord of heaven and earth who, according to St Paul, 'works all things according to the counsel of His will'.[6]

## The absent-landlord God

A useful alternative to the hand-wringing God is the God of deism. According to deism, God is the prime mover who created the universe and set it in motion but then withdrew and no longer takes the slightest interest in his handiwork—he is the archetypical absent landlord. Deism, of course, stands in stark contrast to theism, according to which God is not only the creator but also the sustainer of the universe and is closely involved with everything that goes on in it. Like the hand-wringing God, the absent-landlord God can be excused from responsibility for the bad things that happen on earth simply because they are no longer his problem. If you buy an expensive wrist-watch, the designers and manufacturer take some responsibility if it subsequently malfunctions; you usually get at least a twelve-month warranty. But the God of deism, having fashioned the universe and wound up the spring, no longer answers our calls. He never offered any guarantees in the first place and all complaints bounce back as 'undeliverable'.

The World Union of Deists (slogans: 'God gave us reason not religion' and 'In nature's God we trust') define their beliefs as follows: 'Deism is the recognition of a universal creative force greater than that demonstrated by mankind, supported by personal observation of laws and designs in nature and the universe, perpetuated and validated by the innate ability of human reason coupled with the rejection of claims made by individuals and organised religions of having received special divine revelation.'[7]

Mainstream deism arose during the Age of Enlightenment in the seventeenth to eighteenth centuries, especially in the UK, USA and France. It flourished for a time among disaffected Christians who were unhappy with orthodox beliefs about such things as the Trinity, miracles and the inerrancy of Scripture, but who did nevertheless still believe in one God. Although there were other luminaries in the history of deism, the movement was popularized by British radical and American revolutionary Thomas Paine (1737–1809). His book *The age of reason* quite rightly attacked corruption in organized religion and the efforts of the Christian Church to acquire political power, but it went much further. Elevating reason above revelation, Paine rejected miracles and viewed the Bible as ordinary literature lacking divine inspiration—arguing instead for natural religion and a creator who could be known through reason alone.

Deism's rejection of 'revealed religion' allows deists to explain the conflicting claims of such religions in terms of their all being false—a handy generalization which fails to consider that in real life counterfeit objects only proliferate when there is some valuable genuine article to imitate. It also avoids the embarrassment of individuals being personally answerable to God (man's relationship with God is said to be 'transpersonal') and, like atheism, practises a morality based on reason.

Overall, the predominant theme in deism is reliance on human reason rather than on divine revelation or the intrinsic mind or nature of God (which, says deism, is inaccessible to man). Reason alone, therefore, is the final court of appeal and thus becomes the real 'God' that deism worships. In that respect, and in spite of vigorous denials, deism is a soul-mate of atheism. The only difference is that 'deism teaches that the creator is knowable and discoverable through the creation itself'.[8] Strangely, deism appears to teach that while God is 'discoverable' by reason (you can work out that he exists), he is 'knowable' experientially only through mystical 'spirituality'—not by any *rational* communion between God and man. Confused? Me too.

### The LCD God

I know that some people worship their TV sets, but by LCD I don't mean 'liquid crystal display' but 'lowest common denominator'. Here is a God who puts an end to all disputes, at least among those who believe that he exists. Come to think about it, that is about all they do believe, for this is a malleable deity who can be beaten into any shape you please. He is at one and the same time the God of all religions, of Buddhists, Moslems and Sikhs, of Jews and Christians, of Unitarians and Trinitarians, of theists, deists, pantheists and animists (oops! I almost added 'atheists'). He is indeed 'all things to all men', though that wasn't what St Paul meant when he coined the phrase.

The idea is deceptively simple. As long as there is only one genuine God, all who worship him must, by definition, worship the same God. Different civilizations, different eras, different races and different cultures have all formulated their own individualistic perceptions of this singular God, but these cultural accretions have no real substance and are unimportant. In fact, they are a cause to celebrate rather than despair, because each religious tradition contributes its own special insights, adding unique threads to the one grand religious tapestry and enriching both human culture and life. Never mind that the different traditions are profoundly contradictory as soon as you get down to the detail. The devil is in the detail so it's best not to join him there. Stick to generalities—be good; God loves you; he's not totally in control but he's doing his best. It's OK to be optimistic, pessimistic, paternalistic, fatalistic or whatever else you fancy; there is, after all, a better life to come (isn't there?). That's about all the theology you need if you worship the LCD God. And since one size fits all, there's no need to get out the assorted tape measures of theology, historicity, rationality or self-consistency. We live in a post-modern world—just believe what you like and be happy.

Clearly, Isaiah is so 'yesterday' when he records God's words: "'To whom then will you liken Me, or to whom shall I be equal?" says the Holy One. Lift up your eyes on high, and see who has created these things ... by the greatness of His might and the strength of His power.'[9] And again, 'Look to Me, and be saved, all you ends of the earth! For I am God, and there is no other.'[10]

## The Bible's God

Isaiah's God is, of course, the God of the Bible—and that's the definition of God I intend to adopt throughout the remainder of this book. Our hypothesis, then, is that the God of the Bible exists, and I shall seek to demonstrate that this hypothesis explains human observation and experience far better than atheism or even science can ever do—and remember that I write as a scientist as well as a Christian.

The Bible's opening words are these: 'In the beginning God created the heavens and the earth.'[11] I said at the end of chapter 4 that this statement constitutes the hypothesis of God because it is the foundational assumption on which is built all that follows in the Bible (and in the Christian faith). Notice that the Bible doesn't set out to prove the existence of God. The nearest it gets to that is Psalm 14:1: 'The fool has said in his heart, "There is no God."' Rather, the Judaeo-Christian Scriptures adopt what I have called the 'hypothetic' approach, in which the existence of God is advanced as a premise from which conclusions are then drawn. It is, I think, a misreading of Genesis 1 to turn the statement around and produce from it (like a rabbit out of a hat) a version of the cosmological argument—namely, that since the universe exists, someone called God must have caused it to exist. On the contrary, Genesis 1 *begins* with God, who is said to have created not only the 'heavens and the earth' but also, as the chapter unfolds, their constituent parts. God is always the subject of the sentence while the things created are always its predicate.

Having correctly juxtaposed horse and cart, we can see that Genesis 1:1 is making three distinct claims. Firstly, it asserts that there existed 'in the beginning' an entity (God) who *of necessity* stood outside the universe and was prior to it. Secondly, this God is further characterized as being *capable* of creating the universe *ex nihilo*—out of nothing. Thirdly, we are told that he did in fact create the universe in just this manner. We shall look more closely at these three claims in chapter 7.

**Progressive revelation**

Obviously, the statement of Genesis 1:1 cannot be verified by human observation or thought. In spite of persuasive scientific evidence pointing to a genuine starting point for the universe—the famous 'big bang'—science is incapable of telling us why it happened or who or what 'happened' it. Nor can philosophical 'cosmological arguments' prove by what agency the universe was formed; at best they can argue in favour of a 'first cause'. The Genesis statement goes much further than to assert that the universe was caused by an uncaused prior cause (because otherwise 'it's turtles all the way down'). So where does this extra information come from? It comes to us by *revelation* or not at all. Put simply, because we weren't there, God who *was* there must tell us about these things. Otherwise we could never know. And if there is no God, we *shall* never know. Of course, some will deny the very possibility of revelation, but don't forget that this is my hypothesis not theirs.

The concept of revelation is fundamental to the Bible's definition of God—which is why it comes under such withering fire from atheists. Sadly, Christian apologists often duck their heads below the parapet when this happens, fearing that to appeal to revelation is somehow sub-intellectual and exposes them to the charge of superstition. Accordingly, they fall back upon philosophical, scientific and pragmatic arguments, often falling *over* in the process. But by adopting the hypothetic approach we have no need to apologize for the obvious—that revelation is integral to the Bible's teaching about both God and creation. If we hypothesize the Bible's God we take on board everything implied in Genesis 1:1—the prior existence of God; the transcendence of God (he is outside the material and temporal universe); the ability of God to create the universe; the fact that he did create it; and the realization that we can only know these things by revelation from God himself.

Let me reiterate; I am not here assuming what I set out to prove. The hypothesis is not itself proof of anything. The proof will lie in the consistency of what is hypothesized with human experience and observation.

Returning to the subject of revelation, the Bible presents us with what theologians call 'progressive revelation'—a gradual unveiling of the nature and purposes of God. The first chapter of Genesis contains much more truth than we often realize but it doesn't contain the whole truth about God and the cosmos. For example, it tells us that God created man but only later do we learn that, in a spiritual sense, he both talks and 'walks' with men.[12] In the course of time, the great flood of Noah's day demonstrated that God was ready to judge all mankind for its wickedness. Centuries later, as biblical history unfolds, God reveals himself to Moses as the self-existent one: 'I am that I am'[13]—and as the source and giver of moral law.[14] At the same time, through the types and shadows afforded by Old Testament religion, he revealed himself as the one who forgives sin, but only through the instrumentality of atonement. Finally, in the coming of the promised Messiah, Jesus Christ, God revealed the fulness of his purpose to redeem sinners from judgement and reconcile them to himself.

The opening words of the New Testament book of Hebrews summarize the concept of progressive revelation with both verbal and conceptual felicity: 'God, who at various times and in various ways spoke in time past to the fathers by the prophets, has in these last days spoken to us by His Son, whom He has appointed heir of all things, through whom also He made the worlds; who being the brightness of His glory and the express image of His person, and upholding all things by the word of His power, when He had by Himself purged our sins, sat down at the right hand of the Majesty on high.'[15]

It follows, therefore, that the Bible's concept of God cannot be boiled down to a dictionary definition or creedal formula. In biblical terms, the definition of God is dynamic, evolutionary (unfolding progressively) and in many ways revolutionary. My task in the remainder of this book is to work through the implications of this definition—this hypothesis—against the background of opposing and alternative opinions and, most important of all, of pragmatic human experience.

# CHAPTER SEVEN ...

... in which we turn to serious business and begin to consider things that science, *by its very nature,* will never be able to explain. Let's start with the subject of cosmic creation and explore in layman-friendly terms such topics as Einstein's relativity theories, the expanding universe and the 'background' cosmic radiation. We shall find that all these things imply that the material universe has not always existed, as cosmologists once thought, but that it had a real beginning.

This beginning can be modelled in various ways such as a 'hot big bang' singularity, but all such models point to an origin in which space, time, matter and energy came into being *ex nihilo* (out of nothing)—just as the biblical hypothesis of God predicts.

Current scientific cosmologies thus imply the existence of a non-physical realm (we'll call it 'eternity') that transcends space and time and *within* which the physical universe was created. We shall discover that the hypothesis of God correctly predicts what science is only now beginning to reveal about this non-physical realm.

## New words?

*Boojum and Snark*: Mythical creatures that feature in Lewis Carroll's nonsense poem, *The hunting of the Snark*.

*Cosmology*: the study of the cosmos or universe as a whole.

*Phenomenological*: relating to the way things appear.

*Singularity*: an event or situation in which one or more physical quantities (like temperature or density) become infinite in value.

# 7. Starting with a bang

> The best data we have concerning the big bang are exactly what I
> would have predicted, had I nothing to go on but the five books of
> Moses, the Psalms, the Bible as a whole.
>
> Arno Penzias[1] (astrophysicist and Nobel laureate)
> in *The New York Times*, 12 March 1978

I f you do a Yahoo internet search on 'Huxley Memorial Debate'
(don't forget the inverted commas) you should get around 500
citations[2]—which is a bit surprising considering that the debate
took place over twenty years ago and is now history (in whatever
sense you choose!). The debate was held at the Oxford Union on 14
February 1986 on the motion that 'The doctrine of creation is more
valid than the theory of evolution.' Under the OU's arcane rules, I
spoke first as seconder of the motion, followed by Richard Dawkins
who seconded for the opposition. The proposer, Dr A. E. Wilder-
Smith, followed and the opposer, Prof. John Maynard-Smith, spoke
last. The debate was then thrown open to the floor and the motion was
eventually defeated. But we 'creationists' lost by a surprisingly small
margin considering that many students came to the debate seeking
entertainment at our expense. Unfortunately, the relevant OU minute
book was subsequently and mysteriously lost or stolen, and no written

record remains of the actual result. However, the whole debate was recorded on tape (CD recordings are still available; check the internet) and the result was read out none too clearly by the moderator as 198 against the motion and either 115 or 150 in favour. The final vote was taken very late, long after I had retired to bed, so I can't confirm the matter one way or another. However, to avoid arguments I am content to settle for 115, meaning that significantly more than one third of those voting were persuaded by the case for creation.

My own speech centred on the thesis that, *by their very nature*, certain things cannot be explained by purely material causes. If we want to explain such things, I argued, we must look beyond and behind science to God, and this applies not only to the physical world but even more strongly to the human spirit and human experience. The four scientifically inexplicable things I raised were: (a) the origin of the universe; (b) the origin of the laws of nature; (c) the origin of life; and (d) the origin of mind and thought. As recently as 2007 Richard Dawkins on his web site accused me of 'duplicity' at the debate because, instead of presenting the arguments he had expected, I set out my stall on this higher philosophical ground. I think it rather put him off his stroke—though at the time, I must say, he was quite nice about it all (which may surprise those familiar with his more recent utterances). At various stages in the chapters that follow we are going to revisit my four points, beginning with the origin of the universe itself.

If the God of the Bible does indeed exist, the first consequence we would expect is that the ultimate origin of material things will never be explicable in material terms. In chapters 2 and 3 I fed you with the *seeming* impossibilities of modern physics, but we must now start looking at some things that really are impossible to explain without invoking non-scientific causes.

Of course, atheists (and even some theists) will immediately cry foul, declaring that just because scientific explanations are not currently available it doesn't mean they never will be. Science is progressive and new discoveries are being made all the time, so that what seems scientifically impossible today may be scientifically explicable tomorrow. I recognize the force of this argument but intend to stand my ground. The claim that, given time, science will explain everything is simply the atheist's version of the God of the gaps. The gaps in our knowledge can be plugged, they say, by future (but as yet unknown) scientific advances. Thus the 'God of the gaps' is simply replaced by the 'future science of the gaps'—same gaps, different deity. It's what philosopher of science Karl Popper called 'promissory materialism'.[3],[4]

## Credentials of a creator

As I pointed out in chapter 6, the Bible consistently identifies God as the one who 'created the heavens and the earth'. This identification runs like a refrain through both the Old and New Testaments. Perhaps the best known example is St Paul's speech to the Epicurean and Stoic philosophers on Mars Hill (the Areopagus) in Athens, recorded for us in Acts 17:22–31. It warrants repetition in full:

> 'Men of Athens, I perceive that in all things you are very religious; for as I was passing through and considering the objects of your worship, I even found an altar with this inscription: "to the unknown God". Therefore, the One whom you worship without knowing, Him I proclaim to you: God, who made the world and everything in it, since He is Lord of heaven and earth, does not dwell in temples made with hands. Nor is He worshipped with men's hands, as though He needed anything, since He gives to all life, breath, and all things. And He has made from one blood every nation of men to dwell on all the face of the earth, and has determined their pre-appointed times and the boundaries of their dwellings, so that they should seek the Lord, in the hope that they might grope for Him and find Him—though He is not far from each one of us; for in Him we live and move and have our being, as also some of your own poets have said, "For we are also His offspring." Therefore, since we are the offspring of God, we ought not to think that the Divine Nature is like gold or silver or stone, something shaped by art and man's devising. Truly, these times of ignorance God overlooked, but now commands all men everywhere to repent, because He has appointed a day on which He will judge the world in righteousness

by the Man whom He has ordained. He has given assurance of this to all by raising Him from the dead.'

Clearly, there is much more here than we need in discussing the origin of the universe but we shall have cause to return to Paul's statement later in the book, so it does no harm to put the whole thing in context here. The claim of immediate interest is, of course, that 'God ... made the world and everything in it ... [and] is Lord of heaven and earth'.

It might seem unkind to compare Paul's trenchant theology of two thousand years ago with the waffle of today's atheists, but I'll do it just the same. Victor Stenger's alternative credo runs as follows: 'In short, the natural state of affairs is something [by which he means the universe] rather than nothing. An empty universe requires supernatural intervention—not a full one. Only by the constant action of an agent outside the universe, such as God, could a state of nothingness be maintained. The fact that we have something is just what we would expect if there is no God.'[5] This is philosophical (not to mention scientific) candyfloss—in terms of substance, Paul wins hands down. But quite apart from that, Dr Stenger fails to recognize the inanity of his 'scientific' reasoning.

He begins by utterly confusing the pre-creation 'nothing' that lies *outside* of space-time with the 'nothing' of a vacuum *within* space-time. Next, without making it clear which 'nothing' he is talking about, he claims that 'the transition from nothing to something is a natural one, not requiring any agent'.[6] He then argues that 'nothing' would be evidence for God's existence but the existence of 'something' requires the non-existence of God. His implied (but unavoidable) conclusion is that when 'nothing' became 'something', God—who until then had striven manfully to maintain 'the state of nothingness'—somehow ceased to exist, having become surplus to requirements. Like the ill-fated baker in Lewis Carroll's *The hunting of the Snark*, Victor Stenger's God 'softly and suddenly vanished away' at the very moment of triumphant creation.

In the midst of the word he was trying to say,
In the midst of his laughter and glee,
He had softly and suddenly vanished away—
For the Snark *was* a Boojum, you see.[7]

## There was a beginning

As we saw in chapter 6, the biblical hypothesis of God predicts that
the universe did indeed have a beginning, by which I mean: (1) that it is
not eternally old; and (2) that before its beginning *nothing* of a material
nature existed—neither matter nor energy, neither space nor time. To
put it another way, we are talking about *ex nihilo* creation—creation
out of nothing—a real beginning rather than something happening in
or to some prior physical order. Over the last 100 years, cosmologists
have reluctantly come to terms with the fact that this prediction is
strikingly borne out by their observations and cosmological models.
For some, like Arno Penzias cited at the head of this chapter, this
came as no surprise. But for many others it has become a source of
huge discomfort.

The reason is not hard to find. Stephen Hawking puts it thus: 'So
long as the universe had a beginning, we could suppose it had a creator.
But if the universe is really completely self-contained, having no
boundary or edge, it would have neither beginning nor end; it would
simply be. What place then for a creator?'[8] This quote, triumphantly
reproduced in a variety of atheistic writings, comes at the end of chapter
8 of *A brief history of time* and suggests superficially that Hawking has
finally locked God out of the universe. But not so fast! Let's remember
that the *concluding* chapter of Hawking's book ends rather differently
with the following paragraph:

'However, if we do discover a complete theory, it should in time be
understandable in broad principle by everyone, not just a few scientists.
Then we shall all, philosophers, scientists and just ordinary people, be
able to take part in the discussion of the question of why it is that we
and the universe exist. If we find the answer to that, it would be the

ultimate triumph of human reason—for then we would know the mind of God.'[9]

I remember hearing astrophysicist Fred Hoyle speak at a debate on creation at University College, London, when I was a student there in 1952. At that time he and others (specifically, Hermann Bondi and Thomas Gold) were exciting much interest in cosmological circles by proposing a 'steady state' theory of the universe involving 'continuous creation'. This theory—which suggested that the universe remains the same for all time—was an extension of the accepted 'cosmological principle', namely, that the universe looks roughly the same from every point within it. To explain how this could happen in an *expanding* universe, Bondi, Gold and Hoyle suggested in 1946 that matter was being created continually,[10] so that its average density throughout the universe remained the same in spite of the expansion. To achieve the required balance, matter would have to be created at the rate of about one atom of hydrogen for every litre of space every billion years—not something the casual observer is likely to notice.

Hoyle and his colleagues were motivated at least in part by a reluctance to accept that the universe had a beginning. For entirely philosophical reasons, they were allergic to the idea of a 'big bang' origin. In fact, when Fred Hoyle coined the term 'big bang' he intended it as a term of derision. Eventually, the force of evidence persuaded him to abandon 'continuous creation' but he was never entirely happy with the idea that the universe actually *began*.

So let's take a look at this idea that no one really wanted to know about—the big bang theory of the origin of the universe, also known as the 'standard model' of cosmology. Having done so, we shall then return in the next chapter to the strenuous attempts that are still being made by theoreticians to get around its theological implications.

## Anyone for tennis?

It is a striking fact that even at the start of the twentieth century the book of Genesis was something of a lone voice in proposing that the universe *did* have a beginning. Although the heavens had always displayed frenetic activity in terms of *local* celestial motions (the sun, moon, planets, comets, asteroids and meteorites or 'shooting starts') the more distant 'fixed stars' didn't seem to move at all. Scientists generally believed that, taken as a whole, the universe was static and unchanging. This did not entirely rule out a beginning of some kind but it certainly didn't lend any support to the idea. Indeed, the prevailing belief in an unchanging cosmos was dramatically demonstrated by Einstein himself when he produced his theory of general relativity in 1915. Much to his dismay, he found that his equations were incompatible with a static universe. Picture it like this. When a tennis player throws the ball into the air in the process of serving, the ball rises, stops momentarily at its highest point, and then begins to fall. It is stationary for a split second at the top of its trajectory but this is an unstable state—it can't last. Stability requires that the ball is either rising or falling.

In a similar way, the equations of general relativity said that the universe could be either expanding or shrinking but it could not be static. But instead of accepting this, Einstein's belief in a static universe was such that he added to his equations a fudge factor which he called the 'cosmological constant' and which had the effect of balancing the gravitational attraction that would otherwise cause the universe to collapse. When, later, it was found that the universe actually was expanding, Einstein discarded the cosmological constant, describing its inclusion as his 'biggest blunder'. Ironically, cosmologists have since fished it out of the rubbish bin, dusted it down and put it back on the mantelpiece. There are now reasons to believe that the cosmological constant could play a significant role in cosmology after all, but that's another story.

### The expanding universe

In one sense, as we have seen, the idea of an expanding universe began with Einstein's general relativity theory in 1915 but the elephant in the room was deliberately ignored until Aleksandr Friedmann in 1922 and Georges Lemaître in 1927 independently found solutions to Einstein's equations that described *evolutionary* as opposed to static models of the universe. This implied a beginning which could be represented mathematically as a 'singularity' in Einstein's equations. (A singularity is a point where some physical quantity becomes infinite—in this case the density and temperature of the universe, implying a 'hot big bang' beginning.) Much later, George Gamow, Ralph Alpher and Robert Herman developed the big bang theory of the early universe in a paper titled 'The origin of chemical elements' published in the *Physical Review* on 1 April 1948. In spite of the date it was no 'April fool' spoof and turned out to be one of the most celebrated scientific papers ever.

Even before Friedmann and Lemaître published their ideas, the foundations were being laid for a spectacular *experimental* demonstration of cosmic expansion. During 1908–1912 Henrietta Leavitt, one of America's first women astronomers, found that within a given stellar 'cloud', certain stars (called cepheid variables) fluctuated periodically in brightness in a rather special way—those with greater intrinsic luminosity (light output) also had longer periodicities. The relationship was so precise that the periodicity could be used as a measure of the intrinsic luminosity.

Now, for a given *intrinsic* luminosity, the *apparent* luminosity or brightness of a star depends on its distance from us, just as a distant car headlight looks dimmer than one close up. So the distance to a cepheid variable star could be measured by comparing its true luminosity, obtained from its periodicity, with its apparent luminosity as recorded on a photographic plate. This, of course, gave only a relative distance—a calibration was needed to find the actual distance. Such a calibration was provided by Ejnar Hertzsprung who used a method called parallax (a form of triangulation applicable only to nearby stars) to measure the distance of several cepheids in our own galaxy. Using this calibration, the distance to any cepheid could be determined, no matter how far away it is. Astronomers had found a tape-measure to the stars.

The next actor in the drama was Edwin Hubble (who gave his name to the modern Hubble Space Telescope). Hubble—who was once tipped as a prospective boxing champion—began working in astronomy in 1919 at the Mount Wilson Observatory in California, where the world's largest and most advanced optical telescope had recently been set up. Back in chapter two I mentioned that the spectral lines (discrete colours) in light from a distant source get shifted in frequency if the source is moving relative to the observer. If the light source is approaching us, we observe a shift towards the blue end of the spectrum (that is, to shorter wavelengths); if it is receding from us the shift is towards the red (to longer wavelengths; the so-called 'red shift'). Between 1912 and 1922, Vesto Slipher, working at Arizona's Lowell Observatory, had discovered that the light spectra from many distant galaxies were systematically red-shifted, but it was Hubble who in 1929 first realized that the red shift of some cepheid variable stars was directly related to their distance from us. Not only were the galaxies containing these stars moving away from earth (like a starburst, equally in all directions) but the more distant galaxies were receding faster. In fact, the relationship was linear, the recession speed being proportional to distance. Astronomers found themselves in an expanding universe and modern cosmology was born!

The final piece in the jigsaw puzzle was provided in 1963, when Arno Penzias (cited earlier) and Robert Wilson,[II] working on a satellite designed to measure microwave radiation, found that microwaves were beaming in on us from space, equally from all directions—the very thing that Gamow, Herman and Alpher had predicted in their theory of the big bang. Dubbed 'the cosmic microwave background' it is believed to represent the cooled-down radiation left over from an earlier ultra-hot universe and it convinced most astronomers that the big bang theory was correct. Penzias and Wilson were awarded the 1978 Nobel Prize in Physics for their discovery. By the way, don't worry. These microwaves are far too weak to zap you.

### Evaluating the big bang

From Einstein in 1915 to Penzias and Wilson in 1963 is less than fifty years, but this period saw a revolution in man's perception of the cosmos. Scientists were at last convinced that the universe had a beginning, just as the book of Genesis had always said. But ever since this unavoidable conclusion was reached, there have been tireless

*Who Made God?*

efforts to avoid it! We shall look at some of these evasive strategies in the next chapter, but first we need to understand just what is implied by big bang cosmology.

First, a note of caution is needed. The big bang or 'standard model' of the universe is just that—a scientific model. It is a scenario reached by extrapolating back in time the current observation that space is expanding and is uniformly bathed in a background of microwave radiation—consistent with an original enormously hot condensed universe. The scenario also represents one solution of the equations of general relativity theory. It is thus a highly convincing picture but it remains a model that might not, in the end, correspond to reality. A particular problem is that to explain both the shape and the extreme uniformity of the universe, theoreticians have had to introduce the idea that (in its initial stages) the universe 'inflated' from nothing to one metre in diameter in a period of $10^{-35}$ seconds—a speed of $10^{35}$ m/sec which is a trifling $10^{27}$ (ten followed by 27 zeros) times faster than the speed of light. That's a billion billion billion times faster that the fastest thing we know. However, at present, *some* kind of 'hot big bang' offers the only scenario for the origin of the cosmos that is based on experimental evidence and which therefore constitutes science as distinct from mathematical and philosophical speculation.

Secondly, we need to understand that the big bang was *not* some kind of cosmic-scale explosion in space. If it had been, the universe would be expanding away from some central point at which the explosion occurred—and that point would have to be Earth itself because it is from Earth that we observe a universe expanding equally in all directions. Yet there is no scientific or theological reason to think that the Earth is the physical centre of the universe, and I know no one who suggests that it is.

I once acted as an expert witness in a lawsuit in Helena, Montana. A railway company had carelessly allowed a freight car full of explosives to detonate, inflicting considerable damage on the town, including the cathedral. Its 'marble' pillars had suffered serious cracking and it was my task to show that this could plausibly be attributed to deflection of the building caused by the explosion. This proved to be quite complicated because explosions are funny things and the blast doesn't usually travel equally in all directions from the epicentre. But the consequences attributed to the big bang are amazingly 'isotropic', that is, they are precisely the same in all directions, as witnessed by the red shift and the uniformity of the microwave background radiation. Not your typical explosion, then.

The final nail in the coffin for the idea that the big bang was an explosion in pre-existing space is the fact that if it were, the most distant galaxies would be receding from us at a speed greater than the speed of light. But that cannot be, because this is forbidden by the special theory of relativity, which says that nothing can travel through space faster than light. The resolution of these assorted dilemmas is built into all the big-bang theories. The expansion of the universe we observe is not the flight of galaxies through space, but an expansion of space itself. This is not an easy idea to grasp, so let's make it simple.

Take a round toy balloon and begin to blow it up. The two-dimensional *surface* of the balloon represents the three dimensions of space (this means of course that nothing else about the balloon, like the centre of its spherical shape, has any meaning. The surface represents everything there is). Next, attach small circular stickers all over the balloon's surface to represent galaxies, and continue to inflate the balloon. What happens? As the balloon grows in size, the stickers move away from one another uniformly in all directions. If you were a bug sitting on a sticker you would see exactly the same thing whichever sticker you were on—all the other stickers would be receding from you equally in all directions. What is more, the further away a sticker is, the faster it will move away from you. A green sticker that was originally two inches away recedes at twice the speed of a red sticker that started out only one inch away. As the surface area of the balloon (representing the volume of space) increases, so the stickers (representing galaxies) move relative to one another in precisely the way galaxies actually do move in the expanding universe. This also solves the problem of the rapid recession of distant galaxies. Relativity theory only forbids faster-than-light movement *through* space; it has no problem with space *itself* expanding faster than light!

What our balloon model cannot picture is the actual beginning itself. For this you have to imagine travelling back in time so that the balloon shrinks and shrinks while retaining its spherical shape and curved surface. Eventually, of course, the balloon will vanish to a point and the stickers will all gel into a single mass. In actual big bang cosmology this means that, going back in time, all the matter and energy in the universe gets squeezed together into a pinhead—a process that would make it very, very, very hot. This is why the origin of the universe is often referred to as the 'hot big bang'.

But what lies outside the expanding cosmic space? The answer is truly 'nothing'. Everything that exists materially is contained within the expanding volume of space itself. There isn't even a vacuum or a void outside of space—just nothing at all. And if the big bang theory is correct, and the universe (and space itself) began as an infinitely small, infinitely hot pinhead, then there was at first an awful lot of nothing and not much something (in fact, none). This, of course, is exactly what the biblical hypothesis of God leads us to expect, namely, that creation occurred *ex nihilo*—out of nothing.

In concluding, let me say this. The first chapter of Genesis can be interpreted in a number of ways. Personally, I believe it records genuine history. Perhaps we should call it pre-history, to avoid confusion with human history or geological history, but either way I believe that the events described there actually took place. Clearly, as regards the statement, 'In the beginning God created the heavens and the earth', this is in full accord with current scientific beliefs in a big bang origin for the universe. The language of Genesis, though poetical in style, is clearly historical in intent—an epic poem, if you like.

Unlike some, I have never had any problem reconciling a historical view of Genesis with the big bang theory, and I set out just such a scenario in my 1978 book *From nothing to nature*.[12] Briefly rehearsed, this scenario is that the *ex nihilo* creation of the universe is reported in verse one of Genesis 1—'In the beginning God created the heavens and the earth'—with no reference to how long ago that happened. I also regard the order as significant, the heavens being mentioned (and thus created) before the earth. From verse 2 onwards, the account concentrates squarely on the earth itself, which was at first covered with water. As the waters separated into clouds above the firmament (sky) and liquid water on the earth's surface (the waters under the firmament) the earth was bathed in light from the sun—light that was 'separated' from darkness because only half the globe was illuminated, just as today. As the sky cleared, the heavens became visible from an earthly perspective and the heavenly bodies (having already been created) were 'set' or placed in the sky—a classic use of phenomenological language describing what would have been seen by an observer on earth had anyone been there to see it.

Understood in this way, the Genesis account of creation is fully compatible with the big bang theory and, indeed, predicts some such creation scenario. This will become more apparent when, in the next chapter, we consider how the universe develops with time.

# CHAPTER EIGHT ...

... in which we grapple with time and the hypothesis of God. Beginning with a brief history of time, we undertake an entertaining and (as far as possible) non-technical review of what time is all about.

The scientific view of time has its foundations in entropy and the second law of thermodynamics (don't worry, all will be explained). Unlike space, time allows us to go only in one direction. This one-directional 'arrow of time', says science, is the direction of increasing randomness, and this has profound implications for the origin and fate of the physical universe. It means, for example, that time must have both a beginning and an end—but also that *all* time, past, present and future, still exists. And *that* implies the necessary existence of eternity.

Such are the theological implications of time that many ask, 'Can we get rid of time?' The atheist needs to do so if he is to avoid the event of creation, so we'll watch him trying (unsuccessfully). By contrast, the hypothesis of God accurately describes the evolving cosmos, time and eternity.

### New words?

*Continuum*: An unbroken expanse.

# 8. Steam engine to the stars

> Time is the longest distance between two places.
>> Tennessee Williams, *The glass menagerie* (1945)

> Most of the methods for measuring time have, I believe, been the contrivance of monks and religious recluses who, finding time hangs heavy on their hands, were at some pains to see how they got rid of it.
>> William Hazlitt, 'On a sundial' (*Sketches and essays*, 1839)

L et me introduce you to Wells, Who and Hawking. Don't worry, they are not my solicitors but merely a few of the people who have messed with the mystery of time—and speculated how to get rid of it. In 1888, novelist H. G. Wells published *The chronic argonauts*,[1] a short story featuring time-travellers who visit the past and the future using a time-machine. Wells followed this in 1895 with his better known story *The time machine*.[2] Then there's Doctor Who—British TV's intrepid, perennial and accident-prone 'time-lord'—whose temperamental Tardis (a spaceship-cum-time-machine) lands him in all kinds of uncomfortable times, places and situations. He should need no further introduction. Finally, as we have already seen, Stephen Hawking covered the serious stuff by writing *A brief history of time: from the big bang to black holes*.[3]

When I talk about 'getting rid of time' I don't quite mean what Hazlitt meant by it, but am referring to any attempt to escape the restrictions that time imposes on us. In real life that's impossible. In fiction it's easy; just use a time-machine. In science it's somewhere in between—rather more difficult than for Wells and Who but not conceptually impossible, as Professor Paul Davies has argued in his entertaining but exceedingly far-fetched book *How to build a time machine.*[4] As we shall see, those who seek to escape the implications of a beginning of the universe are actually trying to cast off the shackles of time. And who can blame them? (no pun intended). As the Persian poet Omar Khayyám[5] reminds us, time is the ultimate taskmaster:

The moving finger writes and having writ
Moves on; nor all thy piety nor wit
Shall lure it back to cancel half a line,
Nor all thy tears wash out a word of it.

Nicely put and all too true; but what if we *could* somehow get rid of time? According to our biblical hypothesis, of course, God already has, for having invented time he cannot be subject to it. He was already *there* before time began[6] and time is just as much part of the created material order as are space, matter and energy. As we have seen, this accords entirely with general relativity and basic big bang cosmology. God himself, the Creator, stands outside the created order and thus outside of time. Psalm 90 declares: 'Before the mountains were brought forth, or ever You had formed the earth and the world, even from everlasting to everlasting, You are God. You turn man to destruction, and say, "Return, O children of men." For a thousand years in Your sight are like yesterday when it is past, and like a watch in the night.'[7]

Look at it this way. God is time's cartographer—time for God is spread out like a map. Just as we might study a route map showing villages, townships and cities, together with their environments and the roads that link them, so God surveys all history at a glance—encompassing everything that is to us past, present and future. As Isaiah 46:9–10 puts it: 'For I am God, and there is no other; I am God, and there is none like Me, declaring the end from the beginning, and from ancient times things that are not yet done, saying, "My counsel shall stand, and I will do all My pleasure."'

This implies, of course, the intriguing concept that all time still *exists*. In the three dimensions of space, I can travel from London to Manchester and onwards to Glasgow. In terms of my *experience*, once I reach Manchester, London lies in the past and Glasgow in the future. But this doesn't mean that London has stopped existing or that Glasgow is still a green-field site. So with time. The fact that we are confined to 'now' and can visit neither yesterday nor tomorrow, doesn't mean that yesterday has ceased to exist or tomorrow doesn't yet exist. It is, in fact, one of the inevitable conclusions of relativity theory that the *whole* of space-time must have a real and continuing existence—regardless of our perception of time as being divided into past, present and future. If you doubt my word, physicist Brian Greene sets out detailed arguments to prove this[8] and concludes: 'Just as we envision all of space as *really* being out there, as *really* existing, we should also envision all of time as *really* being out there, as *really* existing too' (his italics). The biblical idea that God surveys all time is therefore predictive of what has only recently become apparent to science.

Isaiah 57:15 provides a further example of the Bible's teaching on this subject, naming God as 'the High and Lofty One *who inhabits eternity*, whose name is Holy' (emphasis added). The Hebrew word translated 'holy' means 'separate' and speaks of the 'otherness' of God, both in a moral sense and in respect of his eternal self-existent and non-material nature. As Frederic Amiel put it: 'Time and space are fragments of the infinite for the use of finite creatures.'[9] That's us, not God. So let's take a look at time—first of all, as science sees it.

### The arrow of time
Einstein's special and general theories of relativity, developed in 1905 and 1915 respectively, caused a seismic shift in science's perception of the universe. Until then, space and time were considered to be the 'given' and unchanging stage on which the drama of existence was

played out. In Newtonian physics, everything happened *in* time and space but nothing ever happened *to* time and space. With Einstein all that changed.

Even before Einstein, physics already viewed time as a 'fourth dimension' and had come to terms with the idea of a four-dimensional 'space-time continuum'. For example, the equations derived by James Clerk Maxwell in 1876—which describe how electromagnetic waves like light, heat and radio waves propagate through space—showed that time behaves like a fourth spatial dimension divided by the speed of light. But even before that, in an 1848 essay on cosmology (appropriately titled *Eureka*), the American poet and writer Edgar Allan Poe had concluded, after ninety pages of philosophical reasoning, that 'space and duration are one'.[10] This was apparently the first time anyone had suggested in print that space and time were linked. Following Poe's pronouncement, H. G. Wells later wrote: 'There is no difference between time and any of the three dimensions of space except that our consciousness moves along it'—adding, 'Scientific people ... know very well that time is only a kind of space.'[11]

So what difference did Einstein make? He showed that the space-time continuum was not the rigid and unchanging 'stage' (or frame of reference) for everything else, as had previously been supposed, but was itself an actor in the cosmic drama. It was part of the fabric of the universe, capable of change and distortion. Thus gravity ceased to be some mysterious action-at-a-distance and became instead the result of massive objects causing curvature in space-time. In a relativistic universe, the three dimensions of space and the one dimension of time are all equally flexible. However, the equivalence of space and time is only partial. We can move freely backwards and forwards in any of the three dimensions of space, but we can only go forwards in the 'pseudo-space' we call 'time'. For convenience we can (and shall) talk about time *itself* being unidirectional, or time 'flowing' in one direction, but strictly speaking it is we who are moving in one direction *through* the pre-existing landscape of time. Except in science fiction, the past is forbidden territory. Conversely, you can remember the past but not the future. This unique unidirectional nature of time is called 'the arrow of time', a term coined in 1927 by British astronomer Sir Arthur Eddington.[12]

Interestingly, almost all the equations and theories of science are symmetrical with respect to time—that is, they hold true whether events are running forwards or backwards in time. For all they care, the clock can go 'tick-tock' or 'tock-tick', it makes no difference. They contain nothing to indicate what we all know to be true, namely, that we can only move in one direction through time. But Eddington identified one glaring exception—a single physical law that is *not* indifferent to the direction of time. The law in question is the 'second law of thermodynamics', a long-established principle that describes and governs growth in randomness. The law states that while the randomness (technically, the 'entropy') of an isolated system may increase with the passage of time or remain unchanged, it can never decrease. Eddington concluded that as far as science is concerned, the arrow of time is a property of entropy alone. So, what's entropy all about?

## By steam engine to the stars

*Per ardua ad astra*. Let's take a journey to the stars by steam engine. I know it sounds like a Wallace and Gromit project, but in fact our companions on this trip will be a child of the French revolution, a Pomeranian ambulance driver, a British baron and the son of a Viennese tax inspector. More respectfully, they were all leaders in the development of the science of thermodynamics—Sadi Carnot, a French military engineer whose father served on the French revolutionary council; Rudolph Clausius, a German scientist born in Pomerania who organized an ambulance service during the Franco-Prussian war; Lord Kelvin who, as William Thomson, was appointed to Glasgow's Chair of Natural Philosophy when he was just twenty-two; and Ludwig Boltzmann who, in 1869, became Professor of Mathematical Physics at the University of Graz at the similarly early age of twenty-five.

Carnot wanted to improve the efficiency of the steam engine and wondered what factors might be involved. To simplify the problem, he imagined an idealized 'heat engine' in which heat flowed from a source at high temperature (like the fire of a steam engine) to a sink or reservoir at a lower temperature (like the steam exhausted from the engine) to produce mechanical work (as the steam moves the engine's piston and turns a shaft). Carnot pictured an ideal engine with no friction or external interference in which the whole process could be reversed by driving the shaft backwards and pumping heat back from the cool reservoir to the hot source. Such a 'reversible' engine could be taken through a complete cycle and brought back to its original state without losing any heat energy. Carnot realized that no heat engine could be more efficient than a reversible one, since if it *were* more efficient it would deliver perpetual motion (it could drive the shaft without expending energy).

Carnot also showed that the efficiency of a reversible heat engine didn't depend on the details but only on the temperature-difference between the heat source and the heat sink. E. T. Jaynes comments: 'Carnot's reasoning is outstandingly beautiful because it deduces so much from so little—and with such a sweeping generality that rises above all tedious details—but at the same time with such a compelling logical force. In this respect I think that Carnot's principle ranks with Einstein's principle of relativity.'[13]

Next, enter William Thomson (later Lord Kelvin), who along with James Joule established that heat and mechanical work are equivalent— each is a form of energy that can be converted into the other. The original idea and measurements are credited to Joule (and independently to Julius von Mayer) but Thomson was the one who analysed, explained and published the results. The Kelvin or 'absolute' temperature scale used by scientists today was a direct result of this work.

Another James—not Joule but Bond—famously required his cocktails to be 'shaken, not stirred'. When you agitate a cocktail shaker you are performing mechanical work on the contents and as a result the liquid warms up (as a thermometer would show). If the shaker were perfectly insulated so that no heat could escape, the heat generated inside the shaker would equal the mechanical energy supplied, and no energy would be lost. (Mind you, James, the same would be true if the drink *were* stirred rather than shaken. In fact Joule first demonstrated the point by using a falling weight to drive a stirrer which, in turn, raised the temperature of a water-bath.)

But it was Clausius who came up with the perfect mix. Taking one part of Carnot's heat engine and adding two parts of Kelvin-Joule's mechanical equivalence of heat, he produced a cocktail that could well be called 'steam engine to the stars'. What did he discover? That if any isolated system goes from one equilibrium state to another, the net heat flow (called Q) divided by the temperature (T) at which it occurs can only increase or remain constant—it cannot decrease.[14] Clausius called this quantity (Q/T) the 'entropy', so whatever happens to such a system either leaves the entropy unchanged (only true for a perfectly reversible system) or causes it to increase. Furthermore, Clausius had the audacity to point out that this applied not only to idealized steam engines but to the ultimate 'isolated system'—the universe itself.

(Note that even in a 'closed' system, where heat but not mass is allowed to pass in or out of the system, the principle of the second law of thermodynamics still applies.)

## Bicycle pumps and rubber bands

Other scientists (notably J. Willard Gibbs and Ludwig Boltzmann) carried the subject further. They showed that entropy has a statistical character—the more ways there are to arrange the components of a system (e.g. a collection of atoms, molecules or soup-bowl fragments, see chapter 1) the higher is its entropy. If you compress a gas (as when pumping up a bicycle tyre) its temperature increases but its entropy decreases because there are fewer places for the air molecules to go in the smaller volume available. The lesson? You have to work hard to decrease entropy.

A rubber band is another example of a closed system where energy must be injected to reduce the entropy. In an unstretched band, each of the long segmented rubber molecules is coiled up randomly into a ball. Since there are a very large number of ways in which its many segments can be arranged in such a coil, the entropy of an unstretched molecule is high. But when you stretch the rubber band the molecules uncoil and elongate, lining up roughly parallel to one another. Since there are only a small number of ways to achieve this highly ordered molecular arrangement, the entropy of the stretched band is correspondingly low.

To go from the unstretched state (high entropy) to the stretched state (low entropy) we have to apply a stretching force and perform work on the rubber band—an energy input is needed to reduce the entropy. Notice that this energy input is not random. We could supply energy randomly by zapping the rubber band in a microwave oven, but that won't make it stretch. To reduce the entropy the energy supplied must be specifically controlled and directed. When the tension is released, the molecules revert to their normal form of random coils and, in the process, the rubber band can give back energy to its surroundings—for example, by driving the propeller of a model aeroplane.

The chief thing I want you to notice here is that rubber bands can't stretch themselves—it takes effort to put the rubber into a state of low entropy (a stretched condition having a high degree of order with all the molecules lined up). Equally, it takes effort to work the bicycle pump that compresses air and reduces its entropy—the gas will not spontaneously compress itself. So in an isolated system like the universe, low overall entropy can no more 'just happen' than can a rubber band stretch itself or a gas compress itself. On the other hand, a state of low entropy (high order) can spontaneously 'unwind' to one of high entropy, releasing energy in the process—just as a stretched rubber band can turn a model propeller or a compressed gas can spontaneously expand (let go of the pump handle at the end of a compression stroke and the handle will spring back as the gas expands).

## Clausius' cocktail hour

In the days when the law required British pubs to close at a fixed hour of the night, the landlord would cry out in a loud voice, 'Time, gentlemen, please' to advise his customers that the statutory moment had arrived. The Clausius cocktail hour also has profound implications for time but on a much grander scale. Put briefly, the only way science can explain the phenomenon of time, with its one-directional 'arrow', is by assuming that the universe began in a highly ordered (low entropy) state. Physicist Brian Greene puts it thus: 'Conditions at the birth of the universe are critical to directing time's arrow. The future is indeed the direction of increasing entropy. The arrow of time—the fact that things start like this and finish like that but never start like that and end like this—began its flight in the highly ordered, low-entropy state of the universe at its inception.'[15]

So, according to science, we experience time in one direction because the universe can only run downhill from high order to low order—the entropy or randomness can increase but never decrease. Scientifically speaking, then, time is simply the measure (and experience) of change, as the universe is transformed progressively from an initial highly ordered state of low entropy to some final condition of maximum entropy. In this final condition the universe would be in a 'reversible' state—entropy would stop increasing and time would cease to flow. The question then arises: what or who provided the energy input that established this low-entropy condition in the early universe?

Basic big bang cosmology can say only that the universe was created that way (in a low entropy state). However, the latest idea is that immediately after the universe originated, it underwent an 'inflationary' stage in which the force of gravity was actually negative, thus pushing apart space and its contents (whatever they were at that point, which is by no means agreed) at a fantastic speed. This inflation, it is argued, smoothed out any irregularities in the chaotic pre-inflationary universe and produced an expanded universe having low entropy. This scenario involves assumptions and speculations which we can't go into here, but it does agree with our conclusion that energy must have been input to create a low-entropy universe. In the inflationary scenario, of course, it was the negative gravitational field (called the 'inflaton field') that donated this energy.

But where did the inflaton field get *its* energy? From 'a statistical fluctuation from primordial chaos',[16] we are told—from an initial nugget of chaos that weighed a mere twenty pounds (9.07kg) and was just $10^{-26}$ cm in diameter (that's about one billionth of one billionth of one billionth of a centimetre). Twenty pounds doesn't sound heavy, but a one-pound jam-jar full of this chaos stuff would weigh a billion billion billion billion billion billion billion billion billion metric tons— and that's not counting the weight of the jar itself.

But whether all this turns out to be true or not, the fact remains that to get the whole process of time and 'creation' going, somewhere back there, someone or something somehow supplied energy *that wasn't already present in some prior shape or form*. It's either God or turtles, so make your choice.

## Full marks for the hypothesis of God

It seems to me that whichever scientific theory you adopt, it accords completely with the predictions of the biblical hypothesis of God. Let's take stock.

Firstly, the scientific scenarios outlined above validate the biblical concept of eternity. 'Before' the origin of the universe, time could not exist. Why not? Because until the universe was *there* in some shape or form it could not be in *any* entropy state, low or otherwise.

Secondly, when the universe originated, it must either have been created *ab initio* in a low entropy state or subsequently put into such a state. Either way, as rubber bands and bicycle pumps teach us, it takes effort to create low entropy—this isn't something that can just happen spontaneously. It follows that an 'energetic' act of creation must have occurred at some stage before time could begin to run.

Thirdly, as entropy began to increase (producing the phenomenon of time) the universe began to change and evolve. Modern cosmology seeks to chart and describe this development, and may or may not have got it right. But the Bible clearly teaches a progressive development of the universe. Not only does the book of Genesis record a progressive creation (including the unfolding of the 'six days of creation') but other Bible passages clearly describe a universe that changes and 'runs down' with the passage of time.

For example:

> Of old You laid the foundation of the earth, and the heavens are the work of Your hands. They will perish, but You will endure; yes, *they will all grow old like a garment*; like a cloak You will *change* them [or fold them up], and they will be *changed*. But You are the same, and Your years will have no end [emphasis added].[17]

Finally, according to the Bible, there was not only a beginning of time but there will be an end. St Peter writes in the New Testament: '...do not forget this one thing, that with the Lord one day is as a thousand years, and a thousand years as one day. The Lord is not slack concerning His promise, as some count slackness, but is longsuffering toward us, not willing that any should perish but that all should come to repentance. But the day of the Lord will come as a thief in the night, in which the heavens will pass away with a great noise, and the elements will melt with fervent heat; both the earth and the works that are in it will be burned up.'[18]

None of this 'proves' the existence of God. What it does do, however, is confirm that the biblical hypothesis of God makes correct predictions—predictions that are only now being confirmed by cosmological research, thousands of years after the hypothesis was first advanced. We are beginning to see, therefore, that our hypothesis survives the acid test—it has predictive power.

## Getting rid of time

Needless to say, many have tried (and are still trying) to get rid of the
theological implications of all this.

So let's see how some scientists try to get rid of time and, specifically,
the idea that it actually started. There are several current ideas, including
the evergreen speculation that the universe has gone through a
succession of big bangs, expansions, contractions and 'big crunches'—
the cycle repeating *ad infinitum*. But where, in this scenario, does the
energy come from to create the low starting entropy necessary to explain
the arrow of time? You might think that the low entropy that started
the present cycle could be supplied by the energy of the collapsing
cosmos as it shrank to a point at the end of the previous cycle. But this
doesn't work. If the net energy of the universe is zero (as Hawking and
others[19] maintain, the 'positive' energy of matter and radiation being
exactly balanced by the 'negative' energy of gravitational attraction)—if,
in other words, the universe is the ultimate 'free lunch'—then any 'big
crunch' would cause the positive and negative energies to annihilate
each other leaving no energy to recreate a low entropy state. The free
lunch would vanish leaving the cupboard completely bare of energy.
But if there was no energy left over to put the newly crunched universe
into a low entropy state—so that the flow of time could start all over
again—how did this low entropy come about?

One answer is that time doesn't *have* to restart following a big crunch.
It could be argued that time continues to flow smoothly throughout
successive expansions, contractions and 'bounces' (or punches, crunches
and free lunches, if you prefer)—with entropy continuing to increase
all the time. Each new big bang would simply begin with the entropy
left over from the previous cosmic cycle without any resetting of the
clock. This would certainly satisfy the second law of thermodynamics
but it fails to explain the existence of time. Why? Because if there was
no beginning, but only an eternal sequence of bangs and crunches,
then entropy would have been increasing for ever. But sooner or
later the entropy of the universe must reach a maximum, which will
happen once complete disorder is established. If entropy had been

increasing for an infinite time, then maximum entropy would have been achieved and time would have ceased to flow. When nothing changes, time stands still.

## Imaginary time

There are other more sophisticated ways of getting rid of time. Dr Stenger, for example, seems somewhat ambivalent on the origin of the universe. On page 133 of *God, the failed hypothesis* he talks about the 'nothing-to-something transition' as if it really happened, but just a few pages earlier he suggests that perhaps there was, after all, 'something' rather than 'nothing' before the big bang. He writes on page 126: 'In *The comprehensible cosmos* I presented a specific scenario for the purely natural origin of the universe ... based on the "no boundary model" of James Hartle and Stephen Hawking. In that model the universe had no beginning or end in space or time. In the scenario I presented, our universe is described as having "tunnelled" through the chaos ... from a prior universe that existed for all previous time.'

The idea that our own universe is just one of a bunch is quite fashionable among those who speculate about time. Read *any* popular book on cosmology or time and you'll find yourself tripping over universes by the dozen. It is almost taken for granted that we exist not so much in a universe as in a 'multiverse'. So, what do we know about these other universes or, in Stenger's case, this eternally prior universe? Precisely and absolutely nothing—which is a good deal less than we know about God. Yet Dr Stenger has the chutzpah to conclude: 'I do not dispute that the *exact* nature of the origin of the universe remains a gap in scientific knowledge, but I deny that we are bereft of any conceivable way to account for that origin *scientifically*' (my italics). The fact is that neither Dr Stenger nor anyone else has a clue—exact or inexact—about how the universe might have originated by material causes. This must be true because if the origin of the universe *did* have a material cause it wasn't the *origin* of the universe at all, but merely a later stage in its development. Watch out for those turtles! Furthermore, to invoke an invisible, inaccessible, eternal and totally unknowable prior universe as the material cause of the one we know, can hardly be dignified as a 'scientific' account of origins. Science fiction and pop-science can get away with such speculations but real science demands a little more evidence.

Finally, Stenger's claim to have found a completely material explanation for the origin of the universe invokes not only alternative universes but also the idea that our own universe is finite but 'unbounded in time', having neither beginning nor end. The idea (the Hartle-Hawking theory) is borrowed from Stephen Hawking, who pictures such a universe as a sphere—like the earth marked with lines of latitude and longitude. The size of the universe at any time is represented by the length of a given line of latitude. Thus, for example, the maximum size of the universe is related to length of the equator. (Of course, in this picture we have to drop two of the dimensions of space, so that the one-dimensional line of latitude actually represents the three-dimensional volume of the universe.)

What about the lines of longitude that run from pole to pole? These represent trajectories in time—but (wait for it) not in 'real' time! What Dr Stenger omits to mention is that you only get a 'universe [that] had no beginning or end in space or time' if you replace time by *imaginary time*—a perfectly legitimate mathematical concept introduced to help solve the equations underlying the model.[20] Hawking emphasizes that 'we may regard our use of imaginary time ... as merely a mathematical device (or trick) to calculate answers about real space-time'.[21] 'Trick' is Hawking's word, not mine.

This 'imaginary time' model suffers no singularities—the laws of science never break down nor do any physical quantities rise to infinity, even at the poles where the size of the universe shrinks to zero. Just as you can walk through the North Pole without anything dreadful happening to you, so the universe could pass back and forth through zero size without any breakdown of the physics that describe it. This is what Hawking means by a finite but unbounded universe. Such a universe could indeed undergo successive collapses and bounces—but only in imaginary time, never in real time, as Hawking is at pains to point out. He writes, 'Only if we could picture the universe in terms of imaginary time would there be no singularities ... When we go back to the real time in which we live, however, there will still be singularities'[22]—of which of course an *ex nihilo* creation of space and time would be a perfect example. And that is bad news for anyone wanting to get rid of time.

Much more could be said about attempts to banish the beginning of time but space forbids. So who should be allowed to have the last word on this subject? Might I suggest we defer to Sir Roger Penrose, the esteemed Oxford mathematician who worked with Stephen Hawking on the theory of black holes and other cosmological problems. Writing in *New Scientist* on 27 April 1996, Gabrielle Walker cites him thus: 'The standard big bang model is agreed, says Oxford mathematician Roger Penrose, and everything else is "embellishments and flights of fancy".'

This should alert us to the danger of being seduced by speculation masquerading as science. Whatever flights of fancy we may undertake, travelling in imagination to other universes in cosmic bubbles or time machines, real science offers no prospect of escaping the inescapable fact that time really did begin!

# Chapter nine ...

... in which we recognize the universality of law—in human conscience, human nature and human society—and mull over its significance. In chapter 10 we're going to explore how the hypothesis of God addresses the laws of nature, but before doing so we're going to pause to notice something that is easily overlooked. This is the fact that God's hand as the lawgiver is seen in every aspect of human society and experience, not just those areas accessible to science.

Beginning with 'bedknobs and broomsticks', with games, sports and families, we see that human social behaviour at all levels is permeated and regulated by rules and laws. Not only does 'law' underpin human society, it also manifests itself in our consciences, as we distinguish 'right' from 'wrong' and act accordingly.

Can all this be the result of evolution? Or does it make more sense to follow the hypothesis of God and see all law as flowing from a transcendent yet paternal lawgiver? We'll get some answers by asking three further questions, namely:

1. Why is law so universal throughout the cosmos?

2. How do laws originate—who makes the rules?

3. Why should we care anyway?

### New words?

*Patria Potestas*: paternal power.

*Ubiquitous*: universal; found everywhere.

# 9. Peeling onions

There is but one law for all, namely that law which governs all law,
the law of our Creator, the law of humanity, justice, equity—the law
of nature and of nations.

> Edmund Burke, 1788, in the opening speech
> for the prosecution at the impeachment
> of Warren Hastings, former governor-general of India

L et's peel an onion. It may make our eyes water but it will
add flavour to our meal. The particular 'onion' we're going
to look at is law, and we shall consider it layer by layer. In
this chapter we'll look at law in human society, experience
and conscience, while in chapter 10 we'll get down to basics and think
about the laws of science and nature.

Philosophers have been studying the concept of 'law' for millennia
and still can't agree, so we too may shed a few tears of frustration over
it. But hopefully the effort will be repaid, for few things affect our
lives more deeply than law in its various forms.

Talking about law, I once acted as an expert witness in the British
High Court for a small Swedish company which was suing a

household-name multinational for patent infringement. Following cross-examination by the opposing counsel our 'own' counsel, as is normal, conducted a short re-examination to tidy up any loose ends. During this re-examination, I was asked a question which, I felt, missed the most important point. So I replied, 'With respect, that's not the right question.' This brought the house down, as they say, and the whole court dissolved in laughter (to his credit, the judge managed to keep a straight face). My response had been both innocent and true but, of course, it is counsel's job to ask questions and the witness' job to answer them. The prospect of a witness telling counsel what he should and shouldn't ask was simply hilarious to the assembled lawyers. When the laughter had subsided the judge said in a kindly tone, 'First answer his question and then answer the question he should have asked.'

I tell the story not just to introduce a chapter on law but because it really is important to ask the right questions. And there are three particular questions that are seldom asked (and therefore seldom answered) but which lie at the heart of the whole debate about the existence and nature of God.

1. Why is law so ubiquitous or universal throughout the cosmos?

2. How do laws originate—who makes the rules?

3. Why should we care anyway?

Let's try to find some answers.

### Peeling the first layer

A simple and familiar concept of law is found in games. If all you knew about soccer was derived from watching the animals in Walt Disney's *Bedknobs and broomsticks*, you would probably think it was a game without rules. Animals compete and play but they don't play *games*, by which I mean contests governed by rules or laws (for the time being I use these two words interchangeably). When we talk about 'the law of the jungle' we don't mean law at all; we mean lawlessness.

By contrast, if you give a ball to a bunch of seven-year-olds, a game will very soon be under way which *does* have rules. They won't be the official laws of soccer; the goalposts may be piles of coats or chalk marks on a wall; all the players may be trying to score in the same goal; and there may be more than two teams. But I guarantee that the game will be played according to rules of one kind or another. Furthermore, though I've never put it to the test, I suspect that the same would be true if the seven-year-olds lived in some remote jungle and had never seen a football in their lives.

Indeed, I would argue that without rules there is no such thing as a 'game'. Have you ever 'cried foul' or complained that someone has 'moved the goalposts'? These common sporting allusions remind us that games deteriorate into chaos unless the players abide by the rules. All may be fair in love, war and the battle for the mind, but the tendency to ignore rules in *these* activities simply shows that they're decidedly not games.

But why must games have rules? Because the rules actually define the game and provide its structure. When, at Rugby School in 1823, William Webb-Ellis allegedly picked up the ball and ran with it, he broke the rules of soccer—and created Rugby football, an entirely *different* game. OK, this incident is almost certainly apocryphal, but the myth serves our purpose well enough—if you change the rules to any significant extent you change the game. As I said, the rules define the game.

Although this may all seem rather trivial, it is in fact quite profound. Laws emerge not as the icing on the cake—something *imposed* on a game—but as the cake itself, the defining essence of the game. Think it through for yourself; in one sense, the laws *are* the game. We invent a new game only when we invent a new set of rules. The rules come first and remain fundamental, although they may be refined, expanded or simplified with the passage of time.

## Laws and society

The fact that laws are so basic in the familiar realm of games and sports has implications at a deeper level—it suggests that rules are also basic to human social interactions. To win *lawfully* you have to play fair by recognizing the rights of others involved in the sport or game. So let's think for a while about the way rules and laws affect the way people interact with one another—which brings us to the second layer of the onion, namely, laws and society.

Just as rules define a game, so in large measure do laws define society—but they do so in two different ways. At the superficial level they define what *kind* of society exists, but at the fundamental level they define the existence of society itself. Concerning the first, it is obvious that societies differ according to the specific laws that govern them. Societies whose laws discriminate against certain categories—women, or racial or religious minorities, for example—are very different from those where all are equal under the law. Again, societies having laws that suppress dissent differ profoundly from those that encourage free-speech.

Let me take that for granted, then, and move on to the second statement, namely, that law—viewed as a principle—defines not so much the character of a particular society but the very existence of society. Mankind has a love-hate relationship to rules and laws. We almost always find them irksome, yet no society can function or survive without them. The same is true, to some degree, of other creatures. From ants to apes, meerkats to monkeys, and bees to basking sharks (yes, honestly, I checked it out[1]), many animals live in 'societies' governed by 'rules'. But how did this almost symbiotic relationship arise between life and law?

That's not so easy to explain. The problem is that human societies are more complex than games. Whereas games are defined solely by their rules, societies are defined first by relationships—such as common descent (ethnicity), common beliefs and common language—and only secondarily by their laws. Jurisprudence (the theory and philosophy of law) traces the history of law in human society from its earliest known forms. The consensus seems to be that societal laws had their origin in what lawyers call *Patria Potestas*, that is, paternal power. The earliest human societies were simply families in which the male progenitor exercised power and authority over his wife or wives and over his offspring and their families. This authority extended also to servants and slaves who were regarded as an extension to the family. In his classic book *Ancient Law*,[2] Sir Henry Maine describes patriarchal society thus:

The eldest male parent—the eldest ascendant—is absolutely supreme in his household. His dominion extends to life and death, and is as unqualified over his children and their houses as over his slaves; indeed the relations of sonship and serfdom appear to differ in little beyond the higher capacity which the child in blood possesses of becoming one day the head of a family himself. The flocks and herds of the children are the flocks and herds of the father, and the possessions of the parent, which he holds in a representative rather than in a proprietary character, are equally divided at his death among his descendants in the first degree, the eldest son sometimes receiving a double share under the name of birthright ...

With the passage of time, however, human society began to develop beyond the immediate confines of family, and Maine continues: 'Scriptural accounts ... [reveal a departure from] the empire of the parent. The families of Jacob and Esau separate and form two nations; but the families of Jacob's children hold together and become a people. This looks like the immature germ of a state or commonwealth, and of an order of rights superior to the claims of family relation.' Of course, it was to Jacob's incipient 'commonwealth' that God gave the Mosaic law at Sinai—a detailed moral, civil and religious code, traditionally dated around 1440 BC, that cemented the twelve tribes of Israel (another name for Jacob) into nationhood.

But although by then law had evolved beyond the family fiefdom, Maine points out that the fundamental *Patria Potestas* concept remained foundational: 'In most of the Greek states and in Rome there long remained the vestiges of an ascending series of groups out of which the State was at first constituted. The Family, House, and Tribe of the Romans may be taken as the type of them, and they are so described to us that we can scarcely help conceiving them as a system of concentric circles which have gradually expanded from the same point. The elementary group is the Family, connected by common subjection to the highest male ascendant. The aggregation of Families forms the Gens or House. The aggregation of Houses makes the Tribe. The aggregation of Tribes constitutes the Commonwealth ... all ancient societies regarded themselves as having proceeded from one original stock ... The history of political ideas begins, in fact, with the assumption that kinship in blood is the sole possible ground of community in political functions.'

Boiling all this down, we see that the basic concept of law in society—as distinct from the various laws and legal systems that grew from this rootstock—derives from the primitive idea of the supremacy of fatherhood.

### Law in the hypothesis of God

Let's pause at this point to see where this leads in relation to our biblical hypothesis. Few would dispute that the Bible presents God as the ultimate paternal lawgiver or that the dual concepts of fatherhood and law run consistently through the pages of Scripture. In Genesis 1 creation itself is described as the result of God's commands, and a command presupposes legal authority: 'Then God said, "Let there be light"; and there was light' (v. 3). The formula 'let there be' is repeated in verses 6, 9, 11, 14, 20, 24, 26. Furthermore, value judgement is engaged as the record adds, 'And God saw the light, that it was good' (v. 4). The sun and the moon are said to 'rule' the day and night respectively; again, the language is that of law, order, regulation.

After man is created 'in the image of God', God commands him to 'Be fruitful and multiply; fill the earth and subdue it; have dominion over ... every living thing that moves on the earth' (v. 28). Just as God's word was 'law' in creation, so man's word would become 'law' as he assumed dominion over the earth. Human law derives from divine law; man as lawgiver reflects the image of God, the supreme lawgiver. However, in accordance with *Patria Potestas*, man remained subject to God's law—'but of the tree of the knowledge of good and evil you shall not eat, for in the day that you eat of it you shall surely die' (Genesis 2:17). The theme of God as lawgiver persists throughout the Bible. In Psalm 119, which is by far the longest of the psalms, almost every one of its 176 verses refers to God's law in one way or another, using words like 'statutes', 'law', 'judgements', 'commandments', 'testimonies', 'word' and 'precepts'. Acts 17:26 claims that God 'has made from one blood every nation of men to dwell on all the face of the earth, and has determined their pre-appointed times and the boundaries of their dwellings'. God not only gives law but enforces it (which is a large subject in itself).

But what about *Patria Potestas* itself? That too is modelled on man's relationship to God, who is not only the ultimate source of law but also the divine Father—from whom, says St Paul, 'the whole family[3] [Greek *patria*] in heaven and earth is named'.[4] That man is made 'in the image of God' represents a form of sonship.[5] In Luke 3:38 the lineage of Jesus Christ is traced back to Adam, who is then declared to be 'the son of God'.[6] Again, when St Paul addressed the Athenian philosophers he concurred with the Greek poet who had written 'For we are also [God's] offspring'[7] and added: 'Therefore, since we are the offspring of God, we ought not to think that the Divine Nature is like ... something shaped by art and man's devising' (a reference to their many idols).

An interesting feature of the Bible chapters cited above (and other biblical texts) is the way natural law (the laws of nature, considered in the next chapter), moral law (what God requires of man) and human law (how man rules the earth) are all presented as different aspects of a unified divine rule. Most people today would see no connection between these three kinds of law since they operate in entirely different realms—nature, conscience and society respectively. But while recognizing these distinctions, the Bible views law of all kinds as divinely imposed. As Nebuchadnezzar declares[8]: '[God's] dominion is an everlasting dominion, and His kingdom is from generation to generation. All the inhabitants of the earth are reputed as nothing; He does according to His will in the army of heaven and among the inhabitants of the earth...' God's dominion over the cosmos ('the army of heaven') is one with his dominion over humanity, both corporately and individually.

## Law and conscience

It's time to peel another layer of the onion, a layer I introduced in the preceding paragraph. According to the biblical hypothesis, God's law affects humanity directly on a personal level—affording further insight into the *Patria Potestas* that, according to Maine, is the root of societal law. So let's consider the uncomfortable subject of law and conscience.

You may remember how wood-carver Gepetto, a lonely old man, creates a puppet called Pinocchio. His wish that Pinocchio should become a real boy is unexpectedly granted by a fairy, but even fairies have their limitations. Being at heart a puppet, Pinocchio has no conscience. So Jiminy Cricket is assigned to fill the gap and keep him out of mischief. As the movie blurb puts it: 'Jiminy is not too successful in this endeavour and most of the film is spent with Pinocchio deep in trouble.' I'm not sure what the moral is, except perhaps that any conscience is better than none.

Interestingly, according to the Bible, that wasn't always so. In Eden's paradise there was no need for conscience and it was precisely 'the knowledge of good and evil' that God denied to Adam and Eve. Commenting on this arrangement, theologian Philip Eveson writes: 'In the only other passage in the books of Moses where the phrase "knowledge of good and evil" is found, it is used of children who cannot be held accountable for their actions. They are dependent on their parents (Deut. 1:39). In like manner, Adam and Eve were to see themselves as children totally dependent on the Creator God, their heavenly Father, for wisdom and understanding.'[9] Our first parents didn't need conscience but they acquired it anyway by disobeying God's only law.[10] Their newfound guilt-awareness was soon put to work as they 'hid themselves from the presence of the LORD God among the trees of the garden'.[11]

So how does the Bible view man's conscience in a morally fallen world? St Paul explains: 'When Gentiles, who do not have the [written Mosaic] law, by nature do the things in the law, these, although not having the law, are a law to themselves, who show the work of the law written in their hearts, their conscience also bearing witness ... their thoughts accusing or else excusing them.'[12] In other words, Paul claims that man has an innate sense of moral law—of what is right and what is wrong in the eyes of God. This is exactly the knowledge our first parents obtained in Eden and it lingers on in what we call 'conscience'. And this is important, because having traced societal law to its root in *Patria Potestas*, we are forced to ask where the 'eldest ascendant' got the ground-rules by which he governed his family. The Bible's answer is that these laws were (and remain) innate in every descendant of Adam—human beings have an *instinctive* knowledge of good and evil, right and wrong. Unlike Pinocchio, they have a built-in conscience and Jiminy Cricket is redundant (or ought to be—see ch. 17).

## Darwinian spectacles

There are those, of course, who insist on viewing everything through Darwinian-tinted spectacles and will attribute the emergence of law in society and human conscience to the 'survival value' of social stability—a stability that stems from rules, taboos, inhibitions, traditions, pecking orders and the like. And, to be fair, it is obvious that laws and legal systems *do* evolve. After all, neither Hammurabi nor the Hyksos Kings required charioteers to hold a valid driving licence.

But we need to bear in mind the distinction made earlier between the *idea* of law and the laws themselves—between law as a concept and the use to which a particular society applies it. The latter is certainly subject to 'evolution' though not necessarily in a Darwinian sense. But the former appears to be hard-wired into the primeval human psyche.

An evolutionary origin of law, like many evolutionary scenarios, doesn't stand up well to scrutiny. To say that 'social stability has survival value' is a tautology—for what else do we mean by 'stability' than the capacity to survive adverse circumstances (wars, natural disasters, internal conflicts and so on)? So the claim reduces to a statement that 'survival has survival value' which, while no doubt true, is also trivial. Stripped down to its underpants, therefore, the evolutionary explanation of societal law must be as follows: 'Laws help a society to survive and are therefore subject to evolution by natural selection.' But is that what actually happens in real life? It's a moot point.

When human societies fall and perish—whether they be ancient dynasties or modern states; tribal communities or nomadic groups; political parties or social classes—it is not usually because they are short on regulation but because they are overwhelmed by things beyond their control. Some succumb to wars and invasions; some to urbanization and industrialization; others to internal tensions and contradictions; yet others to natural disasters like famine, climate change or habitat destruction. Although defensive laws may be enacted to withstand these threats, they are but rearguard actions. A nation threatened with invasion will introduce conscription to boost the strength of its army. A society falling apart through internal dissent may impose draconian laws to suppress the disaffected. But no amount of law-passing can protect a society against overwhelming odds.

It might be argued that the rise of *Patria Potestas* is itself an evolutionary phenomenon. Families bound together by strong parental rule ensured their own survival by working together effectively, whereas fragmented families succumbed more readily to circumstances. But remember that natural selection alone cannot cause evolution; there must also be advantageous traits to be selected. But if such traits are already present, they don't need to evolve. The biological theory of evolution gets around this dilemma by proposing that *new* advantageous traits arise by random beneficial mutations—changes in the genome that were *not* originally present. Could *Patria Potestas*, therefore, be a mutant social 'meme' by analogy with biology's mutant genes? Hardly. Parent power is always present, if only because human offspring are biologically dependent on their parents during their early years. It may need to be reinforced and elaborated but it doesn't need (and cannot have) an evolutionary *origin*.

To summarize, then, the evolutionary survival value of law to a society is pragmatically of a low order and certainly not strong enough to explain societal law as the result of evolution. To explain away the ubiquity of law in human society as nothing more than an evolutionary phenomenon is simplistic. Societies do indeed need laws for stability, but this need grows from an altogether deeper root—a proposition that, according to the 'hypothesis of God', arises naturally from the relationship between God as supreme lawgiver and man as his 'image' and offspring.

## Law and the lawgiver
So let's return to the questions posed at the beginning of this chapter.

1. Why is law so ubiquitous throughout the cosmos?

2. How do laws originate—who makes the rules?

3. Why should we care anyway?

Working from the hypothesis of God, I have argued that all law—whether expressed in nature, society, or in the human conscience—derives from a single divine lawgiver. That is why law is so remarkably ubiquitous in human experience. We have yet to look in detail at the laws of nature, of course, and this we shall do in the next chapter. But so far the evidence strongly supports the sentiments of Edmund Burke—cited in our chapter masthead—that all law is a unity because it is derived from God: 'There is but one law for all, namely that law which governs all law, the law of our Creator, the law of humanity, justice, equity—the law of nature and of nations.' May we not conclude, then, that the *principle* of law permeates the cosmos (and human experience) because it has a single source in the transcendent Lawgiver by whom all things were made? Or is there, after all, some naturalistic explanation of these things?

Arthur Bloch, the American humorist and author of the 'Murphy's law' books, warns that 'A conclusion is the place where you got tired of thinking.' So let's avoid drawing premature conclusions by doing some hard thinking in the next chapter about cosmic law in its most fundamental manifestation—the laws that describe and control the physical universe. These, at least, can have no Darwinian explanation for they have existed since the dawn of time.

# CHAPTER TEN ...

... in which we explore the character and origin of the laws of nature. Without natural laws there could be no science, but where did they come from and how do they work? These are deep questions but we'll keep the treatment light as we consider the universality, elegance, mathematical nature and comprehensibility of the laws of science and nature.

The atheist attempts to explain away the origin of these laws by appealing to yet higher natural laws but that, of course, is turtles all the way up. Alternatively, they claim that we live not in a universe but in a multiverse, inhabiting just one of a possibly infinite multitude of universes, all with different laws of nature. But that can't help either—because whatever the laws may be they have to come from somewhere.

Finally, we examine Victor Stenger's efforts to prove that the laws of nature simply emerged from nothing, but discover that he is confusing two different kinds of 'nothing'—the pre-creation eternity where nothing physical existed and the physical vacuum of space that lies within the created order.

With some relief, we discover that the biblical hypothesis of a transcendent yet immanent God explains both the origin and nature of these laws in a fully satisfying way. It also explains why we can understand them (if we couldn't, there would be no such thing as science in the first place).

# 10. Cosmic chess

> It is a game which has been played for untold ages, every man and woman of us being one of the two players in a game of his or her own. The chess board is the world, the pieces the phenomena of the universe, the rules of the game are what we call the laws of nature. The player on the other side is hidden from us. All we know is that his play is always fair, just and patient. But, also, that he never overlooks a mistake or makes the smallest allowance for ignorance.
>
> T. H. Huxley,
> quoted in 'Professor Huxley's hidden chess player',
> by R. H. Hutton, *The Spectator*, 11 January 1868

L et's now remove the final layer of the onion and consider the laws of nature. These most certainly did not arise by natural selection. At best, natural selection is just one of the multitude of rules that shape the natural world, and it's a Johnny-cum-lately at that. The very existence of science testifies to the fact that the universe is subject to physical laws that have operated from its inception. Unless this were so, all attempts to describe or 'explain' the cosmos *scientifically* would be in vain. Although Huxley was an agnostic (it was he who coined the term) he nevertheless understood that there is a 'game' in town and that it is played according to unchanging rules. The question we have to ask in this chapter is what or who makes these rules?

The oft-repeated claim that science can (or will eventually) 'explain everything' is highly suspect. For in what sense does science explain *anything*? Only by discovering the laws that govern the events to be explained. It is these 'laws of nature' that define the game of cosmic chess.

Of course, when we play chess, the laws determine the moves we *can* make but not the moves we *do* make. That is, the laws are not deterministic; they don't impose a particular outcome for the game. In the same way, the laws of nature determine what is and what is not physically possible, but they do not determine what actually occurs within the multitude of available possibilities. Scientists once thought they did but, as we saw in chapter 2, scientific determinism was abolished by quantum mechanics.

In a very real sense, then, science consists in the search for the rules of cosmic chess—that's what science *is*. But having discovered the laws of nature which constitute its own existence, science cannot then explain them. Put succinctly, science cannot explain itself. Why not? Because to do so it would have to explain natural law in terms of some other more fundamental principle that was not itself natural law—like God or turtles.

We mustn't get confused about this. It is always possible for science to unify, revise, refine or generalize known laws. We have already seen this process of unification at work in the search for a 'theory of everything'. General relativity was a highly successful generalization of Newtonian mechanics, and superstring theory may (or may not) eventually unify the hitherto incompatible laws of quantum theory and gravity—thus 'explaining' these laws in terms of some more fundamental law. But every 'more fundamental law' is still a law of nature that itself needs to be explained. A theory of everything may one day be found that encompasses all other physical laws as special cases of one unified overarching theory. But the unified theory itself will still need to be 'explained' or else simply taken for granted.

Those who promote atheism in the name of science thus fall into a trap. They suppose that they can explain the origin of the laws of nature by appeal to such things as the 'symmetry of empty space' or to events called 'symmetry breaking' or 'cosmic phase transitions'. In such an event, a single all-embracing natural law is supposed to break down into several separate laws—something that might conceivably have happened as the universe cooled down from a big bang. This isn't easy to illustrate, but imagine a smooth mixture of two different liquids which is then cooled until the liquids begins to crystallize. If the crystals of one liquid cannot contain molecules of the other, each liquid will be forced to form its own crystals, and the end product will be a solid mass in which pure crystals of one substance are interspersed with pure crystals of the other. By analogy, it is suggested that single 'homogeneous' laws could have separated out into two or more different laws as the temperature of the early universe dropped. But this is *only* an analogy. And even if such attempts to explain the laws of nature (as we know them today) were successful, it would do nothing to solve the mystery of the ultimate origin of natural law. We are still left with imponderable questions like: Why does 'empty space' possess these supposed symmetries? What higher *but still physical laws* control 'symmetry breaking' or cosmic phase-changes? No one really knows.

### What is 'natural law'?

Before we go any further, let's be sure we understand what we are talking about. I once had a somewhat surreal conversation with a man who told me he drove a coke delivery lorry for a living. Remembering the struggle we had when I was a child to obtain solid fuel to burn in our open grates (fuels like coal, coke, coalite), I discussed with him the problems of supply in those war-time years. When the puzzlement on his face became unmistakable I realized that something was amiss. It then emerged that he had never heard of coke as a fuel and that his job was delivering Coca Cola—carbonated perhaps, but carbon it's not. So, let's be clear what we mean by 'the laws of nature'.

The first distinction we must make is between the laws of nature (or natural law[1]) and the laws of science (scientific law, i.e. the laws of physics, chemistry, biology and so on). The latter are the result of man's scientific endeavour; the former have existed, necessarily, from the beginning of the universe. Martin Rees expresses the matter neatly: 'This progress [in our scientific understanding of the cosmos] is possible only because of the contingency—in principle, remarkable—that the basic physical laws are comprehensible and apply not just to earth but also to the remotest galaxies, and not just now but also in the first few seconds of our universe's expansion. Only in the first millisecond of cosmic expansion, and deep inside black holes, do we confront conditions where the basic physics remains unknown.'[2]

Our scientific understanding is, of course, expressed in terms of scientific laws, but these only reflect the pre-existence of 'the basic physical laws'—the laws of nature that have governed the cosmos since its inception. We can put it another way. The laws of nature *constitute* unchanging reality whereas the laws of science are our frequently imperfect attempts to *describe* reality. It is the business of science to discover laws that describe, more or less accurately, how the universe works. Such discoveries not only deepen our understanding of the cosmos but can often be exploited for man's benefit in what we call 'technology'. But neither science nor technology would be possible without the unchanging substratum of natural law—the ultimate physical reality that science strives to probe and understand.

As we have seen, Einstein and other leading scientists have stressed this difference, pointing out that beneath our scientific descriptions of the universe there may well lie 'realities' that we do not (and perhaps cannot) comprehend. And it is possible, even inevitable, that sometimes science's laws and models lead us *away* from these realities rather than towards them. The long-held belief that light propagated through an omnipresent medium called the 'ether' is a historical example. This idea was genuinely 'scientific', being based on the fact that waves generally occur in some medium—ripples on a pond propagate in water and sound waves propagate through air (or some other fluid or solid medium). But until it was proven wrong, this perfectly reasonable scientific model stood in the way of a true understanding of electromagnetic fields and radiation. Some modern speculations may prove equally false and equally misleading. Science proposes a huge variety of laws, principles and models, ranging from specific quantities like the speed of light and the firmly established principles of optics or electromagnetism, to mathematical constructions such as string theory and speculative models based on multiple universes that verge on science fiction.

A failure to distinguish between the laws of nature and the laws of science lies behind the superiority that atheists often claim for science over theology. Science, they say, unlike theology, is open to change. Its errors can be corrected, its theories refined and its explanatory power continually expanded. All this is true, but it only reflects the fact that the laws of science are an imperfect representation of the changeless reality and perfection of natural law. Similarly, human theology is a search after the changeless truth about God and is notoriously subject to error, revision and refinement. But the revealed realities concerning God, when properly understood, are no more fallible or changeable than the underlying laws of nature that science seeks to uncover (indeed, there is a close connection between the two).

All that said, the laws of science that we establish by *practising* science represent, at any time, our best approximations to the underlying realities of nature. In so far as they can be verified by experiment (and that is an important proviso) they enhance our understanding of the cosmos and should not be despised because they are approximations, liable to refinement and correction. They may not reveal the fullness of 'the mind of God' but, when backed by experiment, they do give us substantial insights into the fundamental laws of nature.

## Comprehensibility
The laws that describe the physical cosmos possess a number of striking properties. First of all, they are almost universally expressed in terms of mathematics, that is, they take the form of algebraic equations rather

than verbal statements. Of course, we can often put into words what the equations are telling us, but the laws can only be stated precisely and definitively using the language of mathematics. For example, Newton's law of gravity says that the force of attraction between two objects is proportional to the product of their masses divided by the square of the distance between them. But these words do nothing more than describe the equation:

$$F = G\{m_1 m_2\}/d^2$$

That is, the law itself *is* a mathematical expression. The whole of nature appears to be built out of mathematical Lego! You may ask why my verbal statement of the law isn't just as good as the mathematical equation. Couldn't the maths be nothing more than shorthand—just a convenient way to write down the law? Actually, no. To be meaningful, the verbal statement has to include words such as 'is' (implying an equality), 'proportional', 'product' and 'squared'—mathematical language which demonstrates that the law is *essentially* mathematical, not verbal.

The fact that the structure of the physical cosmos is fundamentally mathematical is really strange—because mathematics is entirely a construct of the human mind! When I was a child it was popular to build 'cat's whisker' or crystal radio detectors—simple non-powered devices that could pick up the invisible radio waves that filled the room. Success depended on establishing a sensitive contact between a natural mineral crystal such as galena and a thin metal wire (the 'cat's whisker') and was often a matter of luck. So why is the human mind able to 'tune in' to the cosmos in such a remarkable way by using the 'cat's whisker' of mathematics? Is it, like the crystal radio signal, just a matter of luck? Or is there some reason why conscious thought connects us so perfectly with the physical structure of the universe?

I need hardly point out that the hypothesis of God provides a ready answer. If God created the universe and the laws that govern it; and if man is made in the image of God as a rational, intelligent being; then it is clearly possible—even necessary—for man to 'think God's thoughts after him' (Kepler) and 'know the mind of God' (Hawking). If God is a mathematician, man will also be a mathematician. But if there is no God, and man is an accident of evolution, there is not the slightest reason why we should be able to make sense of, or even recognize, the mathematical structure of the universe.

## The symmetry of the universe

A second feature of natural law is one that underlies much of science itself—namely, the concept of symmetry. This is so important that in his book *The fabric of the cosmos* Brian Greene declares: 'During the last few hundred years there have been many upheavals in science, but the most lasting discoveries have a common characteristic; they've identified features of the natural world that remain unchanged even when subjected to a wide range of manipulations. These unchanging attributes are what physicists call symmetries.'[3]

That sounds a bit daunting but the basic idea is actually both simple and familiar. A billiard ball is highly symmetrical because you can rotate it around any axis without changing its appearance (there is nothing to show that the rotation occurred). On the other hand, a pear only displays symmetry if it is rotated around a vertical axis through its core; if you spin it about any other axis (a horizontal one for example) you can immediately see that it has been turned. In other words, the pear has only limited rotational symmetry. Finally, an oddly shaped pebble has no such symmetry; however you rotate it, the movement will be obvious.

But the symmetry of objects rotating in space is only one example of a much more general principle, so let's cut a long story short and get to the interesting bit. The symmetries that most interest physicists are not those of objects in space but of the laws of nature. For example, the laws of nature don't change from place to place. You can perform an experiment in London, Washington, Tokyo, on the moon and in a space station, and you will find that the laws of nature are exactly the same. This means that these laws display 'translational' symmetry—they are not affected as you move from one place to another. Of course, we can only test this kind of symmetry in the limited region of the universe accessible to us. But here is the interesting thing. By assuming that the laws of nature are symmetrical *throughout* the universe—that they do not change as they skip from one galaxy to another—it is possible to set up scientific theories that make testable predictions. Einstein's general theory of relativity is an outstanding example of this, having as its starting point the assumption that all observers—wherever they might be in the universe and however they are moving relative to other observers—will find that the same laws of nature apply unchanged.

Another major symmetry is symmetry with respect to time. As we have noticed previously, almost all the laws of science remain unchanged if time is replaced by negative time—that is, they are mathematically independent of the arrow of time. The only known exceptions are the law of increasing entropy (the second law of thermodynamics) and the behaviour of an obscure quantum particle called a 'kaon'—which seems to know which way the arrow of time is pointing.[4] The 'strange case of the kaon' may have some other explanation that doesn't break time-symmetry, but entropy is highly important since it appears to determine the direction of time. However, time-symmetry is still the overwhelming character displayed by nature's laws.

### Elegance in science

But why, I wonder, does nature love symmetry? That's a difficult question. As Brian Greene comments: *'The laws of physics didn't have to operate in this* [symmetrical] *way'* (his italics).[5] So let's look at the matter in a wider context. Symmetry is closely related to non-material qualities such as beauty and elegance. It is well known, I think, that the human faces we consider beautiful are those having perfect symmetry. In the same way, a symmetrical vase is more pleasing to the eye than a misshapen one, while a well-proportioned edifice such as the Palace of Versailles is deemed the height of classical elegance.

But aren't we drifting away from science? Strangely, no. To be told that science sets great store by the elegance and beauty of its equations and theories may come as a shock to those who think science is mechanistic and unencumbered by aesthetic subjectivity. But anyone who has actually engaged in scientific research or teaching will immediately understand what I am saying. The two compliments I treasure most as a scientist came respectively from a senior scientist at the Bell Telephone Laboratories in New Jersey and the then Research Director of the Dow Chemical Company, USA. Following lectures in which I presented some of my research, each pronounced the work 'elegant'—signifying that, to some degree at least, the research reflected the simplicity and beauty of underlying realities. That is something a scientist values above many other achievements.

At a 2005 conference sponsored by the US National Science Foundation, Sherry Farwell, head of the NSF program to stimulate competitive research, quoted with approval the following words from a participating research professor: 'My work defines me. It enables me to contribute in ways that are entirely holistic. The logic and elegance of science are a compliment to the human state of being.'[6] This striking statement reflects the almost mystical view many scientists have of their discipline. They see it as 'holistic', involving not just the cold logic of the mind but the whole personality, including aesthetic apprehensions of beauty, elegance and fitness. Perhaps few scientists would express themselves quite so emotively, but most confess to an awareness that science—or rather the reality that science seeks to explore—touches the core of their humanity. That, no doubt, is what Huxley was getting at when he personalized the cosmic chess match as something in which we are *individually* engaged as human beings. In less materialistic times this would be recognized as a kind of religious awe—as exemplified by Kepler's exclamation that he was 'thinking God's thoughts after him'.

And this is just what we would expect on the basis of the hypothesis of God. Science's 'book of nature' reflects the nature of nature's Creator. 'The heavens declare the glory of God; and the firmament shows His handiwork,' declares Psalm 19:1, while St Paul contends that 'what may be known of God ... His invisible attributes are clearly seen, being understood by the things that are made, even His eternal power and

Godhead.'[7] In Genesis 1, God declared the created order 'very good' while Ecclesiastes claims that he 'has made everything beautiful in its time'—adding significantly: 'Also He has put eternity in [men's] hearts, except that no one can find out the work that God does from beginning to end.'[8] Solomon seems to be saying here that the beauty of the created order can be appreciated by men because God has put an awareness of eternity into their hearts and minds. However, he appends a caveat: we can never discover everything about everything. The 'work of God' will always transcend our ability to understand it, which is exactly the conclusion we came to in chapters 2 and 3 of this book.

The elegance and beauty we discern in science and mathematics create an acute problem for the atheist. An internet blogger comments thus: 'One of the most exquisite moments on radio for me recently has been to hear [Richard] Dawkins squirm and flounder when asked to explain and justify the existence for humans, or the evolutionary purpose, of anything remotely metaphysical (such as, say, beauty, the effects of music, and the pursuit of philosophical truth) that lie beyond the ken and stricture of his own scientific rationality. He simply cannot do this convincingly, despite his considerable purely intellectual powers.'[9]

It's a fair comment.

### The origin of natural law

So, let's remove the final layer of our legal onion and consider the origin of natural law. The source of *scientific* law is apparent. It is a work of man and, normally at least, the end-product of the hypothetic process applied to physical events and entities. Observation leads sequentially to hypothesis, prediction, testing and either verification or falsification. But our interest here lies not in the fruits of science but in the underlying natural law that makes science possible at all.

Very few writers offer any explanation for the *ultimate* origin of natural law. They simply accept it as 'given'—as the unexplained and probably inexplicable substratum of reality that science seeks to explore and without which it could not exist. Recent authors as diverse as Martin Rees, Stephen Hawking, Brian Greene and Paul Davies, though never afraid to speculate (sometimes wildly) about the origin of the universe and the nature of reality, make no attempt to 'explain' or even discuss how natural law came into being. Nor, indeed, does Richard Dawkins. Victor Stenger is the one exception and we shall catch up with him at the end of this chapter.

Let me clarify what I am saying. I do not mean that laws cannot be explained in terms of deeper physical principles, because they often can. For example, certain important laws of 'conservation' derive from the symmetries we discussed above—and are a direct consequence of 'Noether's first theorem'. Amalie Noether (1882–1935) was a German mathematician famed for her contributions to abstract algebra and theoretical physics. Albert Einstein described her as 'the most important woman in the history of mathematics'. Noether's theorem allows physicists to extract important information by considering the various 'transformations' which leave the laws unchanged.

We hear a lot about 'conservation' these days. We want to conserve the environment, the rain forests or threatened species. Lots of things are conserved in physics too—that is, they are not lost or diminished when circumstances change. Noether's law shows, for example, that because the laws of physics do not vary from place to place (they display 'translational invariance') the total linear momentum of a physical system must be conserved. In the same way, invariance of the laws with respect to rotation leads to a further law—the conservation of angular momentum. Symmetry with respect to time implies the law of energy conservation, while the rotational symmetry between time and space leads to special relativity theory. Symmetry between inertial and gravitational mass results in general relativity, and so on. In quantum field theory, an analogue to Noether's theorem yields further conservation laws, such as the conservation of electric charge.

I'm sorry that was technical, but you don't have to understand the details or even the terms to get the idea. What it means is that many scientific laws are mathematical consequences of the observable simplicities (symmetries) of space, time, motion and so on. It could even be said that the search for the fundamental laws and 'building blocks' of nature boils down to a search for such symmetries in the structure of the natural world.

Let's take as an example the 'inverse square' law that applies to gravitational, magnetic and electrical forces (and 'force-fields' in general). This law states that the force gets weaker as you move away from its source in a very specific way—when you double your distance from the source, the force weakens by a factor of four (that is, two squared) and so on. To help understand this, let's pay a visit to a glassblower and watch him make a hollow glass sphere. As the initial blob of molten glass expands into a sphere, the glass wall gets thinner because a fixed amount of glass is spread out over the increasing area of the sphere's surface. But the quantity of glass doesn't change; its volume is always constant and equal to the wall thickness multiplied by the sphere's surface area. So the thickness must be inversely proportional to the area and thus to the radius squared.

If we now think not of glass but of a force emanating from a point, it is clear that the force will be 'thinned out' over the surface of a sphere (centred on the point) just as the glass is thinned out in my glass-blowing analogy. So the force experienced at a distance 'd' from the source will be proportional to $1/d^2$—which is precisely the inverse square law we observe in nature. It should be obvious that this law arises because space has three-dimensions, since only in three dimensions does the surface of a sphere have an area proportional to the radius squared (don't even try to imagine a four-dimensional glass-blower).

Great! We've explained the origin of inverse square laws. But don't think that we have explained the laws *away*. We have simply replaced them by a deeper and more general principle, namely, the 3D symmetry of space. It didn't have to be that way. For centuries mathematicians have been able to set up and solve equations relating to spaces with *more than* three dimensions and, as we have seen, some scientific theories like string theory can't even get off the ground without assuming that space has ten or eleven dimensions. So why are there only three 'real' space dimensions? What accounts for this particular symmetry in nature? No one knows. And if some day we could explain it we would have to do so in terms of some deeper underlying principle.

And underlying principle is exactly what the hypothesis of God provides, as we shall see in chapter 11. And it's also what science needs because by itself, science will never pick itself up by tugging on the bootstraps of natural law. But perhaps for a little while we should watch it trying.

## Stenger's argument

We've touched on this before but it's time to revisit the one author who claims to know how the laws of nature originated. Victor Stenger's explanation runs as follows:[10] 'So where did the laws of nature come from? They came from nothing!' They 'follow from the symmetries of the void out of which the universe spontaneously arose'.[11]

It's a fine flourish which fully justifies the exclamation mark, but I doubt whether it justifies anything else. There are several problems with Stenger's bold claim. First of all, he confuses 'nothing' with 'nothing'—which is an intellectual feat in itself. Remember that, according to big bang cosmology, the universe began as a tiny object which *contained* space and time within itself. Outside the expanding boundaries of the primordial cosmos there was neither space nor time, so let's call this region *external* to the cosmos 'void-zero'. According to Stenger, this is 'the void out of which the universe spontaneously arose'—the void whose supposed symmetries, says Stenger, gave birth to the laws of nature.

But void-zero has no physical or material properties (such as symmetries) because it has no physical or material existence! By definition it lies outside the physical and material universe. It can only be described theologically, and the Bible calls it 'eternity'. For example we read in Isaiah 57:15: 'For thus says the High and Lofty One who inhabits eternity...' Void-zero is the eternally pre-existent, non-physical framework in which the physical universe began and must, by definition, lie beyond the reach and remit of science. Stenger's claim is thus an unwitting admission that the laws of science had a non-physical, theological origin.

But Stenger doesn't intend to make any such admission. He is simply confusing void-zero ('from which the universe spontaneously arose', as he puts it) with a totally different void—one which lies entirely *within* the material universe. The flexible space-time continuum of general relativity is a *constituent* of the cosmos (its fabric, if you like) and it contains an awful lot of empty space—sometimes called 'the vacuum of outer space'. Let's call this empty space 'void-one' to distinguish it from void-zero. It is, of course, characterized by the absence of matter and energy, at least 'as we know it', but there is more to void-one than meets the eye. According to Heisenberg's uncertainty principle, it must undergo quantum fluctuations that lead to the appearance and disappearance of phantom (or virtual) particles—which are created as particle-antiparticle pairs and immediately vanish again by mutual annihilation. More than that, according to some theories, void-one is actually filled with an 'ocean' of Higgs particles. This 'Higgs field' is a kind of cosmic treacle, resisting the movement of known particles and imparting to them the property of mass.

But all this relates to empty space *within* the space-time fabric of the physical universe—a fabric that has, by definition, existed only from the moment of creation. When Dr Stenger says that the void possesses symmetries, he is talking about void-one. He may be right. After all, if we allow that the vacuum of space is awash with phantom particles and Higgs bosons, it would be a bit mean to say it can't have symmetries as well. In for a penny, in for a pound! And we know from Noether's theorem that certain laws of conservation (like the conservation of energy) are the consequences of symmetry.

So let's suppose for a moment that Stenger is right so far, and that laws of nature originate from the symmetries of void-one. What does that tell us? Since void-one is an integral constituent of the cosmos it tells us that the laws of nature follow naturally from the existence of the cosmos. Put more simply, they are just part of the created physical order. But we already knew that, because science cannot conceive of a physical order which is not governed by rules; laws are built into the very concept of 'physical *order*'. So the symmetries of void-one (if they exist) do nothing to explain the *origin* of the laws of nature, being themselves simply an expression or manifestation of those laws. And it's no good saying (as some do) that in the early moments of the big bang there was chaos rather than order, because scientifically speaking even chaos is governed by laws. James Gleick's book *Chaos*[12] is subtitled 'Making a new science', while the front cover calls it 'the amazing science of the unpredictable'. I hardly need add that where there is science there has to be law.

The third problem with Stenger's thesis is that he seriously misrepresents Noether's theorem. He claims that the theorem proves that the laws of nature originate from the symmetries of void-one.[13] But this is not what Noether's theorem says at all. Let's get the low-down from John Baez, an American mathematical physicist at the University of California, known for his work on loop quantum gravity. He explains: 'Noether's theorem is an amazing result which lets physicists get conserved quantities from symmetries *of the laws of nature*. Time translation symmetry gives conservation of energy; space translation symmetry gives conservation of momentum; rotation symmetry gives conservation of angular momentum, and so on' (my italics).[14]

Thus Noether's theorem only allows you to deduce a new law of nature from the symmetry of *existing laws*. If there are no pre-existing laws you can deduce nothing whatsoever. For example, as we have seen, if a physical system obeys the same laws regardless of how it is oriented in space, Noether's theorem shows that its angular momentum must be conserved—which is the law of conservation of angular momentum. But the physical system itself doesn't need to be symmetric (a rotating space station conserves angular momentum despite being asymmetrical). It is the *laws of motion* that are symmetric. Noether's theorem only works if there are laws already in place.

Victor Stenger called his book *God, the failed hypothesis*. But if you're looking for a failed hypothesis his explanation of the origin of natural law can hardly be bettered.

# CHAPTER ELEVEN ...

... in which Richard Dawkins informs us that miracles do happen but are simply highly improbable natural events. He introduces us to the hand-waving marble statue and the cow that jumps over the moon—and claims that such things really could happen. Looking a little closer, however, we find that his arguments are scientifically vacuous.

But why does the atheist need to engage in such logical contortions, simply to establish that literally anything will happen by natural causation given enough time—false conclusion though this is? Because it's the only way he can account naturalistically for the origin of life (a subject we'll address in later chapters).

Nevertheless, Dawkins has some surprising allies as he argues that nothing can happen except by the strict operation of the laws of nature—people like theist St Augustine and pantheist Baruch Spinoza. Their arguments, however, lead to a god who paints himself into a corner, rendered impotent by the very laws he has himself created. The biblical hypothesis of God, on the other hand, provides us with an altogether more rational and integrated view of providence, miracles and the meaning of life—a view that doesn't imprison God within the confines of natural law.

# 11. Over the moon

For we say that all portents [miracles] are contrary to nature; but they are not so. For how is that contrary to nature which happens by the will of God, since the will of so mighty a Creator is certainly the nature of each created thing? A portent, therefore, happens not contrary to nature, but contrary to what we know as nature.

St Augustine, *The City of God*, Book XXI, ch. 8

The miracles in fact are a retelling in small letters of the very same story which is written across the whole world in letters too large for some of us to see. Of that larger script, part is already visible, part is still unsolved.

C. S. Lewis in *God in the dock*; *essays on theology and ethics* (Eerdmans, 1994), p.29

Hey diddle diddle, the cat and the fiddle,
The cow jumped over the moon;
The little dog laughed to see such fun
And the dish ran away with the spoon.

British nursery rhyme, 1765

I sn't life strange? You look in vain for a good quotation and then three come along together! Unlike buses, however, you don't have to choose which one to take; you can use all three. And that's just as well because we are going to need as much help as we can get as we turn from the laws of nature to consider things that appear to violate them—miracles.

You don't believe in miracles? That's a pity, because Richard Dawkins does. You didn't know that Richard Dawkins believes in miracles? Yes, really, though he would prefer to call them 'extremely improbable events' rather than miracles. But don't take my word for it, read what he says himself.[1] Dawkins writes:

> A miracle is something that happens, but which is exceedingly surprising. If a marble statue of the Virgin Mary suddenly waved its hand at us we should treat it as a miracle, because all our experience and knowledge tells us that marble doesn't behave like that.[2]

He continues:

> In the case of the marble statue, molecules in solid marble are continually jostling against one another in random directions. The jostlings of the different molecules cancel one another out, so that the whole hand of the statue stays still. But if, by sheer coincidence, all the molecules just happened to move in the same direction at the same moment, the hand would move. If they then all reversed direction at the same moment the hand would move back. In this way it is *possible* for a marble statue to wave at us. It could happen. The odds against such a coincidence are unimaginably great but they are not incalculably great. A physicist colleague has kindly calculated them for me. The number is so large that the entire age of the universe so far is too short a time to write out all the noughts! It is theoretically possible for a cow to jump over the moon with something like the same improbability. The conclusion to this part of the argument is that we can *calculate* our way into regions of miraculous improbability far greater than we can *imagine* as plausible.[3]

We'll come to the cow in a moment. Let's first examine the hand-waving. RD seems to be under the illusion that marble is a gas in which molecules move around randomly and can finish up anywhere they like. Unfortunately for his miracle ('It could happen,' he says), marble is not a gas but a crystalline solid composed of calcite, aragonite and/or dolomite crystals. The atoms or ions that compose these crystals are not free to wander where they will but are locked into the crystal lattice and vibrate about their mean position at a frequency that is typically around 15 Teraherz—that is 15,000 billion times per second. Any atom that tried to set off on the long-range journey envisaged in Dawkins' miracle is going to be hauled back to its starting point in short order (exceedingly short order).

But let's suppose for argument's sake that all the atoms in the statue's hand *did* suddenly move in the same direction. What would happen? As soon as they had moved less than their interatomic separation (let's say a hundred millionth of a centimetre or four billionths of an inch) the boundary between the moving hand and the stationary arm would experience a sudden outward pull. Since every action produces an equal and opposite reaction, the unmoving arm will restrain the hand from moving further and will, in fact, pull it back to and beyond its original position—creating an oscillation that would travel throughout both hand and statue as a sound-wave. You might *hear* Dawkins' miracle but you certainly wouldn't see it.

A second problem is that a spontaneous movement of the statue's hand would violate the laws of conservation of energy and linear momentum (the velocity of a body in a straight line multiplied by its mass). Prior to the Dawkins miracle, the hand has neither linear momentum nor kinetic energy (the energy of motion). Suddenly the atoms all move upwards in the same direction and the whole hand takes off towards the ceiling. It now has both linear momentum and kinetic energy, neither of which it had before. Two basic physical laws of conservation have been broken and Thomas Huxley's chess master wouldn't like that at all.

It's no use saying that the new momentum and energy come from the motion of atoms within the hand. Before the miracle, the collective momentum of the assembled atoms is zero because the atoms vibrate randomly and their movements cancel out. So if the hand moves and acquires linear momentum, this momentum has appeared from nowhere. Likewise, the kinetic energy of the hand cannot come from the vibrational motion of the atoms, because this energy simply reflects the temperature of the solid and is not available to move anything.

We'll leave aside other naivities—such as the implication that marble, if not exactly gaseous, is at least made of plasticine so that the statue's wrist can flex without snapping off—and get to the point. Dawkins says 'it could happen' but he is wrong. It couldn't. The idea that the *internal* motion of atoms in a lump of crystalline rock could somehow cause that lump to move from here to there is scientifically ridiculous. Harry Potter it may be, but science it is not. Which brings me to the moo-cow and the moon.

## The kinetic cow

Can the cow really jump over the moon? According to Richard Dawkins, yes, it can. 'It is theoretically possible,' he avers, with more solemnity than I can muster on the subject. Personally, I'm with the little dog in the nursery rhyme, so let's have some fun ('sport' in the American version of the rhyme). Let's begin by giving credit where it is due. Even without the help of Harry Potter, Dawkins has at his disposal three possible lines of argument—bootstrap-elevation, the bovine wave function, or telekinesis. Let's take a look at all three.

We have already seen one fine example of bootstrap-elevation (picking yourself up by your bootstraps) in the strange case of the waving statue. Let's try another. I'm sure Richard D and I can agree that the cow's unaided muscle power couldn't propel it over a haystack, let alone the moon. So how does our bovine astronaut acquire her kinetic energy and achieve escape velocity without the services of NASA? Ah, you might reply, consider an equatorial cow. Being located on the surface of the earth at the equator, it already has a huge velocity, travelling through space at more than 1000 mph due to the rotation of the earth. Could this not launch the cow into space by a kind of slingshot effect? Well, hardly. If it could, we would *all* be over the moon (as they say) along with the cow. But even worse, the moon itself would be travelling away from us as fast as we could approach it. There's something called gravity that keeps both cows and speculations in their place (and moons too).

How about an appeal to quantum mechanics (QM) then? Perhaps this is what Richard Dawkins has in mind (he doesn't give much detail about his moo miracle). If electrons and photons can have wave-functions, why not cows? You will remember from chapter 2 that subatomic particles behave in strange ways that can only be explained by assuming that they are not located in a single place but only have a certain probability of being somewhere. This probability is specified by the wave function which varies in strength from place to place but exists everywhere—so there is a non-zero probability that the particle could be anywhere in the universe.

If we apply this idea to the cow, then her presence beyond the moon, though highly improbable, is not impossible. Furthermore, QM actually does teach that each and every object has a wave function that spreads throughout space. Wow! Perhaps RD really has hit the bullseye (or the cow's) this time? Sadly, no. We'll let his friend Victor Stenger put him right: 'Quantum mechanics changes smoothly into classical mechanics when the parameters of the system, such as masses, distances, and speeds, approach the classical [large-scale] regime. When that happens, quantum probabilities collapse to either zero or 100%, which then gives us certainty at that level.'[4] Stenger is here referring to a phenomenon in QM known as 'decoherence'. For reasons not well understood, quantum particles that exhibit wave function behaviour when isolated from other particles (or when coherent with them) cease to do so when they interact with the environment.[5] If there are too many particles of different kinds knocking around, all their wave functions get nervous and 'collapse'—meaning that instead of having the freedom to turn up anywhere, each particle decides where it wants to be with 100% certainty. Perhaps we shouldn't be surprised. After all, as we saw in chapter 2, you only have to *look* at a quantum particle to make its wave function collapse in this way.

The outcome of all this is that every particle—electron, quark, atom and so on—in our long-suffering cow (or any other massive object) knows exactly where it is, even before we look at it. It's right there in the cow and *nowhere else* (which is what we mean by classical or non-quantum behaviour). But if all the constituent parts of the cow know they are localized in a field on a farm in (say) Filey or Farnborough, it is evident that neither the cow nor any part of it will be found on the other side of the moon. There really is no such thing as a cosmic cow.

## Telekinesis

OK; how about telekinesis? Telekinesis or psychokinesis refers to the alleged movement of solid objects by pure thought. Could Richard Dawkins be trying to *think* the cow over the moon—or simply wish it there? I believe this could be the answer to the conundrum. But why would he want to do that? The answer takes us to the heart of his thinking.

The problem for Richard Dawkins and his fellow atheists is this. They face serious difficulty in explaining the 'miracle' of the origin of life in a purely materialistic way. Indeed, the problem appears insuperable, as we shall see in the next chapter. But let's just accept for the moment that atheism currently has no answer to the riddle. The careful atheist will not appeal to as-yet-unknown scientific discoveries for an explanation, because he recognizes that such an argument is a mirror-image of the God of the gaps theory he so despises. So what can he do? His first strategy is to 'prove' that even the most bizarre events imaginable—like marble motility or bovine ballistics—could conceivably occur by natural causation. Of course, his explanations fail miserably at the scientific level, but that will not worry him unduly as long as he succeeds in planting in our minds the hazy idea that any 'miracle' *may* have a natural explanation.

But then comes the tricky bit. He now needs to make an agile leap from 'miracles *may* have a natural cause' to 'miracles *must* have a natural cause'. This he attempts to do using our old friend 'probability'. Specifically, he advances the thesis that everything imaginable in the physical universe will surely happen by natural causation if you wait long enough, provided only that its mathematical probability is not zero. And this sounds plausible because, having rejected the old Newtonian idea of a deterministic universe, we can rule out nothing in principle. But although plausible, the thesis is false, because mathematical probabilities bear no necessary relationship to physical possibilities, as we saw in chapter 1. It is *mathematically* possible to build an infinitely tall tower of bricks but it is *physically* impossible to do so, because sooner or later the weight of the tower will crush the bottom brick to powder and the whole (non-infinite) tower will collapse. Before mathematical probabilities can be applied to the real world they have to be passed through the twin filters of logic and physical reality.

The fact is that we can imagine very few physical events that are mathematically impossible. 'Impossibilities' arise in the physical universe not from mathematical constraints but from the laws of nature (such as the non-infinite compressive strength of bricks). It's not mathematics that prevents statues waving or cows jumping over the moon, but the stubborn facts that energy and momentum must be conserved and that QM wave functions decohere in massive objects.

## Augustine and Spinoza
Dawkins insists that 'miracles' are perfectly in accord with the laws of nature but are simply events having very low mathematical probabilities. Although his appeal to probability fails to impress for the reasons already discussed, there are other ways to avoid the awkward idea that miracles transcend the laws of nature. St Augustine of Hippo and seventeenth-century savant Baruch Spinoza are Dawkins' unlikely allies in this cause.

Augustine (see chapter-head quote) maintained that the laws of nature can never really be transgressed because everything that happens according to God's will occurs by natural process. So, to break a law of nature would be to overthrow the divine will, which is not possible. No event can, therefore, contradict natural law but may *appear* to do so because our understanding of that law is imperfect.

Benedict (Baruch) De Spinoza (1632–1677) advances essentially the same argument, maintaining that miracles are not transgressions of natural or scientific laws but only transgress those laws *as we currently understand them.* A 'miracle' is simply an event we cannot explain—a natural event that transcends our limited comprehension. To a being with perfect understanding, nothing would appear miraculous. He puts it like this:

Further, as nothing happens in nature which does not follow from her laws, and as her laws embrace everything conceived by the Divine intellect, and lastly, as nature preserves a fixed and immutable order; it most clearly follows that miracles are only intelligible as in relation to human opinions, and merely mean events of which the natural cause cannot be explained by a reference to any ordinary occurrence, either by us, or at any rate, by the writer and narrator of the miracle.[6]

Spinoza's contemporary, René Descartes (1596–1650), was of the same mind. He wrote: 'Even if in the beginning God ... established the laws of nature and then lent his concurrence to enable nature to operate as it normally does, we may believe without impugning the miracle of creation that by this means alone all purely material things could in the course of time have come to be just as we now see them ...'[7] Cornelius Hunter comments: 'In later years Descartes' call for strictly naturalistic explanations would be canonised in science, but his justification would be replaced by another form of rationalism.'[8] Hunter goes on to show that other influential theists such as Thomas Burnet, Gottfried Leibniz, John Ray, Immanuel Kant, James Hutton, John Playfair and Charles Lyell were 'calling for naturalistic explanations in the years leading up to 1859 when Darwin published his theory of evolution'.[9]

What I find interesting is that Augustine (and his fellow theists), Spinoza (a pantheist) and Dawkins (an atheist) find so much common ground. They all insist that everything that happens in the material universe must conform to the laws of nature. They are not alone, for this is also the position of many Christians today. For example, distinguished scientist and clergyman Sir John Polkinghorne,[10],[11] envisages the possibility of 'a new regime' of natural law which 'expresses itself in totally unprecedented, totally unexpected consequences'. This is also the position, whether stated or not, of many who embrace 'theistic evolution'.

Although it is eminently logical to assume that physical events normally follow natural causes, we create a significant problem if we rigidly exclude all alternatives. Such blanket naturalism puts God in the classic position of the man who, in staining a floor, paints himself into a corner from which there is no escape (until the stain dries). Of course, for the atheist, there is nobody in the corner anyway because the floor paints itself, but all agree that God, if he exists at all, has imprisoned himself within his own laws and cannot act in the material universe except through the medium of natural causes. In other words, there is no such thing as a genuine miracle—by which I mean an event that *cannot* be explained as the outcome of natural law.

Dawkins arrives at his position by imposing on the laws of nature a plasticity that they do not possess, being happy to violate those laws with a wave of the hand in the very act of appealing to them. Augustine and Spinoza avoid this pitfall by invoking unknown *but still natural* laws to eliminate the truly miraculous. However, in doing so they argue in a circle. What, to them, is a miracle? An event governed by unknown laws of nature. What are these unknown natural laws? Those that facilitate miraculous events. The logic is underwhelming.

The fact is that these distinguished persons, and many others, all begin by assuming what they seek to prove. They all declare—in one way or another and as an *a priori* philosophical principle—that no event can occur in the physical and material realm that does not itself have a physical and material cause (it must obey laws of nature, known or unknown). As a reductionist, Dawkins and his friends see nothing beyond natural law. On the other hand, Augustine, Spinoza and their philosophical heirs, base their assumption on the nature of God—asserting that the will or decrees of God can only be implemented in strict accordance with the laws of nature. This is a basic fallacy, for while the laws of nature can be considered as *an expression* of the mind of God (as we shall see) there is no logic in supposing that they *exhaust* the divine potential in regard to physical events. But having assumed at the outset that the will and purpose of God in relation to the material world is expressed *exclusively* through the laws he has established to govern nature, they leave God sitting in the corner watching paint that never dries.

C. S. Lewis[12] has a clearer view of the miraculous, pointing out that if a non-material (or spiritual) realm exists at all, there must of necessity be an interface between this realm and the natural world—as a shoreline marks the interface between land and sea. And just as the sea may sometimes flood across that interface and invade the land, so the spiritual may from time to time invade the physical world. This enables a miracle to occur in which non-physical spiritual causes temporarily overrule the laws of nature. However, it seems to me that even Lewis fails to grasp the biblical concept of miracles. So what has the hypothesis of God to say on this disputed subject?

## Miracles and the hypothesis of God

Let me try to clarify matters by making an important distinction—between miracles and providence. The biblical hypothesis of God makes the difference very plain. Providence is God's sovereign control of nature (and human history) to bring about certain ends, and involves no suspension or violation of natural law. I have already cited St Paul's classic statement of the doctrine of providence in Acts 17:24–28: 'God, who made the world and everything in it … gives to all life, breath, and all things. And He has made from one blood every nation of men to dwell on all the face of the earth, and has determined their pre-appointed times and the boundaries of their dwellings … for in Him we live and move and have our being.' In like manner Paul also states that 'all things work together for good to those who love God...'[13]

Nebuchadnezzar, king of Babylon, declared: '[God] does according to His will in the army of heaven [i.e. the heavenly bodies] and among the inhabitants of the earth. No one can restrain His hand or say to Him, "What have You done?"'[14] A further example is the way Joseph forgave his brothers who sold him into slavery: '...you meant evil against me; but God meant it for good ... to save many people alive.'[15] God's providential control over nature is emphasized constantly in the Psalms; for example:

You visit the earth and water it, You greatly enrich it;
The river of God is full of water; You provide their grain,
For so You have prepared it.

You water its ridges abundantly, You settle its furrows;
You make it soft with showers, You bless its growth.
You crown the year with Your goodness.[16]

Some well-known biblical 'miracles' should really be classified as providence, a prime example being the crossing of the Red Sea by the Israelites as they fled from Egypt. The book of Exodus records that 'the LORD caused the sea to go back by a strong east wind all that night, and made the sea into dry land, and the waters were divided'.[17] The wind in question must have been a most unusual phenomenon, but nevertheless it offers a *natural* explanation for the dividing of the waters—though not, of course, for the timing of the 'miracle'. Clearly, any attempt to understand supernatural miracles in terms of the hypothesis of God needs to take into account God's providential control of natural processes.

## Real miracles

So, what does the Bible mean when it refers to miracles? The Hebrew Old Testament uses words that mean literally 'signs' or 'wonders', while the Greek New Testament refers to 'acts of power' and 'signs'.

The Bible, therefore, emphasizes the 'sign meaning' or significance of the event, together with the evident power displayed and the wonder evoked in those who witness it. In most cases, the power referred to is the power of God rather than that of any human agent who may be involved, and the 'sign meaning' usually relates to God's testimony to (or approval of) some teaching or person. For example, we read of the 'salvation, which at the first began to be spoken by the Lord [Jesus Christ], and was confirmed to us by those who heard Him, *God also bearing witness both with signs and wonders, with various miracles, and gifts of the Holy Spirit*, according to His own will' (emphasis added).[18]

It is clear that biblical miracles are identified in terms of their effects on the observer rather than their causation. A miracle of healing, for example, is not specifically labelled 'supernatural'—a fact that provides some wriggle-room for the Augustinian idea of unknown natural causes. However, when the Bible attributes a miracle to the direct action of God it can only intend supernatural causation, the first and greatest such miracle being the *ex nihilo* creation of the universe itself. Other examples abound, including the resurrection of Christ from the dead ('whom God raised up, having loosed the pains of death, because it was not possible that [Christ] should be held by it'[19]) and the healing of the lame man at the temple gate ('let it be known ... that by the name of Jesus Christ of Nazareth, whom you crucified, whom God raised from the dead, by Him this man stands here before you whole [i.e. restored to health]'[20]). The biblical hypothesis of God does, therefore, provide for events to occur, albeit rarely and for a specific purpose, in which supernatural causation replaces natural causation. In other words, natural law can be augmented or overruled by divine fiat.

Such supernatural involvement with the physical realm is *intrinsic* to the biblical record and therefore to the historic Christian faith. As C. S. Lewis points out: 'The mind which asks for a non-miraculous Christianity is a mind in process of relapsing from Christianity into mere "religion".'[21] Only a sanitized non-biblical 'Christianity' can dispense with this miraculous dimension, and such a faith lacks both pedigree and plausibility. Furthermore, to be internally consistent, this bowdlerized religion must deny many other biblical claims—such as the *ex nihilo* creation; the divine creation of life; the special creation of man; the resurrection, ascension and return of Christ; and every other eschatological teaching of Scripture including a coming day of judgement. There really would be little left to believe. How, then, does our biblical hypothesis of God reconcile the pervasive operation of natural laws established by God, with miraculous events in which those laws are superseded by divine fiat? The answer lies in the Bible's view of natural law.

## The word of God's power

When I first visited the USA in the early 1960s, I stayed with an American family. One morning my host remarked in passing that the central heating system had just switched itself on for the first time that autumn. I had never before come across a heating system that worked automatically and I was suitably impressed! 'You mean you didn't have to switch it on yourself?' I asked. Now, of course, we take it for granted that many systems work automatically. When I turn on the ignition of my new car on a frosty morning, it automatically activates front and rear window heaters, wing mirror heaters, air conditioning, windscreen wipers and icy road alert—all of which is quite disconcerting when you first encounter it.

Perhaps it's not surprising, then, that even theists tend to think of the laws of nature as a self-actuating, stand-alone control system—originally set up by God, perhaps, but somehow subsequently independent of him. But that is not how the Bible views the matter. Our brief consideration of providence should alert us to the idea that natural law operates in such a way as to give expression to the purposes of God—suggesting that this law does not enjoy the hands-off independence that we often ascribe to it but rather is subject to the will of God.

This principle is stated plainly in a key Bible passage where Christ, as God, is said to 'uphold all things by the word of His power'. The statement is found in Hebrews 1:1–3 and reads as follows: 'God ... has in these last days spoken to us by His Son, whom He has appointed heir of all things, through whom also He made the worlds; who being the brightness of His glory and the express image of His person, and upholding all things by the word of His power, when He had by Himself purged our sins, sat down at the right hand of the Majesty on high.' The 'cosmic' nature of this statement is self-evident and the conclusion unavoidable—it teaches that the physical universe was first created by God in Christ and is now sustained in the same way. And if this aspect of the hypothesis of God is true, it means that we must equate the system of natural law that upholds the cosmos with the real-time, present-tense 'word' of Christ.

The concept is supported by St Paul, who states that, 'All things were created through [Christ] and for Him. And He is before all things, and in Him all things consist.'[22] The Greek verb translated 'consist' means 'put together' or 'hold together' and, when linked (as it is here) to the act and purpose of creation, can only refer to the structural and functional integrity of the physical universe. Notice specially the contrast between the past event of creating ('*were* created') and the present tense phenomenon of holding together ('consist'). Since, scientifically speaking, this ongoing integrity derives from the laws of nature, we again find natural law equated in some way to the power of Christ.

One way to understand this is to say that the divine will is *immanent* in nature. While the God of the Bible necessarily transcends nature as its creator, he also pervades nature as (1) the upholder of all things; and (2) the provider of all things. As regards (1) he ordains and maintains the laws of nature through the moment-by-moment action of his mind and will, while as regards (2) he employs these same laws providentially to bring about his purposes in the material world. However, the point to grasp here is that because of (1) he is not limited to (2)! If the laws of nature are indeed the present tense expression of the mind of God, as opposed to some system independent of God, there is no reason why he should not override them locally in space and time to cause a miracle to occur.

Let me illustrate. When I worked in London I commuted daily from my home in Hertfordshire. Suppose a visitor from outer space was sent secretly to study human behaviour and allotted the task of discovering what rules governed my movements day by day. The hidden observer would soon see that I left my house at a given time, walked to the railway station a mile away and boarded a train to London. However, this only happened for five days in succession and then for two days I did not travel. This pattern was repeated in a cyclic fashion and could be written down as a formula. Happy with his findings, the alien sociologist is about to report his results when, unexpectedly and without warning, I get into my car one day and drive to London instead. A 'miracle' has occurred—a deviation from the established and well-documented 'law'. But that is only in the perception of the observer. In my own mind both rail travel and car travel are conscious decisions made daily in the light of circumstances; they are not qualitatively different. Normally the hassle of heavy traffic made rail travel preferable, but if I had to haul home a heavy load of books or papers it made sense to use door-to-door transport.

In the same way, it normally suits God's purpose, as 'Lord of heaven and earth'[23] to work providentially by employing his own natural laws. Why should he bother to do so if he is in moment-by-moment control of everything? Because there is much benefit in this mode of operation. As we have seen, the consistency and elegance of these laws testifies to the existence, intelligence, power and orderly nature of God as creator. Romans 1:20 states: 'For since the creation of the world [God's] invisible attributes are clearly seen, being understood by the things that are made, even His eternal power and Godhead, so that [unbelieving men] are without excuse.' Furthermore, the laws of nature also serve mankind because their predictability allows civilization and technology to flourish, to name but one benefit. On rare occasions, however, God perceives that a departure from normality is needed and he overrides natural law to effect a non-natural or miraculous event. In either case, however, whether events occur by natural process or by miraculous fiat, it is the present-tense mind and will of God that operates. The miracle is real but differs from a natural event only in the eyes of the observer, not of the ever-immanent God.

The biblical hypothesis of God thus predicts three things. Firstly, it leads us to expect the cosmos to be 'ruled' by consistent, rational and universal laws of nature—because the universe is the product of a rational, omnipresent and almighty creator whose nature 'do[es] not change'.[24] Secondly, it posits that these laws of nature are not self-standing independent principles that exist apart from their originator, but are rather the moment-by-moment expression of his mind and will. As a result, in providence, he causes these laws to 'work together' in such a way that his purposes are fulfilled through them. But, thirdly, our hypothesis also allows that while God normally directs the laws of nature to accomplish his ends *providentially*, he nevertheless has complete freedom to 'change his mind' and operate within the natural world in a different mode, namely *miraculously*.

## Objections

A number of objections will, of course, be raised. One problem is that this view makes incredible demands upon God. It is one thing, say the deists and their theistic fellow-travellers, for God to create the laws of nature and leave them to do their stuff without further divine intervention, but quite another to monitor continually every atom in the cosmos. Yes, I accept that this degree of control is beyond our comprehension, but let's not forget that modern physics lives with equally mind-blowing speculations, as I have tried to demonstrate in earlier chapters. For example, scientists continue to toy with the fantastic 'many worlds' hypothesis which seeks to circumvent the contradictions of quantum theory (and rescue Schrödinger's cat from limbo) by proposing that every subatomic event that has two possible outcomes in QM (the cat is either dead or alive) actually gives rise to two new universes in which each outcome is realized respectively. According to this idea, an incalculable number of new universes have been created since I started writing this sentence—and presumably each of *those* universes is busy splitting itself into countless others. There can't be enough cats to go round.

Furthermore, if God merely set up the laws of nature and then withdrew from all involvement with them (or even if they set themselves up without divine assistance) what power *does* maintain them in such intricate and pristine order? Why should they remain in place, immutable and rock-like in a universe that otherwise is constantly changing? The Roman poet Juvenal asked *Quis custodiet ipsos custodes?* (Who will guard the guards?) It demands an answer from nature as well as from society.

A different kind of objection is that offered by many theists— miracles are inadmissable because God is perfect in orderliness and any deviation from natural law would violate his perfection. For a full discussion of this matter you're going to have to read Cornelius Hunter's excellent analysis in *Science's blind spot*,[25] but put briefly the objection is based on a non-biblical and rationalistic concept of what constitutes 'perfection'. It is, in fact, an idea that actually detracts from God's perfection because it gravely restricts his freedom of action. The biblical hypothesis of God proposes instead a much more satisfactory reality, namely, that absolute power and absolute perfection go hand in hand. It certainly won't let us bind God in a straight-jacket designed by the feeble mind of man.

# CHAPTER TWELVE ...

... in which a dysfunctional moon-rover introduces us to information theory and leads us in a search for the ingredients of life. Following a brief 'layman-friendly' explanation—in which we 'meet the molecules' that constitute the basis of life—we consider the scientific impossibility of life arising by chance.

We'll see how information is *stored* on DNA molecules, *transcribed* onto RNA molecules and *translated* into proteins (which are the work-horses of the living cell). The processes of storage, transcription and translation closely mimic an advanced human language, involving codes, syntax and semantics. This 'language of God' (as Francis Collins, leader of the Human Genome Project, calls it) is present in all living systems and without it no life would be possible. It follows that the essence of life resides not in chemistry but in *information and communication*—things that can only be the product of intelligence, not chance, and which the hypothesis of God leads us to expect.

## New words?

Yes, quite a few, but they are all explained in the text.

# 12. Information, stupid!

If the minimal organism involves not only the code for its one or more proteins, but also twenty types of soluble RNA, one for each amino-acid, and the equivalent of ribosomal RNA, our descendants may be able to make one, but we must give up the idea that such an organism could have been produced in the past, except by a similar pre-existing organism or by an agent, natural or supernatural, at least as intelligent as ourselves, and with a good deal more knowledge.

J. B. S. Haldane; *Data needed for a blueprint of the first organism*, 1965¹

**W**e used to call them proverbs or *bons mots* but today they're 'sound-bites'—short pithy sayings which stick in the memory and convey some significant idea. Such was the slogan, 'It's the economy, stupid,' coined by Bill Clinton's campaign strategist James Carville during the US presidential campaign of 1991. By zeroing in on the plight of the US economy, Clinton unseated the incumbent George H. W. Bush—who had been thought unassailable because of the recent end of the 'cold war' and the successful Persian Gulf campaign. For the Clinton team the faltering economy was a winner; to overlook it would have been easy but stupid.

The same is true of 'information' as we turn to the important subject of the nature and origin of life. We are often told that life consists of nothing more than organic chemistry and that we must discard the idea that it is in some way mysterious or 'special'. But this dismissive statement ignores the inconvenient fact that life depends crucially upon the storage and transmission of detailed information. Easy to overlook, perhaps, but nonetheless stupid to do so.

## Information theory

In digging deeper into the matter of information, people often appeal to 'information theory', so it might be useful to get a grasp of this before going any further. Imagine you are a robot moon-rover sitting on the moon waiting for instructions. However, there is a problem. Your radio tuning device has malfunctioned, so that instead of tuning in selectively to the Houston control centre, your sensitive antenna picks up every passing signal whatever its source. You're tuned in to the universe—impressive but confusing.

Basic (statistical) information theory treats every input signal as equivalent and calls it 'information'—simply because it's new to you. Regardless of whether it is random radio noise from a distant galaxy or a frantic plea from Houston to wake up, it counts as information and can be analysed statistically by the theory. Clearly, information theory at this level isn't going to tell us very much.

Even if you do identify a meaningful message, the statistical theory of information turns up some odd results. Suppose Houston sends a message consisting of the following sequence of letters: findthemaninthemoon. The theory allows us to calculate the 'information content' of this sequence of letters as (approximately) 77 bits. But if precisely the same message had been sent in German instead of English it would have contained 99 bits—nearly 30% more information. This helps us to see both the value and the weakness of the statistical theory. It allows us to *quantify* the amount of information that must be transmitted to convey a message, and thus to identify the most efficient way of sending it (in the example, English is more efficient than German). On the downside, because it considers only the number and frequency of symbols, the theory tells us nothing about the meaning of the message.

The source of the problem is clear. By simply counting symbols the theory pays no regard to the syntax or structure of the message. Any ten letters of the English alphabet would have (almost) the same statistical 'information content', regardless of whether or not they spelled out anything meaningful. Clearly, we need to move up a notch in our search for information.

## The concept of code

The first step beyond 'statistical information' necessitates a code. A code is simply a kind of alphabet—something in which symbols are assigned agreed meanings or functions. In linguistics and language theory, a 'symbol' is defined as something that has meaning in isolation and in the absence of an object. However, I shall employ it in the broader sense used in information theory, where it can include not only meaningful written signs but also recognizable sounds, scents, actions and so on.

Many—perhaps all—animals communicate using codes, which range from simple alarm cries or a hen's call to her chicks, to the complex array of whistles by which dolphins keep in touch. Honey bees perform a 'dance' to tell the hive where nectar is to be found, the 'steps' in the dance indicating both the direction and distance of the hoard. This too is a code. Animal scents may also provide a primitive communication system between members of a species. Ant colonies, for example, use pheromones to pass information around. While none of these animal codes amount to a language in the conventional sense, they all use signs or symbols to pass useful information from one creature to another. Finally, there are human languages in which specific utterances or written characters are endowed with significance. The written English language uses twenty-six symbols (twenty-seven if you include a space), while written Chinese, I am told, employs more than 50,000 characters, each representing a single word. The symbols in the English alphabet are totally different from Arabic or Chinese characters but as long as each symbol is assigned a meaning, each of the three languages can convey the same message.

Although codes come in all shapes and sizes, they all share certain indispensable features. First, they must contain at least two symbols. No meaningful message can be conveyed using a single symbol, but a two-symbol 'alphabet' has enormous potential—witness the Morse code with its 'dot' and 'dash' symbols, and the binary code of 'ones' and 'zeros' on which all computing is currently based. The secret of such codes lies, of course, in the sequences in which the symbols are arranged. Interestingly, to convey information, these arrangements must be neither regular nor random.

A second condition that must be met by a code is that each symbol (or group of symbols such as a word) must have a significance that is *agreed* between those using the code. I was once speaking by translation at a church in Germany when I told the congregation that they should regard their pastor as God's gift to them. The pastor himself was interpreting, but being equally at home in both English and German he failed to translate the word 'gift' but simply repeated it as 'gift'. Now 'gift' *is* a German word but unfortunately it means 'poison' in that language. I'm pleased to say that the congregation saw the funny side of it. The point of the story is, of course, that although both languages use the word 'gift' they don't agree on what it means, leading to the transmission of disinformation rather than information.

'Agreement' is basic to the creation and transmission of information, and all such agreement involves intelligence. In animal communication 'agreement' may involve instinctive recognition of the meaning of symbols or it may be arrived at by a learning process. But either way there can be no agreement without intelligence—by which I mean brain or nervous system activity at some level or another.

## Using codes to send messages

Clearly, the symbols of an alphabet or other code do not themselves constitute messages. A string of symbols that reads abababab... employs the English alphabet code but conveys no meaningful information. For that we need language, in which the code symbols are arranged in 'words' or groups that themselves possess an agreed significance—a significance which transcends that of the symbols forming the words. In my 'gift' story, both English and German agree on the symbols, using and pronouncing the letters 'g', 'i', 'f' and 't' in exactly the same way. But they disagree profoundly about the meaning of the whole word. When we consider the use of codes to express meaning, therefore, we enter a new level of information called 'morphology'—which decrees how basic symbols should be joined together to produce the elements of language (such as words in a written or spoken language).

At the next higher level of information—called syntax—the language elements (I'll call them 'words' for simplicity) can be arranged in sequences that spell out instructions and messages. The arrangement is important. 'Find the man in the moon' means one thing but 'Find the moon in the man', if it means anything at all, conveys a quite different message.[2] This leads immediately to the next level of information known as 'semantics', which is the study of meaning and is involved in the transmission and understanding of ideas. It must always feature when instructions are given.

There are yet higher levels of information[3] that are, perhaps, of less concern to us in this chapter. All human language involves 'pragmatics'—the interpretation of messages according to contextual constraints. For example, an instruction must specify the action requested. Houston *tells* the moon-rover to carry out some pre-ordained task, like picking up moon rocks or analysing soil samples. But why? Therein lies the highest level of information—apobetics—which delineate the purpose or intent of the message. In Houston's case the purpose of its instructions is not really to find the man in the moon but rather to discover the geological properties of the satellite's surface.

Although I have illustrated the various levels of communication in the context of a written human language, they can in principle be found in all forms of information transfer—not least in the workings of a living cell, as we shall now see.

## The living factory

In the chapter-head quote, published posthumously, the geneticist and evolutionary biologist John Haldane (1892–1964) refers to the 'minimal organism'—meaning the simplest object that could be considered 'alive'. The smallest living entity known to us is the single biological cell, and if we stick to fact rather than fantasy, this is the closest thing we can imagine to a 'minimal organism'. (Note that viruses are not truly alive because they can't multiply without hijacking the reproductive machinery of a cell. They could not, therefore, have been precursors to cells.) Some single cells are living creatures in their own right, like bacteria or amoeba. Others function together in multi-cellular organisms such as plants and animals. Either way, the secret of physical life can be traced back to the inner workings of single cells.

Even the simplest single cell is a highly organized and complex structure. The living cell has aptly been likened to a factory, complete with a boundary fence (the cell wall); gates, docking bays and security systems; entry facilities for raw materials; shipping facilities for finished products; internal transport systems; power plants (mitochondria); waste disposal plants (proteasomes); machines for manufacturing proteins (ribosomes); an army of workers with many different skills (enzymes); messengers (mRNA); stock-pickers (tRNA) and blueprints (DNA).

Furthermore, the cell can and must do something that no man-made factory can achieve, namely, reproduce its entire self to order. It is this level of complexity that persuaded Haldane, contrary to all his evolutionary convictions, that the first living organism could never have come into existence by chance. And in the half-century since he made this assertion, nothing has happened to show he was wrong. Indeed, the more we discover about the fantastic complexity of a single living cell, the more obvious his statement becomes.

It would take a molecular biology textbook to tell the whole story, so in this chapter we'll concentrate on just one aspect of the life process—one that drives every other function of the cell. I refer to the storage and use of meaningful information. Enormous strides have been made in understanding how life 'works' since James Watson and Francis Crick discovered the double-helix structure of DNA in 1953, and to benefit from the rest of this chapter you'll need to know something about 'the molecular basis of life'. If you majored in chemistry or molecular biology you can skip a few pages, but for the benefit of ordinary mortals we'll take a moment to sketch out the essentials. So let's meet the molecules!

## Meet the molecules

What are molecules? They are groups of atoms linked together by strong chemical bonds. Thus a molecule of water, having the familiar chemical formula $H_2O$, contains an oxygen atom linked to two hydrogen atoms. But the molecules you are going to meet now are much larger and usually form long flexible chains. You can picture them as strings of popper beads in which the individual beads represent small clusters of atoms (not single atoms). These long-chain molecules are called 'polymers' because they consist of many (*poly*) units (*mers*) and the ones that specially interest us are called 'biopolymers' because they occur naturally only in living organisms. There are many different biopolymers but I'm going to introduce you to the leading actors in the drama of life—three kinds of biopolymer called respectively protein, DNA and RNA.

## Proteins

You already know about proteins because you have to consume them to stay healthy. Meat, fish (nuts and seeds, if you're a vegetarian), cheese, eggs, milk, legumes and many other protein-rich foods form an essential part of our diet. When we ingest proteins the body breaks them down into their component parts—the popper-beads are pulled apart. In proteins these 'beads' are small molecules called amino-acids and there are twenty different kinds of amino-acid used by living organisms.[4] These amino-acids, however, are then used by the cells in our bodies to synthesize new protein molecules.

A typical living cell contains several thousand different proteins, each playing its own role in the life of the cell. Proteins provide all the cellular structural material, they control cell growth and metabolism, and they include hundreds of worker 'enzymes' that carry out activity tasks within the cell—by catalysing chemical reactions that would otherwise occur only slowly or not at all.

But proteins are not just random strings of amino-acids. The *sequence* of different amino-acids along a protein chain is vital because it makes that particular protein molecule fold up into a unique and complex shape, one that is different from any other protein. It is this folded shape that allows a given protein to perform its own special function in the overall life process—much as a uniquely shaped key is needed to operate a particular lock.

## DNA

The second polymer molecule you need to meet is DNA, which stands for deoxyribonucleic acid (so let's stick to DNA). You will almost certainly read about DNA in your newspaper tomorrow because in recent years it has become an essential tool in crime detection, genetic diseases and the determination of parentage. Each of us has a unique 'DNA profile' which can be derived from our skin, blood, hair, saliva or any other source of body cells.

Like protein, DNA is a long-chain biopolymer but it has a completely different chemical structure. Whereas the units or *mers* in proteins are amino-acids, those in DNA are called 'nucleotides'—chemical clusters that contain a phosphate, a sugar and a protruding chemical side-group called a 'base'. There are just four different bases in DNA, their chemical names being cytosine, guanine, adenine and thymine (thankfully abbreviated C, G, A and T).

The nucleotides are linked together into long chains, and two such chains combine to form the famous double helix. Think of a spiral staircase with its two spiralling side-rails linked at regular intervals by the rungs or steps themselves. Each side-rail is a standard nucleotide chain, while a step on the staircase is formed when a base protruding from one rail sticks or bonds to one protruding from the other. Thus each 'step' in the DNA spiral staircase actually consists of two halves, each half being a base and a complete step being a 'base pair'. In forming base pairs, C always bonds with G and A with T, so that there are only four different possible 'steps' on the spiral staircase (C-G, G-C, A-T and T-A).

The bases are normally linked together as base pairs to form complete 'steps' which firmly connect the two rails and so stabilize the double helix. However, the cell has special enzyme molecules that can work their way along the DNA spiral, unfastening the bonds between the step-halves and thus unzipping the double helix (partly or wholly) into two separate strands. Imagine someone taking a chain saw and running it down the middle of an ordinary ladder, cutting all the rungs in half and producing two giant coat-racks! In this picture (which, of course, ignores the helical twist), the protruding coat-pegs represent the unpaired bases. Each of the two exposed strands can then act as a template for the assembly of a new matching strand. The new strand is built by new nucleotides attaching themselves to the template via their own bases—reconstituting base-pair linkages and creating a new double helix.

## RNA

When a cell divides into two daughter cells, this unzipping and duplicating process travels all the way along each DNA molecule, producing two identical double helices, one for each of the two new cells. However, when the cell just wants to make a new protein molecule, the DNA double helix unravels only along part of its length (a section called a gene) and one of the exposed single strands is used as a template to construct a new molecule that copies the gene, base by base. This process is called 'transcription' and the resulting new molecule is called 'messenger ribonucleic acid' (mRNA). It really is a messenger because it copies information from the gene and carries it to where it can be used.

Although RNA and DNA are first cousins, they differ in three ways. Firstly, RNA has a different sugar molecule in its 'popper-bead' units, a fact which makes it less stable than DNA. That's a good thing because, unlike DNA which acts as a permanent store of information, the mRNA serves only a temporary purpose. Secondly, RNA spends its life as a single strand (it never forms a double helix *in vivo*). Again that's just as well because its 'coat-peg' bases need to remain exposed, as we shall see. Thirdly, the base thymine (T) that occurs in DNA is replaced in RNA by a different base called uracil (U).

Once formed, the mRNA molecule detaches from its DNA template and, remaining as a single strand, like the 'coat-rack' mentioned above, it makes its way to the cell's protoplasm. There it is captured by protein-manufacturing 'machines' called ribosomes. Meanwhile, the original DNA double helix is restored as if nothing had happened.

The ribosome 'machine' uses the mRNA 'coat-rack' as a template on which to assemble a matching protein molecule. It does this by recognizing the 'pegs' (bases) on the coat-rack and attaching the appropriate amino-acid at that site. This is a closely regulated process in which it takes three successive bases to specify any particular amino-acid (see later).

The amino-acids needed to build the protein molecule are just hanging around in the cell like unemployed workers in a dole queue. But once the ribosome recognizes the first (triple-base) site on the mRNA, it sends out a request for the corresponding amino-acid. Yet another small molecule of nucleic acid, called 'transfer RNA' (tRNA) is immediately summoned to fetch the required amino-acid from among all those available. It acts like a stock-picker in a factory, first finding the correct amino-acid and then bringing it to the ribosome to start the protein chain.

As the template mRNA feeds through the ribosome, so the process is repeated. The next site is recognized and its corresponding amino-acid is fetched and added to the growing protein molecule. Eventually the ribosome encounters a stop-sign and its job is done. The newly formed protein chain is released, folded into its own special shape and sent on its way to perform its function in the cell—or is 'exported' for use elsewhere in a multi-cellular organism.

The double template copying action—gene to mRNA then mRNA to protein—means that the final result is a *particular* protein, containing a unique sequence of amino-acids that corresponds precisely to the unravelled section (gene) on the DNA.

## So where's the information?
We saw earlier that DNA contains four different bases (C, G, A, T) which stick out like 'pegs' along a DNA single strand 'coat-rack' when the DNA double helix is unravelled. The four pegs can occur in any order and it is their *sequence* that stores genetic information. In effect, the four bases constitute the four-symbol alphabet of the language of life.

'The cat sat on the mat' is a sequence of twenty-two symbols (letters and spaces) which, however trite, constitutes information. How else would we know the cat's posture and position? But notice that although the information is conveyed by twenty-two symbols, there are only ten *different* symbols present. This should come as no surprise because we know that an infinite number of meaningful messages can be written using the English language which, with commendable economy, employs only twenty-seven symbols (including a space; forget the punctuation).

DNA stores information in essentially the same way, though with even greater economy since its 'alphabet' has only four symbols. However, the principle is exactly the same as in a written language. For example, 'the cat sat on the mat' provides useful information but exactly the same symbols arranged in a different order—'tth aem sec ta aht tno'—make complete nonsense. In fact the essence of written language is that only a relatively small number of symbol sequences actually do make sense, while random sequences never spell out meaningful messages. In the same way, the bases (symbols) on each strand of the DNA are not strung along the molecule in a random manner—as they would be if their sequence were determined simply by chemistry during DNA chain-building. On the contrary, just as a language first organizes its alphabetic symbols into words and then arranges words into sentences (to make statements or give instructions), so also does the cell's genetic language. The bases in DNA are first arranged into word-like triplets called 'codons', and each codon corresponds to (or codes for) a specific amino-acid. For example, the triplet sequence GCA specifies an amino-acid called 'alanine'. This is the first level of organization and without it life could not exist. If there were no base triplets, there would be no way of knowing which amino-acids to select to make proteins. No proteins, no life. It's as simple as that. The way specific codons specify (or 'code for') particular amino-acids is what we call the genetic code.[5]

But it's not enough to specify the amino-acids in a protein. As we have seen, to make a working protein molecule the *right* amino-acids must be arranged in the *right* sequence. So the codons on the DNA gene must themselves be organized at a higher level to spell out instructions for the manufacture of the required protein—just as word sequences spell out a message in a written language. This is the second level of organization. Clearly, the arrangement of bases along a DNA gene exhibits the essential features of language—using a code to contain (and store) information at the levels of morphology (codon 'words'), syntax (codon sequence) and semantics (the meaningful instruction to make a *particular* protein). In other words, the DNA of living things is imprinted with information in a manner reminiscent of an advanced language.

Finally, the two levels of organization (codons and instructions) are preserved in the go-between mRNA molecule—so that when the mRNA acts as the final template for the assembly of a protein molecule, the latter corresponds exactly to the instructions encoded in the gene (the length of DNA replicated to make that particular protein). Furthermore, protein synthesis involves not only transcription—making a copy of the language-like information on the gene—but also requires *translation*. At the first level of organization, codons are 'translated' into the corresponding amino-acids in the protein. At the second level of organization, the codon sequences are translated into valid protein structures. This translation process again mirrors the behaviour of written languages, which can be translated into one another using appropriate dictionaries and rules.

Before we move on I need to add one thing—the description I have given of the life process in a single cell is highly simplified and incomplete. The amazing complexity of cell life must also provide answers to many other questions, such as:

- How does the cell know it needs a new batch of a particular protein?

- How does it know where to look for the appropriate gene among the cell's enormous collection of DNA? After all, only a fraction of the total DNA in a cell codes for proteins (varying from 2–3% in humans to 20% or more in bacteria). Until recently, the remaining DNA was called 'junk DNA' and supposed to be the detritus of failed evolutionary experiments. However, this view is changing, as more and more function is being identified within this 'non-coding' DNA.

- How does the cell know where to start unravelling the double helix and where to stop? Clearly, individual genes must be demarcated by 'punctuation' just as, in written English, capital letters and full stops tell us where sentences begin and end. But who thoughtfully put the punctuation in place?

- We know that genes can be 'switched on' to make proteins or 'switched off' to prevent protein manufacture. This involves regulatory proteins which are surprisingly similar in simple and complex organisms and which seem able to 'switch on' not only single genes but the instructions to make entire anatomical structures (though not novel ones).[6] This constitutes a whole new level of complexity. How is it done?

- DNA must also provide the information needed to produce RNA, not just proteins. Where is this information stored?

- It is known that the cell has a capacity for 'proof-reading' molecular transcriptions and correcting errors. How do these facilities function and how did they arise?

- What mechanisms are involved in cell division?

Molecular biology *does* have answers to many of these questions; my point is that the complexity and sophistication of the simplest form of life is almost overwhelming.

## The language of God

I was brought up to believe the duck theorem—'If it looks like a duck, walks like a duck and quacks like a duck it probably *is* a duck.' That is why I have problems with those who (1) admit that nature gives every evidence of being intelligently designed; (2) introduce an alternative materialistic explanation for the *appearance* of design; and then (3) without further discussion conclude that only their alternative explanation can be true. Meet the neo-duckians, whose logic demands that 'If it looks like a duck, walks like a duck and quacks like a duck it is indubitably a chicken.' Such are those who tell us that the cell's molecular language is merely an accident of nature. We have seen that the storage and use of information in the living cell exhibits many, if not all, of the characteristics of human language. Let's set this out clearly:

1. As in human language, the cell employs a code, specifically a four-symbol alphabet.

2. As in human language, the cell organizes its symbols into words (codons).

3. As in human language, the words have an agreed meaning so that they can be recognized by the ribosomes and 'translated' into an alternative amino-acid 'language'.

4. As in many human languages, punctuation is used to demarcate genes.

5. As in human language, words are organized into instructions that specify which one of many possible proteins is to be made by copying a given gene.

6. As in human language, the cell's language has a purpose—namely to construct protein sequences that will fold in specific ways to provide functional keys and catalysts to operate the cell.

In other words, the molecular information system in living cells not only resembles a language—it *is* a language and it all looks remarkably like intelligent design. The neo-duckist will disagree, however. Human and animal languages have evolved, they argue, and are still evolving. Why should the cell's genetic language not also be the product of naturalistic evolution? Indeed, many ingenious but so far unconvincing attempts have been made to hypothesize chemical routes by which the cell's chemical language might have arisen by chance, with a little help from (you guessed it) natural selection.

But while the correspondence between genetic language and human language is solid, any analogy between their respective 'evolutions' is an illusion, and that for one very simple reason. For language to evolve requires the prior existence of intelligence at some level. This is true both of human language and of animal communication systems, whether learnt or instinctive. The development of a language of any kind requires that the information sender has 'intention' and the receiver has 'comprehension'. In a primitive organism the 'intention' may not, of course, be conscious. It could be, for example, a colour change that warns a predator away. But the sender has to have some kind of nervous system that detects the predator and switches on the warning sign. Similarly, no communication occurs unless the predator itself has a nervous system able to detect the warning, interpret it, and keep its distance.

No such possibility exists in the origin of molecular language. If natural chemical processes gave birth to such language (and thus to life) there was no pre-existent *material* intelligence to provide midwifery services. And if intelligence is necessary to prevent still-birth, it had to be that of 'supernature' not nature, making the language of the living cell *The language of God*—to borrow the title of Francis Collins' book.[7]

To summarize, therefore, the locus of development of all animal and human language systems is the brain or nervous system. Such 'evolution' is not a physical process but a mental one capable of generating and recognizing symbols and agreeing on their meaning. There are no such things as clever molecules.

### The hypothesis of God

So let us finally ask what the biblical hypothesis of God has to say about the language of life. You won't find much in the Bible about molecular biology, because the biblical writers knew nothing about it. What we do find in the Bible, however, are two inter-related principles. The first is the idea that God is the source of all life, and the second that God 'speaks' (uses language) both to create and sustain the material universe. Let's look at them in turn.

Firstly, from a biblical perspective, life is inseparable from God. 'He gives to all life, breath, and all things,' declares St Paul, for 'in Him we live and move and have our being'.[8] Of Christ, St John tells us: 'All things were made through Him, and without Him nothing was made that was made. In Him was life, and the life was the light of men.'[9] Again, Jesus himself said, 'For as the Father has life in Himself, so He has granted the Son to have life in Himself,'[10] while Acts 3:15 calls

Christ 'the Prince of life'. Of course, when the Bible speaks of 'life' it can refer to either physical life or spiritual life and we have to determine from the context which is intended. But there can be no question that physical life is often in view—as in the above quotation from Paul and when Jesus explained his power to raise Lazarus *physically* from the dead by asserting, 'I am the resurrection and the life.'[11]

The biblical concept is that all life, whether physical or spiritual, resides in God and flows from God—so that the life of all living things, including ourselves, is derivative from his. Many other texts demonstrate this perception. According to Genesis 2:7: 'the LORD God formed man of the dust of the ground, and breathed into his nostrils the breath of life; and man became a living being.' In the book of Job, Elihu declares: 'The Spirit of God has made me, and the breath of the Almighty gives me life.'[12] We are told in the Psalms that 'the fountain of life' is with God,[13] while Job asks: 'Who among all these [creatures] does not know that the hand of the LORD has done this, in whose hand is the life of every living thing, and the breath of all mankind?'[14]

Secondly, if all life derives from God it is hardly surprising that the biblical hypothesis attributes the *origin* of life to the direct action of God. We read in Genesis 2:19: 'Out of the ground the LORD God formed every beast of the field and every bird of the air, and brought them to Adam to see what he would call them.' But what is particularly germane for us here is that the creation of the biosphere is attributed to the *voice* of God: 'Then God said, "Let the earth bring forth grass, the herb that yields seed, and the fruit tree that yields fruit according to its kind, whose seed is in itself, on the earth"; and it was so.'[15] As Genesis 1 continues, the refrain is repeated for the creation of all other living things, and finally of man himself—in every case we read, 'Then God *said'*. The words suggest not some audible disembodied voice but rather the twin ideas of divine command and communication. We have already noticed in chapters 10 and 11 that our hypothesis identifies the laws of nature (and thus the workings of providence) as the 'word of [Christ's] power'. We now see that creation is *also* attributed to 'the voice of God'. The idea that God is 'speaking' in nature is woven into the fabric of the Judaeo-Christian Scriptures. It leads to the thesis that God has first created and now sustains the physical universe by acts of divine *communication*—using whatever 'language' is appropriate for the task in hand (the word 'language' meaning any vehicle of efficient communication).

If this is so, we would expect God's use of language to be reflected in his works in nature. Thus the ability of creatures of all kinds to (1) communicate using symbols with agreed meaning; (2) to learn from such communication and act upon it; and (3) in the case of man, to develop elevated language skills; are all derivable from the basic idea that God, the Creator and sustainer of all things, is a speaking God who uses language of one kind or another in all his interaction with the created order. This same principle also emerges in the concept of divine revelation, to which we referred in chapter 6.

To this perspective we can now add (as a result of this chapter) the fact that all physical life consists essentially of language—coded information that is in turn constructed, stored, communicated, interpreted and acted upon. What else would we expect of a Creator who 'speaks' all things into existence?

This insight helps also to explain why all life is based upon the *same* molecular mechanisms and the *same* genetic code. Evolution claims that this commonality can only be explained in terms of common descent—that the first life form came into being by chance and that all other life forms share identical life processes because they have descended from this one 'primal organism'. But the hypothesis of God provides us with another, and I believe more rational, explanation. Where physical life is concerned God speaks just one language—giving rise to a single molecular basis of life, a single genetic code and a single system by which that language is expressed in a great diversity of creatures. Commonality is a fact, but it lies in the language God employs. It doesn't have to be explained by Darwinian common descent.

# CHAPTER THIRTEEN ...

... in which we pursue the jellypod, seeking to understand how the first living organism might have come into existence spontaneously by a chance combination of chemicals. We'll follow the work of Craig Venter who builds artificial DNA but only by using sophisticated chemistry and high intelligence, not by tipping the ingredients into a cake mixer.

We introduce 'glove soup' and discover why undirected chemistry can never create biopolymer molecules that actually work, let alone the complex molecular machines present in even the simplest living cell. We examine the naturalistic idea that these structures could just happen spontaneously by some kind of self-organization but find it utterly implausible and devoid of scientific content.

Turning to the hypothesis of God, however, we do finally identify an organizing principle—the mind of God—that is more than adequate to explain how life began.

## New words?

*Jellypod*: My pet name for what Haldane called the 'minimal organism'—the simplest life-form that could exist.

*Panspermia*: The idea that life did not evolve on earth but arrived from outer space. 'Directed panspermia' claims that intelligent beings were responsible for such an event.

# 13. Life in a cake mixer

An honest man, armed with all the knowledge available to us now, could only state that in some sense, the origin of life appears at the moment to be almost a miracle, so many are the conditions which would have had to have been satisfied to get it going.

Francis Crick, Nobel Prize winner
and co-discoverer of the double helix, in *Life itself* (1981)[1]

First he was a jellypod beginning to begin,
Then he was a tadpole with his tail tucked in;
Then he was a monkey in a banyan tree,
And now he's a scientist with a PhD.          Anon.

We shall spend this chapter in pursuit of the jellypod. That's my pet name for Haldane's 'minimal organism'— the simplest entity that could be called 'living' and which we discussed briefly at the start of chapter 12. No disrespect is intended; jellypod is just more memorable than 'minimal organism'.

In chapter 12, having pointed out the enormous complexity of even the simplest life-form known to us today, we put the jellypod on one side to seek out the essence of physical life. This turned out to be organized information—something, moreover, that cannot be stored, transmitted or put to work without the use of communication or 'language'. This is just what we would expect on the biblical hypothesis of God, since the Bible attributes both the origin and maintenance of the natural world to God's 'spoken word'—a metaphor that embraces the twin ideas of command and communication. It is no surprise, therefore, that the molecular foundations of life are stacked full of information and bear all the marks of advanced language.

But now we must let the jellypods have their day and the atheists their say—for they claim (the atheists, that is, not the jellypods) that not only was the origin of molecular information and language a purely material accident but so was the whole jellypod caboodle. Science writer Paul Davies declares: 'Science takes as its starting point the assumption that life wasn't made by a god or supernatural being: it happened unaided and spontaneously, as a natural process.'[2] Let's see if this highly questionable claim stands up.

## Baking bacteria

We have already seen that our jellypod must have resembled a tiny though highly sophisticated factory, but we must now look deeper into its inner workings to see how it might have arisen by chance (or not, as the case may be). How could we prove that, in one giant leap for jellypods, the first 'minimal organism' just happened? Actually, we never could, but we might be able to render the idea plausible. One way would be to manufacture such an entity in the laboratory using only undirected chemistry and materials that could have been present on an ancient lifeless earth. In fact, Haldane envisaged just such a project when he said, '...our descendants may be able to make one' (ch. 12 headline quote). But let's not forget how he went on: 'but we must give up the idea that such an organism could have been produced in the past, except by a similar pre-existing organism or by an agent, natural or supernatural, at least as intelligent as ourselves, and with a good deal more knowledge'. However, when it comes to jellypods, materialists do not lack for optimism, and the 'idea' that Haldane says we should 'give up' has, in fact, been pursued to this day with great vigour and expense. Here's an example.

In January 2008, *The Times* published an article headlined, 'The life-giving miracle of Dr Venter'.[3] It celebrated the achievement of US scientist Craig Venter and co-workers in synthesizing in the laboratory a bacterial DNA sequence containing over 580,000 base pairs. Among other things, the article claimed that chemistry has abolished the idea that life is something special. It declared: 'Dr Venter ... is simply the latest in a long line of biochemists who have punctured life's claims to specialness. Until 1828 it was believed that life, with its so-called "vital forces", owed nothing to science...' The idea being promoted in the article is, of course, that life is just complicated chemistry, nothing more. That is why (they say) life was able to evolve by the chance combination of ordinary non-living chemicals. But there are several basic fallacies in this 'reductionist' approach to life's origin.

Firstly, Dr Venter's chemical *tour de force* demonstrates that to produce a meaningful string of DNA requires a lot of hard work by highly skilled and intelligent chemists. No one suggests that he and his team simply poured the necessary chemical ingredients into a cake mixer, set it on automatic and took a vacation. And that is just to copy an *existing* DNA molecule. To create the first such molecule from scratch would, I suggest, have required an infinitely greater input of intelligence. It simply isn't good enough to claim that the cake mixer actually will produce a 'life-giving miracle' as long as you run it for a thousand million years or so before you bake the cake. Yet that, in effect, is what the atheist is compelled to claim—as Richard Dawkins seems to confirm in the following passage: 'Suppose we want to suggest, for instance, that life began when both DNA and its protein-based replication machinery *spontaneously chanced to come into existence*. We can allow ourselves the luxury of such an extravagant theory, provided that the odds against this coincidence occurring on a planet do not exceed 100 billion billion to one' (emphasis added).[4] We can now see more clearly why Dawkins needs hand-waving statues and ballistic cows. He first maintains that there is some non-zero *mathematical* probability that all the chemical 'components' required to build a jellypod will join together—in the correct sequence, at the same time and in the same place. He then assumes that this *must* happen given sufficient time. Finally, he cleverly reduces the time required by allowing the process to proceed simultaneously on a billion planets, any one of which could get lucky. However, he is still lost in the never-never land of mathematical probabilities and ignores completely the world of chemical reality.

## Jellypod blues

Our quotes from Haldane in the previous chapter, and from double-helix discoverer Francis Crick in this, confirm that any prospect of building a jellypod from scratch by accidental chemical reactions must be viewed with the deepest scepticism. I'll call this gloomy prognosis the jellypod blues.

In September 1972 I was privileged to be one of four specially invited speakers at the dedication symposium of the Michigan Molecular Institute—the others being Nobel Prize winners Paul Flory and Melvin Calvin (both chemists) and medical scientist Dr Donald J. Lyman.[5] Melvin Calvin's lecture addressed the puzzling 'origin of life' problem concerning how amino-acids might have linked together to form protein-like molecules in an aqueous pre-biological world. Basically, they can't, because water always disrupts such linkages. The only way the problem can be overcome is by providing highly specialized catalyst molecules that help the amino-acids link together in spite of the effects of water (this, of course, is what happens in the living cell, but we're talking here about a time before living cells existed). Calvin showed how such pre-biological catalysts might have worked—but was well aware that they could only assist if they happened to be *there* in the right place at the right time (a highly improbable scenario).

The jellypod blues begin, therefore, when we realize that to create a jellypod spontaneously would require *real* chemistry to take place in some primeval chemical soup or similar environment. Not only would amino-acids have to link together to form protein chains but *at the same time and place,* nucleotides (the building blocks of DNA) would also have to link together into polymer chains, again in the presence of water. But water works against chain formation in both proteins and nucleic acids, so that such molecules could only be built from scratch if a variety of highly specific catalysts just happened to be conveniently on hand. In short, the chance creation of proteins and DNA invokes extremely implausible chemistry. Recognizing this problem, some have suggested that the first biopolymers were formed in dry conditions on mineral surfaces, but the idea has never really caught on. Whenever biologists look for signs of extra-terrestrial life, the first thing they want to see is water, since life as we know it cannot exist without it.

But could mineral surfaces provide the catalytic 'muscle' to overcome the effects of water and allow biopolymers to be built up? It is known that certain crystalline minerals such as zeolites do display catalytic activity and can facilitate polymer formation (chain-building), but they only work under carefully controlled conditions. Some technical publications have explored this route to the formation of polymers of amino-acids and bases. For example, computer modelling has been used to predict how amino-acids might behave within the microscopic pores of zeolites,[6] while studies of the adsorption of bases on graphite have shown that some are adsorbed more strongly than others.[7] But the relevance of such results to the origin of life is both remote and speculative, and to date nothing resembling a protein or nucleic acid polymer has ever been produced by such methods.

As a consultant to the Dow Chemical Company for more than thirty years, I frequently worked with chemists whose job it was to synthesize novel long-chain polymers. Anyone involved in such endeavours knows that success depends on using highly purified starting materials and specialized catalysts. It is impossible to build small molecules into long-chain polymers if there are impurities in the system, because the impurities 'poison' the chemical reaction and contaminate the catalysts. It is ludicrous to suggest that amino-acids or nucleotides (even if present in sufficient concentrations) could spontaneously link together in long chains in a chemical environment containing a random assortment of chemicals.

## Glove soup

The jellypod blues deepen when you realize that any particular amino-acid or nucleotide would be present in a 'primeval soup' in several different forms called 'isomers'. What is an isomer? The word means 'same unit' and isomers are molecules that contain exactly the same atoms but have them arranged in different ways. Imagine a pair of tailored gloves. Each glove has four fingers and a thumb and the two gloves match exactly except for one thing—they are mirror images. One glove fits your right hand and the other your left, and there's nothing you can do to change that arrangement. In the same way, most amino-acids occur as both 'left-handed' or 'right-handed' isomers and (like the gloves) you cannot turn one into the other however much you twist them around.[8,9] Any randomly created 'primeval soup' would contain roughly equal amounts of left- and right-handed isomers, and if these *did* somehow link together, the two forms would crop up more or less randomly along the chain.

But such a polymer would not be a protein molecule because proteins consist *exclusively* of left-handed isomers. Similar considerations apply to nucleic acids and other important biopolymers like starch and cellulose—they are all composed of units having the same 'handedness'. Think of making a 'daisy chain' out of identical gloves by joining the thumb of one glove to the little finger of the next, and so on. A protein is like a chain made up exclusively of left gloves while a strand of nucleic acid resembles a chain of right gloves. Any chain that is a mixture of right and left gloves cannot represent a biopolymer. Nor can there be any exceptions to this rule, because the crucial overall *shape* of the molecule depends on it. For example, DNA could not form a double helix unless all its nucleotides had the same 'handedness', nor could proteins fold up to provide guaranteed 'key shapes' if they were not composed exclusively of one-handed amino-acids.

## Lost in translation

But let's imagine (I know it's hard, but do try) that Richard Dawkins' chemical fantasia is enacted, and a genuine protein molecule and a genuine nucleic acid molecule pop into existence accidentally, side by side, in the same place and at the same time. He is still left with a serious problem. Since the *independent* formation of proteins and DNA would have occurred by random chemical reaction (look, no templates!), the sequence of amino-acids in the proteins, and of base pairs in the DNA, would bear no relation to each other. There would be no match between codons on the DNA (assuming them to be present at all) and the amino-acids for which they need to code. In other words, the 'dictionary' required to translate base-pair sequences into amino-acid sequences would be missing.

Suppose two people independently each created a new 'language' by replacing the letters of the English alphabet by colours. One language might use red for 'A', yellow for 'B', and so on. You could then construct words and sentences by lining up differently coloured balls. The second person does the same but, not knowing what his counterpart is up to, chooses entirely different colours—blue for 'A', pink for 'B' and so on. This is how it would be with proteins and nucleic acids formed independently. Unless someone provides a dictionary telling us which colour in the first language corresponds to which colour in the second, it would never be possible for the two languages to communicate with each other. In the same way, it's not enough to have a 'base-pair language' and an 'amino-acid language' created independently; you have to be able to translate from one to the other. Otherwise life never gets started—it is lost in translation.

Such was Francis Crick's belief that life could never have originated on earth that he seriously advanced the theory of 'directed panspermia'—the idea that life was seeded on earth by extraterrestrial beings of superior cosmic intelligence[10] (but for some reason not by God; Crick was an atheist). However, following the discovery of catalytic action in certain RNA molecules (called ribozymes) he became more optimistic about speculations that a form of life based on RNA (as distinct from DNA and proteins) might have originated on earth.[11] The idea that life began in a mythical 'RNA world' is quite popular because it avoids some of the problems outlined above. But you then have to explain how an RNA world was transformed into the DNA/protein/informational world we know today. The problem of 'translation' re-emerges in a different and equally insoluble form.

## Information isn't chemistry

Which brings us back to information. The second fallacy in *The Times* article lies in claiming that life is nothing but chemistry. This is even more nonsensical than the belief that life arose by spontaneous and accidental generation. It is true that science has removed the need for a mystical 'vital force' to explain why life is special, but what they don't tell you is that science has replaced 'vital force' by something even more amazing—organized information. This we saw in the previous chapter, but let's pursue it a little further.

You may have been given a joke book bearing on its cover the bold title, *What men understand about women* (or similar). On opening the book, however, you discover that all the pages are completely blank. You hold the media (paper pages) in your hand but they contain no message. So it would be with randomly formed DNA molecules because there would be no information stored within them. They would be blank media, like the featureless pages of the book. It is perfectly possible— as a matter of chemistry—to string base pairs together *randomly* to create a pseudo-DNA molecule. But such a molecule would make biological 'nonsense' and could contribute nothing to the life-process (unless like Dr Venter you painstakingly copy the DNA of some existing organism). It is not the chemistry of DNA that underwrites life but the information stored in the DNA—information that is encoded by the meaningful *sequence* of base pairs and which spells out instructions that the living cell can read, translate and use. Life, therefore, consists not in molecular chemistry but in the information stored by the molecular chemistry—which is altogether different.

This book chapter could be stored in many different ways—words printed on paper, binary code stored on a computer, magnetic 'marks' on a tape, microscopic pits on a CD, or even radio waves endlessly circling the globe. The media on which the words are stored are necessary as carriers but they are not the information that constitutes the message. The same media could be blank or used to store a meaningless jumble of letters. Conversely, the meaningful message of this book is indifferent to—and independent of—the particular medium used to store it. Life is still as special as it ever was, because it resides not in the chemical media but in the information stored on the chemical media.

If this is so, we are faced with an intriguing problem. Where did the information come from? Certainly not from physics or chemistry. Some scientists suggest that biomolecules were originally seeded with information because (for example) different amino-acids react chemically at different rates. An amino-acid chain generated by simple chemistry, they say, would not be random but would be rich in fast-reacting amino-acids. This non-random feature might have been the first dawning of information—presumably by the law of unintended consequences. But such reasoning really doesn't hold up. Paul Davies, to give him credit, sees the fallacy and puts it like this: 'If we accept that the genome [the totality of genes] is random and information-rich, then appealing to non-random chemistry to make life is a clear contradiction ... The whole point of the genetic code, for example, is to *free* life from the shackles of non-random chemical bonding. A genome can choose whichever amino-acid sequence it wants, oblivious of the chemical preferences of molecules.'[12]

## The making of a jellypod

Although proteins and nucleic acids are essential to life, they do not *constitute* life. For life to exist requires an organism—our single-cell jellypod. At the beginning of the previous chapter, we saw that even the simplest life form known to us resembles a fully functioning factory. Given DNA (or even RNA) and proteins, how could such a life-form come into existence by chance? It is Dr Venter's ambition, of course, to build a living organism in the laboratory—his successful attempts to copy bacterial DNA is just the first step on a very long journey. But no one knows better than Dr Venter himself that he will never complete that journey by using his cake mixer. If he carefully measured out, in their correct proportions, all the molecular constituents of a bacterial cell and stirred them together, he knows that they would not and could not organize themselves spontaneously into a living organism. That would be no more possible than building a house by piling together all the bricks, timber, mortar, concrete, glass, pipes, cables and so on found in the average dwelling. It isn't enough to get all the ingredients together in one place and expect spontaneous generation to occur. And this applies to even the simplest system *within* the cell, let alone the whole living cell. The easiest way to express this self-evident truth is to say that the creation of a living cell (or a house for that matter) requires ingredients *plus* organization. The materialist could hardly disagree, but would insist that the ingredients have the potential for self-organization. The hypothesis of God, by contrast, traces the organizing principle to divine intelligence. So who is right?

Let's consider just one example of organization within a simple living cell—the molecular machines called 'ribosomes' which make new protein molecules when the cell requires them. What do these 'machines' consist of and how do they work? When an mRNA molecule appears, carrying the instructions for a new protein molecule, it is latched onto by a ribosome consisting of two sub-units, one large and the other small. These sit on either side of the mRNA chain and close around it like a clenched fist. The ribosome then runs along the mRNA template, like the slider on a zip-fastener, first calling for and then adding the appropriate amino-acids one by one. At the same time, a growing protein chain is stripped away in the ribosome and folded into the correct shape, often with the assistance of 'chaperone' proteins. In bacteria, the large sub-unit consists of two different molecules of ribosomal RNA and thirty-four different proteins; the small sub-unit of one molecule of ribosomal RNA and twenty-one different proteins (other kinds of cell have different numbers of proteins). The ribosome is truly a machine and, needless to say, every single component is necessary for it to function correctly.

Of course, evolutionary biology claims that the system by which the cell manufactures proteins has 'evolved' from some simpler arrangement by natural selection. As mentioned earlier, one popular speculation is that of 'the RNA world'[13] in which life was initially based on RNA rather than DNA and protein as now. The main evidence for this idea is that the agent that catalyses protein synthesis in ribosomes is RNA rather than proteins (enzymes). But as I have stressed before, natural selection can only operate once there is a working system already in place. What is at issue here is not how the ribosome acquired its bells and whistles (if it has any) but how the *first protein-making machine* came to exist. Stripped to bare essentials, this primal ribosome would have had to perform these minimal functions:

1. It must recognize an mRNA molecule (or other molecule to be used as a template) when it sees one.

2. It must not only latch on to this molecule but also acquire the ability to run along it like a toy train on a track.

3. As it does so, it must recognize each codon (base triplet) on the mRNA.

4. It must then summon the *appropriate* tRNA molecule to bring the right amino-acid to match the codon it has recognized.

5. It must put the amino-acid in place and attach it to the growing protein chain.

6. It must release the protein chain and, possibly, help it fold into the right shape.

7. It must arise spontaneously by chance because until it starts to do its job it won't get any help from natural selection.

That's an awful lot to ask of a bunch of bewildered molecules. As far as I can see, self-organization doesn't get off the ground. And this applies not only to structures within the cell but also to the amazing coordination that must occur *between* all the intra-cellular structures if the cell is to function efficiently or at all. Just as information is the name of the molecular game, so organization is the name of the cellular game.

## Self-organization

Nevertheless, the materialist has no alternative but to ascribe the jellypod's origin to some form of self-organization, but little headway has been made scientifically. We need to be careful about the term 'self-organization' because it is used to describe a variety of quite different things. For example, it can be applied to the amazing coordinated behaviour often seen in shoals of fish and flocks of birds which spin and wheel as one, as if directed by some invisible choreographer. There is, of course, no such unseen hand. The behaviour results from the uncanny ability of the individual fish or bird to maintain a precise distance from its nearest neighbours and respond to changes instantly. A human 'Mexican wave' at a football stadium is a crude parallel in which individual spectators respond to the actions of people next to them.

So, can molecules do the Mexican wave? Could the seemingly miraculous things that molecules accomplish in a living cell be down to their ability to coordinate with nearby molecules? No, because the analogy is false. What the jellypod needs are not transient molecular *actions* but permanent molecular *structures*. We're talking about the origin of machines not choreographed dances.

Another example of self-organization in nature is crystallization where we do find organized structure. Most solid substances are crystalline, though the individual crystals that compose them are often too small to see with the naked eye. Both solid crystal and liquid crystals display a high degree of order, with every atom or molecule in its place (well, nearly every one) and with exquisite symmetry. And who makes crystals? They make themselves. As a molten substance cools down (or as a solution evaporates) there comes a point when the hitherto free-moving atoms or molecules begin to arrange themselves into crystalline arrays. Once locked into this 'crystal lattice' they are no longer free to wander around but 'stand to attention' in serried ranks like soldiers on a parade-ground. Here, then, is self-organization of a high degree. So why can't molecules organize themselves into similar high-order (low entropy) structures in the cell?

Well, occasionally they do. Some living cells secrete crystalline bone-mineral. Others contain small crystals, including magnetite which, being a magnetic substance, allows migratory creatures like birds and fish to navigate by the earth's magnetic field. Chains of magnetite crystals are also present in certain bacteria[14] where their formation is controlled with some precision by the molecular machinery of the living cell. But this last point also demonstrates the difference between the self-ordering of a crystal and the kind of organization exhibited by the biomolecules in living cells—they are entirely different kinds of organization.

Crystallization is driven exclusively by thermodynamics and is fully understood in terms of the tendency of all physical systems to minimize their 'free energy'. Living cells must also obey thermodynamics, of course, but what happens when molecules get together to create molecular machines is quite different from crystallization. To start with, such machines involve special combinations of *different* molecules. Far from lowering the free energy of the system, mixing different polymers together actually raises it.[15] This means that assembling molecular machines cannot happen spontaneously (if it did, it could be done in a cake mixer). Building a molecular machine is like making water run uphill—something that can't happen of its own accord but can be done by using a pump. Machines such as ribosomes *can* be assembled but only with help from enzyme 'pumps' that work against the thermodynamic tendencies. That calls for a higher layer of organization which must itself be organized. Rather than 'turtles all the way down' it's organization all the way up.

But there is an even more profound reason why crystallization and other natural self-ordering phenomena cannot explain the creation of a jellypod and its constituent molecular machinery. You may have heard the expression, 'the wrong kind of snow'—a by-word for lame excuses. This became something of a proverb in February 1991 when British Railways blamed powdery snow for the frequent breakdown of their diesel-electric locomotives. 'Self-organization' also hits the buffers as an explanation because it is the wrong kind of organization, namely, one which is void of information. Paul Davies puts it this way: 'chemical reactions are easy and thermodynamically favoured [but by contrast] life ... fabricates the necessary catalysts ... to drive against thermodynamic gradients ... Life opts out of the strictures of chemistry by employing an information control channel ... The secret of life lies not in its chemical basis but in the logical and informational rules it exploits.'[16] This, of course, brings us back to the previous chapter. To press the railway analogy, any molecular self-organization that bypasses the need for information and algorithms (instructions), even if it could occur, would be a branch line to nowhere. It could not lead to life *because the only life we know is based on information.*

## The ultimate organizer

The God of the Bible is the ultimate organizer. You may have read science-fiction stories in which some distant and inhospitable planet is 'terraformed' by feats of mega-engineering, turning it into an earth-like sanctuary fit for life. But long before Isaac Asimov and Arthur C. Clarke thought of it, the Bible described the terraforming of earth itself—telling how God took a dark water-covered planet that was 'without form, and void'[17] and transformed it into the kind of world we know. In turn he created light, day and night, sky, geography (land and sea) and an abundance of life—a veritable garden of Eden. Furthermore, he didn't create life in a higgledy-piggledy manner but in a hierarchy of self-propagating 'kinds' (perhaps Linnaeus didn't invent classification after all). The most common Greek term for 'world' in the New Testament is 'cosmos', which has the basic meaning of 'order' or 'arrangement', signifying something both organized and beautiful.

You won't find the word 'organize' in the English Bible but what you will find is the repeated assertion that God 'ordains' both the natural universe (see e.g. Psalm 8) and the 'wisdom' that sustains it: 'He has made the earth by His power, He has established the world by His wisdom, and has stretched out the heavens at His discretion.'[18] In doing so, says the Bible, he 'works all things according to the counsel of His will'[19] and 'does according to His will in the army of heaven and among the inhabitants of the earth'.[20] Furthermore, 'He gives to all life, breath, and all things. And He has made from one blood every nation of men to dwell on all the face of the earth, and has determined their pre-appointed times and the boundaries of their dwellings.'[21] The Lord says, 'I appointed the ancient people. And the things that are coming and shall come.'[22] The powers that be, declares St Paul, are appointed (the Greek word means 'set in array') by God.[23] If that's not organization, I don't know what is.

God's covenants with man provide special evidence that God is the supreme organizer. The word 'covenant' occurs some 250 times in the Bible and the concept looms large in its theology. It would be no exaggeration to say that God's covenants provide the connective tissue that unifies the biblical writings from Genesis to Revelation. Put simply, the Bible reveals a covenant-making and covenant-keeping God. He made covenants[24] with Adam, Noah, Abraham, Isaac, Jacob, Moses and David—who wrote: 'He has made with me an everlasting covenant, ordered in all things and secure.'[25] Above all, God has established his 'new covenant' (the references are almost too numerous to list) under which people of all kinds are reconciled to God on the basis of Christ's death, atonement and resurrection.[26]

The Greek word for 'covenant' means simply 'arrangement' and demonstrates that the biblical Deity habitually ordains things, arranges them and sets them in array. He is the sovereign controller of heaven and earth, the supreme organizer of the cosmos and all that transpires in it. So teaches the hypothesis of God. I appreciate that the Bible says nothing about microbiological organization, but it certainly presents the mind and will of God as the organizing principle that has marshalled the natural world from its outset. No area of existence lies outside its remit. The hypothesis of God, therefore, leads us to expect that, at every level, life should exhibit organization of a high order.

## Intelligent design?

At this point my critics will catch the scent of Intelligent Design (ID) and cry heresy. But are they right? Yes and no. I am indeed proposing that life is intelligently designed but I do not capitalize these words—it's 'id' not ID. Although the proponents of ID have made valuable contributions to this whole debate, there are a number of problems with ID as a theory of origins. Firstly, it embroils people in a pointless debate over whether or not ID is 'science'. My own view is that ID is an inference drawn from science rather than part of science itself. It is not alone in this respect. There is a vast amount of speculation concerning the nature of reality that, because it is promoted by scientists, is thought to *be* science when it is nothing of the kind. One glaring example is the 'multiverse' concept often advanced to 'solve' the riddles of quantum mechanics or to account for the anthropic principle (the fact that our universe is ideally suited for intelligent life). There is not the slightest scientific evidence—or any other kind of evidence if you rule out UFOs—to support the multiverse concept. It can never be more than an inference from scientific data. It might or might not be true, but that is something we shall never know.

Science leads us to its boundaries where it introduces us to philosophy. For example, it tells us that the laws of nature exist, what those laws are, and what they accomplish. But it can never tell us why they are *as* they are—for that we need God, turtles or the multiverse (take your pick). ID as an inference from science is just as legitimate as the multiverse and, in my view, much more so. Of course, you are free to define science in such a way as to include its philosophical implications, but if you do you cannot be selective—you must admit ID alongside the multiverse and any other theory that can be neither proven nor falsified by scientific data. Or else you must exclude *all* such theories from your definition of science.

A second problem with ID is that it lacks any philosophical bedrock, such as the hypothesis of God—the foundation I am striving to establish in this book. Thus ID can be accused of adopting a God-of-the-gaps mentality because it concentrates on the intractability of complex biological systems while leaving the rest of the universe to naturalism. This narrow focus leaves it vulnerable to such accusations and means that it is just as compatible with life from Mars or little green men as with divine creation. I find that rather unsatisfactory.

The hypothesis of God does not suffer from these objections. It sees intelligent design in everything, from bacteria to battleships, allowing God the freedom to work through law, providence, miracle and the mind of man. Furthermore, it is not an inference from science but rather provides the foundation of science—the law-abiding nature of the universe—but does so without imprisoning God by the laws he has himself created. That I find satisfying.

# CHAPTER FOURTEEN ...

... in which Rudyard Kipling and blind fish prompt us to take a closer look at the basics of Darwinian evolution, which hails natural selection as the new deity—the blind watchmaker. But it turns out to be a god with feet of clay as we discover the shortcomings and limitations of natural selection as an agent for biological change. To start with, natural selection tends to eliminate variations, not multiply them as evolution requires. We see that get-outs like geographical isolation and biological 'arms races' don't work either. Then there are alternative mechanisms to natural selection, such as genetic drift.

We'll visit the supermarket to demonstrate that natural selection can only select what is already present—it has no creative power. Even worse, new species can only originate by natural selection through the *loss* of genetic information (leading at best to self-limiting micro-evolution). Macro-evolution, involving the creation of new organs and animal types, cannot therefore occur by natural selection. The creative power of evolution, if it exists, must lie elsewhere—as we shall see in chapter 15.

## New words?

*Alleles*: Different versions of the same gene, such as the two alleles of the human eye-colour gene that produce brown and blue eyes respectively.

*Gene pool*: The total genetic information of a species or sub-species.

*Genome*: The total genetic information of an individual member of a species.

*Pachyderm*: A thick-skinned non-ruminant animal such as the elephant, hippopotamus and rhinoceros. (From the Greek for 'thick' and 'skin'.)

# 14. The tidy pachyderm

The Elephant's Child sat there for three days waiting for his nose to shrink. But it never grew any shorter ... For, O best beloved, you will see and understand that the Crocodile had pulled it out into a really truly trunk same as all elephants have today. At the end of the third day a fly came and stung him on the shoulder and before he knew what he was doing he lifted up his trunk and hit that fly dead with the end of it. 'Vantage number one!' said the Bi-Coloured-Python-Rock-Snake. 'You couldn't have done that with a mere-smear nose.'

Rudyard Kipling, *Just so stories* (The elephant's child)[1]

Kipling's tales, written for his daughter Josephine, were published in 1902, just forty-three years after Darwin beat him to it with *The origin of species*. If you read the stories carefully, it is difficult to avoid the impression that Kipling was (playfully) either echoing Darwin or getting back at him. Set in an exceedingly young world, where all the animals were related and lacked many of their current features, the story of the Elephant's Child is specially redolent of the great biologist's theories. It is, of course, the story of how the elephant got his trunk—and how greatly he was advantaged by this novel, useful and yet altogether accidental acquisition. Not only could the trunk be used to squash flies but it also served to pick fruit, swish water, spank trunkless animals and hoover up the melon rinds he had dropped on his way to the Limpopo river—which is why Kipling called him a 'tidy pachyderm'.

Of course, Kipling's animal world is more Lamarckian than Darwinian. Jean-Baptiste Lamarck (1744–1829) proposed that evolution occurred by the inheritance of acquired characteristics, and is not without his disciples today. Many years ago I debated evolution and creation with the popular British TV botanist David Bellamy, who confessed himself to be more a neo-Lamarckian than a Darwinist. Either way, the 'just so' stories do serve a valuable cautionary purpose. They remind us that a theory of origins that, with a little imagination, can explain *anything*, actually explains nothing.

## To see or not to see

I can best illustrate my point by an example. Various fish species have been discovered that live in caves where light does not penetrate. They are blind and their condition is ascribed to Darwinian evolution. Relative to its surface-dwelling counterpart the blind form of the Mexican tetra has an enhanced olfactory sense and can store four times more energy as fat. While it is not a new species, it can obviously make use of these advantages rather than sight. But why should sight have been lost? One Darwinian explanation is that for all their usefulness, fish eyes have the disadvantage of being prone to infection (if you've ever kept fish you'll know how true this is). In the blind tetra the eye is covered by an overgrowth of skin, which prevents such infection, decreases mortality, and thus imparts a selective advantage. We might note in passing that the genetic basis of sight is not totally lost. In one experiment[2] blind fish from two different locations were interbred and some of the fry possessed at least partial sight. The explanation given is that the two blind fish populations had lost their sight by different genetic mutations and that in some offspring genetic losses in one population were compensated by genes persisting in the other (and vice versa). In any case, Darwinian mechanisms can explain the blindness of the cave-fish.

But consider now another recent discovery, reported in an article in *The Times*[3] and based on a paper in the *Journal of Current Biology*. I quote: 'A bizarre "four-eyed" fish has been found to use a unique system of mirrors to protect itself from being eaten in the dark depths of the sea.' The creature (which rejoices in the name of the brownsnout spookfish) is 'the only backboned creature known to use mirrors rather than lenses to get images into focus ... at low light levels ... Arrangements of mirrors have been found in a few crustaceans, but the spookfish is the first vertebrate to have evolved them to help it to see.' The fish has normal eyes but also possesses extra downward pointing 'mirror eyes'—which are supposed to provide a selective advantage by providing sharp images of light flashes emitted by predators in the dark ocean depths. Fascinating.

However, my purpose here is not to debate the Darwinian explanations offered for these various features but to point out something, well, fishy—evolutionary theory has explained opposite effects with equal facility, maintaining that the *same* selective pressure (a dark environment) causes sight to be lost in one species but enhanced in another. I realize, of course, that no two environments are precisely the same. There may be no light-emitting predators in the caves, so the tetra wouldn't need extra eyes to see them. But exactly what defines whether or not a particular environmental factor is 'selective' in evolutionary terms? Why would flash-torch predators be selective only for spookfish and not for every other denizen of the deep dark ocean? In other words, why haven't *all* vulnerable deep-sea fish evolved elaborate detection mechanisms similar to the spookfish? And why weren't the spookfish's normal eyes good enough to spot something as elementary, optically speaking, as a light flash? The questions are endless. Or perhaps not. Perhaps they lead to one big final question—is there *any* feature of *any* creature that could not be explained by one evolutionary scenario or another?

Let's get back to elephants. Their elongated trunks enable them to reach food that would otherwise be inaccessible. But so does the long neck of the giraffe. Why don't giraffes have trunks instead of long necks? This would avoid the quite literal headache that an evolving giraffe might experience—as a result of blood-pressure changes—when going from a head-up position to a head-down position. In fact, the modern giraffe has a special system of valves in its long neck that eliminate this problem, but why go to all that evolutionary hassle when a trunk would provide the same benefit without valves? And how do gazelles and wildebeests survive and prosper in the same environment as giraffes without having long necks (or trunks for that matter)?

The problem I have is that evolution can *always* contrive an answer to these questions and can therefore never be falsified. Yet the capacity for falsification is essential for any truly scientific theory. So pervasive is the belief that evolution can be the only truth, that today it is simply assumed. Our friendly spookfish provides a good example. *The Times* article states: 'Brownsnout spookfish were discovered 120 years ago but little was known about them until one was pulled up from 2000-2600ft during a scientific trawl in the Tonga Trench in the southern Pacific 18 months ago. It was the first live specimen to be studied by researchers.'

At the time of writing, and after only eighteen months, I greatly doubt whether any research has yet been carried out on the *evolution* of the brownsnout spookfish—such as attempts to trace its evolutionary ancestry and, in particular, the evolutionary pathways that led to its amazing mirror eyes. Yet those concerned do not hesitate to state, as a matter of established fact, that the spookfish is 'the first vertebrate to have evolved [the extra eyes] to help it to see'. How can anyone be so sure *ab initio* that the fish has 'evolved them'? That's easy. Because Darwinism dictates that evolution is the *only* way that *any* living organism can acquire *any* characteristic.

Writing in the journal *Nature*, biologists Paul R. Ehrlich and L. C. Birch (respectively from the Universities of Stanford, California; and Sydney, Australia) stated: 'Our theory of evolution has become … one which cannot be refuted by any possible observations. Every conceivable observation can be fitted into it. It is thus "outside of empirical science" but not necessarily false. No one can think of ways in which to test it [that is, falsify it]. Ideas, either without basis or based on a few laboratory experiments carried out in extremely simplified systems have attained currency far beyond their validity. They have become part of an evolutionary dogma accepted by most of us as part of our training.'[4] Although these words were written in 1967, and may express a minority view, nothing has happened since to invalidate them.

As far as life is concerned, evolution's dictum is, 'I am, therefore I evolved.' So is it a genuine science? Or might it be a materialistic philosophy-of-being balanced precariously on a narrow base of scientific fact? Heresy? Let's take a look.

## Evolutionary basics

Although evolution receives blanket coverage in schools and the media, there is a surprising amount of confusion about it among ordinary folk. So we need to review briefly the basics of the neo-Darwinian 'synthesis' current today. The theory attributes evolution (from jellypods to jazz pianists) to the interplay of two simple processes—random genetic mutations (accidental changes in the genes) and natural selection (the survival of the fittest). Clearly, random mutations as such can have no 'directional' effect, such as the inexorable drive to greater complexity in living things that the theory sets out to explain. So that leaves natural selection to impose directionality and be the real driving force behind evolution. Richard Dawkins puts it thus: 'Chance is not a solution, given the high level of improbability we see in living organisms, and no sane biologist ever suggested that it was ... of course it didn't happen by chance ... Natural selection is not only a parsimonious, plausible and elegant solution; it is the only workable alternative to chance that has ever been suggested.'[5] It is, he adds, 'not only a workable solution, it is a solution of stunning elegance and power'.[6] One has to wonder how Dawkins can find chance so obnoxious when it comes to the evolution of advanced organisms but so attractive as an explanation for the origin of complex genetic codes and cell machinery. Remember what he said in reference 4 of our previous chapter? 'Suppose ... life began when both DNA and its protein-based replication machinery spontaneously chanced to come into existence' (which is exactly what he does suppose). Nevertheless, let us imagine that, as far as evolution is concerned, natural selection is king (if not actually God) and concentrate for the moment on the natural selection of traits (as did Darwin himself, knowing nothing at that time of mutations).

Let's revisit the rapid rabbit we met briefly in chapter 5. Imagine that farmer Brown's land is home to a rabbit warren but that the rabbits are kept in check by a family of foxes. Suppose that a mother rabbit has a litter of ten babies, one of which can run much faster than its siblings. In the course of time, five of the others get caught by foxes before they themselves produce offspring. By luck, four others survive, but the rapid rabbit (let's call him RR) always escapes by outrunning the foxes. The five surviving members of the generation each lives to produce ten offspring of its own. The ten RR bunnies all inherit the RR trait and survive their allotted span. The other forty members of this second generation, however, are still rabbit dawdlers (let's label them RD; they are not so lucky and only half of them survive to reproduce). This leaves us with a *reproducing* group of fifty rabbits, but now 20% of them have the RR trait (instead of 10% in the first generation). If exactly the same rules of predation and reproduction apply to the next generation, it is easy to see that the reproducing family will contain 100 RRs and 200 RDs—a rapid rabbit proportion of 33%. As generation follows generation, the 'selective advantage' of the RR trait means that it will eventually spread through and dominate the whole warren. A population of ordinary rabbits will have been transformed almost entirely into super-rabbits as a result of a genetic difference in a single bunny. The details of the story are contrived, of course, but it illustrates the principle. That is Darwinian evolution in a nutshell (or a rabbit hole).

But now let your imagination run on. At first the foxes notice nothing untoward because there are still lots of RDs out there for them to catch. But as the RRs gradually take over the warren, and RDs become a scarce commodity, some of the foxes begin to go hungry. There is now a selective pressure on the foxes—that of starvation. But evolution again rides to the rescue, and a fox is born that itself has a fast-running trait. We'll call him the fast fox (FF) and he always catches his rabbits, even rapid ones. This gives the FF a selective advantage over his siblings, half of whom die of malnutrition before they can reproduce. It is easy to see that the evolution of the RR variety is followed, after due delay, by the rise of a FF variety of fox. As Michael Behe[7] points out, evolutionists liken such inter-dependent evolution to an arms race between two nations—every time one gets a step ahead in the battle for survival the other responds and even overtakes it. Richard Dawkins declares: 'I regard arms races as of the utmost importance because it is largely arms races that have injected such "progressiveness" as there is in evolution. For contrary to earlier prejudices, there is nothing inherently progressive about evolution.'[8] And again, 'The arms race idea remains by far the most satisfactory explanation for the existence of the advanced and complex machinery that animals and plants possess.'[9]

However, Dawkins' sweeping scenario is even more contrived than my RR-FF story. For one thing, there must always be a limit to an evolutionary 'arms race'. Rabbits don't turn into hares under predator-pressure, nor do foxes develop into racehorses. We all have our limitations; rabbits remain rabbits and foxes are still foxes. All that can happen is that they 'evolve' to the limit of their capacity for speed, as rabbits and foxes respectively. This phenomenon of thus-far-and-no-further is familiar to animal and plant breeders who practise artificial rather than natural selection. New or improved traits can be bred into a species almost at will (faster racehorses, for instance) but there is always a limit beyond which genetic in-breeding or other effects start to cause degeneration rather than enhancement. Similarly, many different varieties of a species can be produced artificially, but there are always boundaries that cannot be crossed. Darwin himself fully understood this.

Another reason that arms races are unlikely to rack up the technological triumphs in nature that Dawkins claims for them is that organisms are generally too adaptable to be caught up in such follies. Instead of just running faster and faster, for example, our rabbits might hone their burrowing skills—to such an extent that they dig themselves out of reach within seconds of sensing danger. Or they could achieve better camouflage or discard the odours by which the foxes scent them. In other words, the same selective pressure (in this case, predators) can induce a wide variety of adaptations—none of which is predictable but any of which serves to relieve the pressure. Of course, the foxes might follow them through every twist and turn of this adaptational maze, but I suspect that in reality they would give up on rabbits (being quite adaptable themselves, you see) and raid chicken sheds or dustbins instead. My point is not that arms races never happen in nature but that they are hardly sufficient to explain 'the existence of the advanced and complex machinery that animals and plants possess', as Dawkins claims.

Before we leave our RDs, RRs and FFs, just notice one other curious thing. As long as we focus on a single adaptation (such as running ability) it seems eminently plausible that natural selection might produce super-rabbits—giving their species a leg up the evolutionary tree with foxes not far behind them. But this is less clear when you consider the whole spectrum of alternative responses that could be induced in the rabbit population. In the end, all we can know, as observers, is that some rabbits survive and reproduce successfully. Exactly *why* they do so cannot normally be explained by any particular adaptation or, for that matter, any particular selective pressure (disease, habitat losses, food supply problems or climate changes could also threaten their survival). How, then, do we know which rabbits are best fitted to survive? Is it the fastest, or the strongest excavators, or the best camouflaged, or the most disease-resistant, or the furriest, or those adventurous souls willing to seek new pastures when necessary? Or is it some or all of the above? All we can really say is that those best fitted to survive are those who actually do survive. If this is true, then to define Darwinian evolution by natural selection as 'the survival of the fittest' becomes a mere tautology—those survive who are best fitted to survive. True, of course, but altogether lacking in *explanatory* power.

## Geography matters

So is natural selection all it is cracked up to be? Many biologists believe otherwise. One great problem with natural selection is that, in itself, it causes convergence, forcing a species into a cul-de-sac where all its protective armoury has evolved to the limit and it has nowhere else to go. Rather than cause rabbits to diverge into two different species, and so promote new growth in the evolutionary tree, we end up with highly specialized rabbits that *all* run fast, dig deep, keep warm, don't get sick, and are invisible to fox radar. Their original diversity has been *eliminated* by natural selection, not increased. Evolutionists are, of course, well aware of this problem and introduce a compensating factor—'geographical isolation' (or some other form of segregation between sub-populations in a species).

Farmer Green's land adjoins farmer Brown's but Green keeps chickens and is understandably allergic to foxes. Accordingly, he has his men out every night shooting foxes on sight—with the result that Green rabbits are spared the predation suffered by Brown rabbits. However, farmer Green likes not only chickens but adores birds of all kinds and encourages birds of prey to hunt his fields. Green rabbits, therefore, suffer a selective pressure to which camouflage is a better response than speed. Natural selection thus produces a breed of camouflaged rabbits that freeze rather than flee when danger threatens. A different selective environment has produced rabbits of a different kind and divergence is re-established. Furthermore, the rapid rabbits may well not fancy their funny-looking piebald cousins, so that even where the two farms abut, Brown rabbits and Green rabbits decline to interbreed. We now have two species rather than one. Neat.

But there are crucial down-sides to this scenario. First, of course, geographical isolation becomes king. It usurps the throne first occupied by natural selection because selection now needs its 'permission' to work any transformational magic. And geographical isolation is, in fact, a very chancy business. What happens if Green sells his farm to Brown? The isolation disappears, of course. In real life, evolution identifies various causes of geographical isolation, such as mountain ranges, seas and oceans. The herring gull and the closely related lesser black-backed gull may have evolved from common stock when they became separated by the Ural Mountains.[10] Darwin's finches developed different characteristics on different islands in the Galapagos because they couldn't be bothered to fly from one island to another. As will become clear, I have no problem with this kind of 'micro-evolution'. My point is that geographical isolation is a chance process which, almost by definition, cannot impart directionality to evolution over long periods of time—it is altogether too *ad hoc* to drive ever-increasing complexity over millions of years, as required by Darwinian theory. Gulls are gulls, whatever their plumage. Finches are finches whatever shape their beaks.

## The genetic supermarket

But there is an even bigger problem with natural selection. It can only work by reducing the gene pool of a species. What's a gene pool? Imagine a garden gnome sitting patiently by a pool with his fishing line in the water. The picture says it all. The fish in the pool are genes and the pool itself is the entire genetic content of a given species. The gnome is any individual member of that species and (with apologies) the fish he has caught make up his genome (the totality of genetic material in that individual). Each of us has one genome and thousands of genes, but possesses only a fraction of the gene pool of our species. If there are two gnomes they will each catch a somewhat different range of fish and thus derive different genomes from the same gene pool. It is these 'genomic' differences that allow natural selection to operate.

The term 'natural selection' means what it says—it can only occur if some genetic traits are selected rather than others. Let's change the picture and visit the supermarket. On arrival you are confronted with probably thousands of different products but you don't want them all. So what do you do? You make a selection. Waiting at the checkout you notice idly that the people in front of you and behind you have made entirely different selections, though perhaps with a little overlap. One person may be subject to the 'selective pressure' of a low bank balance, so has chosen only the cheapest goods. Another's basket might be filled with foods beloved of children, due to the selective pressure of a large family. There are three lessons here.

Firstly, even though the total range of in-store products may not change from week to week, there is an almost infinite variety of different baskets that can pass through the check-out tills over a period of time. So also, the inheritance of different genes and gene combinations as one generation follows another can give rise to many different genomes—variations within a species that all derive from the same gene pool. Among humans, for example, different racial groups have arisen. But even within a racial group, no two of us are identical (unless we're identical twins).

The second lesson is that no one carries from the store more than a fraction of the goods available. As far as the shopper is concerned, the remaining products are left behind and 'lost'. If that were not so, every shopping basket would be the same (and heavy). Likewise, selective pressures in nature can only produce diversification by the *loss* of genetic information. If natural selection causes a species to evolve into two separate species, each of the new species must lack some of the genetic content of the parent genome. Otherwise nothing new has been produced. Natural selection, even when guided by geographical isolation, therefore, can never create *new* genetic information. All it can do is *select* different genetic baskets from the gene-pool supermarket, leaving the rest behind. Well might Richard Dawkins admit that 'contrary to earlier prejudices, there is nothing inherently progressive about evolution' (reference 8). Don't worry; I haven't forgotten mutations and we'll come to them in due course.

## Sparrow spread

Biologists agree that natural selection isn't the whole story. There are other mechanisms that sometimes account better for observed changes in living creatures than selection. One such mechanism is 'genetic drift', a process that occurs because in a given gene pool many genes exist in different forms or 'alleles'. Let me explain this by returning briefly to the supermarket for its third lesson.

Just as the supermarket offers several brands of soap powder, so also any gene in the gene pool may come in several versions. Different versions of the same gene are called alleles. A familiar example is the human gene that determines eye colour, which exists in a brown-eye version and a blue-eye version. There is a different gene that gives green eyes. It works along with the blue/brown gene and also determines lightness or darkness of eye colour, but ignore this for the moment.

Each individual has two copies of the primary eye-colour gene and this offers three possibilities—two brown alleles (BB); two blue alleles (bb); or one blue and one brown allele (Bb). A baby also has two alleles, one inherited from its father and one from its mother, but which of the father's alleles is passed on is a matter of chance (likewise for the mother's allele). So a baby with a bb father and a Bb mother might be Bb (giving brown eyes because B is a 'dominant' allele) or bb (giving blue eyes). Likewise, a second child born to the same parents might also be blue or brown eyed. Let's call this process of gene sorting 'mixing and matching'. Clearly, if we now bring the green/lightness gene into the picture we get a significantly expanded range of eye-colour possibilities (though this applies mainly to people of European descent—most others have brown eyes).[11]

The importance of genetic mixing and matching is that it accounts for almost all the variations between races and individuals within a given species—and that brings us back to genetic drift. An interesting example is given by naturalist David Swift.[12] The house sparrow was not a native of North America but was introduced in 1852 at Brooklyn, NY. Like most immigrants to the USA it prospered and spread, colonizing the continent during the next hundred years. As it did so, says Swift, 'quite distinct subspecies or races appeared—varying especially in colour and size—some so different from the originating birds that they may not be immediately recognized as house sparrows by European ornithologists'. Was this variability the result of natural selection? On the contrary, it almost certainly arose because only a small number of birds found their way to a particular area, carrying a corresponding small part of the gene pool of the species. As a result, many alleles present in the species as a whole were 'lost' and unavailable to the local breeding population. A different but equally small breeding population somewhere else also lost alleles but (this being a random effect) they lost different ones—producing a permanent difference in the genetic make-up of the two populations. This is what is meant by genetic drift.

So the alleles available in Kansas might well be different from those expressed in Kentucky, with the result that the two populations of birds exhibit different characteristics (of size and plumage, for example). This can be explained entirely in terms of the mixing, matching and loss of alleles. No natural selection needs to be invoked. Of course, we can always embellish the picture with natural selection scenarios. Perhaps Kansas cats prefer sparrows while Kentucky cats prefer mice, creating a selection pressure in one state that is absent from the other and chasing Kansas sparrows higher up the evolutionary tree. But that is pure Kipling—genetic drift is all the explanation we need.

The 'neutral theory of molecular evolution' proposed by Kimura and King and Jukes in the late 1960s[13] also claims that evolution at the molecular level of DNA and proteins is dominated by random drift—although it assumes that new alleles are continually being generated by random mutations (which we'll consider later). It does not claim that random drift accounts for all evolutionary change—natural selection is still needed to explain clear-cut cases of adaptation (for example, if experiments proved that *only* rapid rabbits outfoxed foxes). The theory does, however, maintain that significant evolutionary changes occur at the molecular level without the intervention of natural selection. Not surprisingly, a dispute still rages over the relative importance of selection and drift in 'speciation' (the creation of new species). However, one thing is blindingly obvious—when new species are formed, whether by natural selection or genetic drift, genetic information is lost. If, for example, one species branches into two new species, these only differ from each other in having *lost* different genes.

## Mutations to the rescue?

Let's take stock. We have seen that:

1.  Random drift, by definition, cannot push evolution along any particular developmental pathway;

2.  Even Richard Dawkins admits that 'there is nothing inherently progressive about evolution' (ref. 8);

3.  Natural selection can only move evolution forward at the whim of geographical (or some other kind of) isolation of breeding populations;

4.  Every speciation event, however it occurs, results in the loss of genetic information from the gene pool of the original species.

This being so, we are entitled to ask whence arises the inexorable progress over vast periods of time—from simple life forms to highly complex ones like you and me—that evolution claims to explain. The answer we are offered is random genetic mutations. When it comes down to brass tacks, mutations are king and evolution goes nowhere unless new genes are being continually invented. This happens, we are assured, by the chance errors and damage accumulation sustained by DNA sequences and inherited as one generation gives rise to the next. How credible is this scenario? Now that we know who really is king of evolution's castle, our enquiry calls for a new chapter—in which we shall also see what the hypothesis of God has to say about the origin and development of the teeming biosphere we know today.

# CHAPTER FIFTEEN ...

... in which we ask whether random genetic mutations really have the creative power assigned to them in the evolutionary scheme of life. In doing so, we'll get involved in the fascinating world of 'junk DNA'—which may not be junk after all.

Having identified mutations as the *only* factor in evolution theory that might conceivably introduce new genetic information into the biosphere, we look in vain for evidence that they actually do so. This leads us to examine the whole idea of 'beneficial' mutations.

Such mutations, it is claimed, include the cases of sickle-cell anaemia (malaria resistance) and bacterial drug resistance, so we take a specially close look at these. They turn out to be beneficial only in a restricted sense, involving a *loss* of genetic information that just happens to protect the organism from specific threats. But these mutations are not 'beneficial' in the constructive sense needed by evolution—of giving rise to increased biological complexity or sophistication. Quite the reverse.

We'll find that the evidence from mutations points to genome degradation rather than upward evolution. The biblical hypothesis of God accounts for this scenario in terms of the fall of man and nature.

## New words?

*Biosphere*: The realm of living things.

*Industrial melanism*: Dark colouration in organisms, allegedly caused by industrial pollution.

# 15. The mighty mutation

Swift to its close ebbs out life's little day;
Earth's joys grow dim, its glories fade away;
Change and decay in all around I see;
O thou who changest not, abide with me.

From the hymn *Abide with me*

L ike his contemporary Charles Darwin, Henry Lyte knew nothing about genetic mutations. Nevertheless, his famous hymn still reflects an underlying reality—that left to themselves, things undergo 'change and decay'. Genomes are no exception and the word 'mutation', derived from Latin, simply means 'change'. Of course, change may occur without decay. Under the right circumstances it can bring improvement rather than deterioration. But experience shows that to make *positive* changes takes determined effort (like painting your house) while negative changes happen entirely of their own accord (like neglecting to paint your house). This goes to the heart of our enquiry in this chapter; do accidental genetic mutations have creative potential or are they essentially degenerative?

There are many different kinds of genetic mutation. These range from 'point mutations' in which a single base in the DNA molecule is replaced by a different one, to 'transposition' where a whole section of DNA is moved to a different place in the genome and 'duplication' in which an extra copy of a gene is added to the genome. There is even an instance in baker's yeast (classified as a fungus) in which the entire genome is believed to have been accidentally duplicated, providing the offspring with a 'two-for-the-price-of-one' supermarket bargain. Assuming this really happened, did two genomes prove better than one? Apparently not; although the organism in question has the ability to manufacture alcohol, it is otherwise almost indistinguishable from its supposed parent. Even such a massive mutation didn't allow it to rise significantly higher in the kingdom of life, and many of the extra genes have since disappeared, presumably eliminated by natural selection.[1]

In spite of the elaborate proof-reading and repair mechanisms possessed by living cells, genetic mutations undoubtedly do happen. Ask the long-suffering fruit fly *Drosophila melanogaster*, of which millions of generations have been bred in hundreds of laboratories and subjected to every conceivable indignity—from radiation to toxic chemicals—to induce and study mutations.[2] The results have included a regiment of monsters (tiny but technically still monsters) with all manner of bizarre bodily features like extra legs where the antennae should be[3] and missing hearts in embryos. But none of the flies was any better off for the experience, not even those which acquired an extra pair of useless wings. And, of course, the mutated *Drosophila* are still nothing but fruit flies.

The details of the different kinds of genetic mutation that can occur are not important for our present purpose. What is important is the creative power with which evolutionary theory endows these molecular accidents of nature. We must not be deterred by loud protestations that the creative power resides in natural selection rather than mutations. Remember the supermarket? Natural selection can only select what is present. It can never create what is absent. Of course, if something really useful *were* created by mutations, then natural selection could in principle stop it being overwhelmed by negative effects such as genetic drift. Imagine a flower bed in which you plant a cultivated seedling, purchased at great expense from your local garden centre. Sadly, it soon becomes choked by weeds and begins to wilt. You can protect the seedling and help it prosper by continually clearing away the weeds—effectively selecting the seedling by destroying its competitors. But just clearing weeds from your original patch will never bring the cultivated seedling into existence. That requires the 'creative' act of introducing it from elsewhere. What will eventually develop into a flowering shrub can be *protected* by weed-clearing but it can't be *caused* by weed-clearing.

So it is with mutations and natural selection; only the former can (in principle) create new genetic information with its potential to advance biological complexity. Apply this logic to the vaunted 'arms race' to which Richard Dawkins and others attribute the development of advanced biological systems. Declaring war never *created* bows and arrows, gunpowder or nuclear missiles. You can't have an arms race without arms but a war doesn't in itself produce weapons. *They* have to come from somewhere else, and if you exclude intelligent design, 'somewhere else' in molecular biology means random and entirely fortuitous mutations. The outbreak of wars among humans may stimulate the invention of new weapons and counter-weapons, but that is an *intelligent* response which is not available to unguided evolution. And since natural selection cannot invent biological armaments, it must hang around until a useful weapon-forming mutation just happens to come along (it could be a long wait; not nice when selective-pressure missiles are raining down around you). Who now is king of the evolutionary castle? Natural selection? Geographical isolation? Genetic drift? None of these. The lowly mutation is king, for without it (according to neo-Darwinism) the biosphere would consist entirely of jellypods.

Now that's a thought. Numerically speaking, the vast majority of living things on planet earth are simple organisms like bacteria. These creatures are so well adapted to a huge variety of environments that they exhibit neither the need nor the tendency to evolve into earthworms or earwigs—nor yet to vanish into evolutionary obscurity as they are superseded by later models. If, as is alleged, evolution is driven solely by reproductive efficiency and optimized survival, then by rights all life forms should be striving to become bacteria, which perform superbly by these criteria. Yet in spite of having near perfect adaptation as a class of living creatures, evolutionary theory insists that bacteria (or something very like them) *did* evolve—otherwise you and I would not be here. Laboriously, they hoisted themselves up the evolutionary tree, becoming all the while decidedly more complex and environmentally 'picky'. That is, they evolved into *vulnerable* creatures that, according to the fossil record, regularly got themselves snuffed out by extinction. Why, I wonder, would they do that, seeing that their un-evolved bacterial cousins lived on in happy adaptation to every conceivable environment, sublimely unaware of the hazards of climbing trees?

### Mutations—harmful and beneficial

But let's get back to genetic mutations. These occur when genomes are either damaged (as by ionizing radiation or toxic chemicals) or, more generally, when they fail to copy-over faithfully as one generation gives rise to the next. Consider again the humble bacterium which reproduces by splitting itself in two. The two daughter cells should be identical but in practice the act of copying the bacterial DNA to provide for a new cell may introduce copying errors, much as a typist copying a document may make typographical mistakes. Compared with typists, DNA transcription is amazingly accurate—yielding but one 'point' mutation for every one to ten million DNA bases. And because the bacterial genome is relatively small (perhaps five million or so bases), and depending on population size, each new generation may contain a handful of mistakes in the genetic transcript.

Most of these errors are harmful and are quickly eliminated because the cells concerned just die. Other mutations are neutral and produce no apparent effects. Furthermore, even simple cells like bacteria contain protein molecules that 'proof-read' and repair the copied genetic text as necessary. However, in spite of all this, bacteria may reproduce so fast (like once every nine minutes) that genetic changes can and do accumulate and spread in bacterial populations. Such persistent mutations are labelled 'beneficial mutations' but we need to watch the rhetoric here. Generally, the organism exhibits no identifiable 'benefit' and the mutation is called 'beneficial' simply because it *does* persist and spread. In a Darwinian scenario, this can only mean that the mutation in question *must* have conferred some selectable benefit on the organism, even though we usually have no idea what it is (I consider exceptions below). The mutation is labelled 'beneficial' simply because it survives to be passed on to a new generation—yet another case of the fittest turning out to be the fittest.

Bear with me while I develop my point with a brief excursion into some original literature. You don't need to understand everything in the quotes because I will point out the key implications. Writing in 2003, David Houle of the Department of Biological Science, Florida State University, and Alexey Kondrashov of the National Center for Biotechnology Information, Bethesda, explain the problem of pinning down beneficial mutations.

'The difficulties of the study of mutation stem largely from one simple fact: individually, mutations are very rare events at the level of a site within the DNA sequence or even of the whole gene. This has always made the direct study of mutation, consisting of recording new mutations as they arise, exceptionally tedious. For example, one of the best direct studies of mutation in mammals is that of Russell and Russell (1996), who report examinations of over 1,000,000 mice to find just 46 visible mutations [of all kinds]. The alternative to this tedium is to fit a model to genetic variation within a population or to the variation found among populations or species. These model-based approaches utilize data on contemporary variation, which are relatively easy to gather, in order to obtain information about mutations which happened in the past, over a considerable period of time. Consequently, much of what we know about mutation comes from model-fitting. Such efforts have a very important Achilles heel—if the model is not correct, the results can be very misleading ... This tension between direct observation and indirect, assumption-based approaches is very common in evolutionary biology.'[4]

Again, there is the implicit assumption that if a mutation persists it must, by definition, be 'beneficial'. But what is more significant is the extent to which biologists rely on computer models when they make pronouncements about mutations. Such models are constructed on evolutionary assumptions and the *experimental* basis for their conclusions is often slender and sometimes absent altogether.

Here's a second revealing example. Writing in the *Proceedings of the National Academy of Sciences*, Marianne Imhof and Christian Schlotterer reported their research into beneficial mutations in the common bacterium *Escherichia coli*. They say:[5] 'The central role of beneficial mutations for adaptive processes in natural populations is well established. Thus, there has been a long-standing interest to study the nature of beneficial mutations. Their low frequency, however, has made this class of mutations almost inaccessible for systematic studies. In the absence of experimental data, the distribution of the fitness effects of beneficial mutations was assumed to resemble that of deleterious mutations. For an experimental proof of this assumption, we used a novel marker system to trace adaptive events in an evolving *Escherichia coli* culture and to determine the selective advantage of those beneficial mutations. Ten parallel cultures were propagated for about 1,000 generations ... and 66 adaptive events were identified. From this data set, we estimate the rate of beneficial mutations to be $4 \times 10^{-9}$ per cell and generation. Consistent with an exponential distribution of the fitness effects, we observed a large fraction of advantageous mutations with a small effect and only few with large effect. The mean selection coefficient of advantageous mutations in our experiment was 0.02.'

Although the authors claim that the 'central role of beneficial mutations ... is well established' they immediately confess that such mutations occur so seldom as to be 'almost inaccessible' for systematic (i.e. scientific) study and that the 'absence of experimental data' means that the behaviour of beneficial mutations has to be inferred from that of deleterious mutations. However, the point of their research was to justify such inferences, and this they sought to do by following mutations in a genetic 'marker'—a length of DNA that was known to mutate rapidly and which was taken from a completely different organism (a plant). This 'marker' was artificially inserted into a 'plasmid' (itself artificial) incorporated into the bacterium. In other words, they were not studying mutations in *Escherichia coli* at all, but in an inserted DNA sequence that reproduced along with the bacterium. Furthermore, 'beneficial' mutations were defined as those that persisted in subsequent generations; there was no indication of any actual *benefit* to the bacteria. Mutations? Yes. Beneficial mutations? The scientific evidence is tentative to say the least.

However, there are a few known cases where it seems fair to claim that mutations have proved genuinely beneficial, and the best known of these is sickle-cell anaemia in humans—which can confer a degree of immunity to malaria during childhood. So we need to consider this and certain other examples before drawing final conclusions. But first, let's take a look at the idea that mutations occurring over millions of years of evolution have left a heavy footprint in the genomes of all species. I refer to the so-called 'junk DNA' that seems to clutter up every living cell on earth.

## Junk DNA

I am constantly amazed (and occasionally impressed) by the way some modern artists can take pieces of junk and transform them into high-priced works of art. Things found yesterday on the scrapheap or in the waste bin are today displayed on plinths in up-market galleries and feted as artistic masterpieces. Stuckists[6]—a group of traditional artists who deplore such 'conceptual' trends in modern art and are proud to be 'stuck' in the past—are not impressed. In the best traditions of duckism, they believe that if an object originated as rubbish, looks like rubbish and behaves like rubbish, it probably is rubbish.

What *should* impress us, however, is the entirely different junk-to-jewellery story now emerging from the study of 'genome sequencing' in living species (genome sequencing is the determination of the precise sequence of bases throughout an organism's *entire* DNA). When sequencing began[7] in the 1980s it was a very slow process, and workers concentrated on the genes that code for proteins and RNA. The remainder of the DNA didn't seem to have any useful function and was labelled 'junk DNA'. Thus not so long ago, we were assured that the very existence of junk DNA—ranging roughly from 98% of the total DNA in advanced organisms to 80% in bacteria—was clear evidence of evolution. It represented the rubbish left over from failed evolutionary 'experiments'. For example, Francis Collins employs an interesting argument in support of evolution based on the unimportance of junk DNA.[8] He gives figures suggesting that historical mutation rates were significantly higher in the junk DNA of various species than in their protein-coding DNA. He then attributes this to natural selection weeding out mutations in the functional genes while leaving the useless junk DNA to its mutational fate. It all sounds convincing until you hear the latest news—junk DNA is probably not junk after all!

When automated DNA sequencing techniques became available during the 2000s and it became possible to sequence entire genomes, including the massive 'junk' ingredient, some curious things were noticed. First came the unwelcome surprise that humans had only 25,000 to 30,000 genes—compared with a similar number in a small plant called *Arabidopsis* and over 40,000 in rice and poplar trees. It's a bit humbling to think that a city full of human beings has a smaller gene pool than a paddy field.

We also now know that humans share 96% of their DNA with chimpanzees (it used to be claimed as 98%). What this proves, of course, is not that chimps are 96% human, any more than rice is 133% human,[9] but that genes and sequences *as such* are by no means the whole story. It is becoming increasingly clear that much if not most of the 'story' resides in the junk DNA. As *ScienceDaily* points out: 'Most of the big differences between human and chimpanzee DNA lie in regions that do not code for genes, according to a new study. Instead, they may contain DNA sequences that control how gene-coding regions are activated and read.'[10]

In fact, the word 'junk' has itself been junked, and this apparently redundant DNA is now referred to as 'non-coding' DNA. Even this may prove to be a temporary title—because although these regions don't code for proteins or RNA, it now seems that they *do* contain control codes that govern such things as gene expression, foetal development and much more which, at the time of writing, is still not understood.

On 26 October 2007, another *ScienceDaily* article reported a study of a recently discovered class of tiny RNAs (called piRNAs) which reveals that they play an important role in controlling gene function. The article states: 'Haifan Lin, director of the Stem Cell Center and professor of cell biology at Yale School of Medicine, heads the laboratory that originally identified piRNAs. Derived mostly from so-called "junk DNA", piRNAs had escaped the attention of generations of geneticists and molecular biologists until last year when Lin's team discovered them in mammalian reproductive cells ... The lab's current work suggests that piRNAs have crucial functions in controlling stem cell fate and other processes of tissue development.'

The researchers found more than 13,000 piRNAs in fruit flies. As an example of their importance, one such RNA forms a complex with a protein known as 'Piwi', which then binds to chromatin—an important region of the genome that packages and strengthens DNA, allowing cell division and controlling gene expression. Dr Lin said, 'This finding revealed a surprisingly important role for piRNAs, as well as junk DNA, in stem cell division. It calls upon biologists to look for answers beyond the one per cent of the genome with protein-coding capacity to the vast land of junk DNA, which constitutes 99 per cent of the genome.'[11]

Frank J. Slack sums up the situation in a paper entitled '*Regulatory RNAs and the demise of "junk" DNA*': 'We are fast learning that large portions of the genome that do not code for proteins are in fact transcribed, and that these regions, previously thought to be "junk", may be useful after all."[12] Far from being a graveyard for unwanted mutations, the non-coding regions that make up the vast majority of our DNA could be the repository of untold genetic treasures.

## Beneficial mutations

Nevertheless, those who believe in the mighty mutation narrative do have some ammunition left. There are a small number of cases where a mutation has imparted acknowledged survival advantages, and sickle-cell (SC) anaemia in humans is the most frequently quoted example. SC anaemia is a genetic disease caused by the substitution of a single amino-acid on the beta chain of the blood protein haemoglobin. This mutation prevents the proper folding of the protein and leads to misshapen red blood cells. Persons having two copies (alleles) of the mutated gene suffer full-blown sickle-cell disease, leading to disability and early death, and clearly enjoy no selective advantage. However, those who have only one copy of the defective gene (the other allele being normal) suffer no ill effects and, as a bonus, are protected from malaria during their childhood years. One explanation is that changes in the blood cells caused by the mutation make it difficult for the malaria parasite to latch on to them—an essential step in the parasite's life-cycle.

As a result, instead of being eliminated by natural selection, as would normally be the case with a debilitating disease, the sickle-cell mutation has become established in regions where malaria is rife, and those with a single SC allele survive in greater numbers to pass on their 'beneficial' mutation. But before we get too excited about this example, we need to look a little closer. Firstly, of course, the mutation is clearly not beneficial in those who have two mutated genes and suffer the full-blown disease. Secondly, it is not beneficial to anyone in regions that are free from malaria. Thirdly, the benefit is self-limiting. As long as only a small proportion of a population has the SC mutation, most of those who inherit it will have only one mutated gene and will reap the benefits of its anti-malarial effects.

However, as the mutated gene spreads through the population, more and more people will inherit two such alleles and become victims of full-blown SC anaemia. The expected (and observed) result is that the gene pool will stabilize at a certain level of SC carriers, but the SC gene will never 'take over' completely from the un-mutated gene. Yet evolution cannot occur unless such genetic takeovers *do* become total and complete.

Unless this happens, different 'varieties' of the organism simply co-exist and a dynamic equilibrium is reached between them which shifts as selective pressures change. The famous case of industrial melanism in the peppered moth is an example of this dynamic equilibrium between varieties within a species. During the industrial revolution in Britain, the dark ('melanistic') variety of the moth prospered relative to the light-coloured variety—allegedly because it was better camouflaged against dark backgrounds.[13] With the introduction of clean-air regulations, however, the light form regained dominance. No new species emerged and no genuine evolution occurred. This needs to be emphasized because such changes in the balance between varieties of a single species are often hailed as 'evolution'. But at best it is micro-evolution, occurring overwhelmingly *within* species, though occasionally giving rise to new closely related species (depending on how you define 'species'). But there is nothing here that can account for macro-evolution—meaning the creation of new organs, a rise in biological complexity or the bridging of genuine gaps between different types of organism. Evolution simply assumes that many micro-evolution steps can be extrapolated to account for macro-evolution but this claim has no scientific justification. For example, environmentalist David Swift points out that the *functional* sites in proteins, and thus the shapes into which proteins fold, are virtually identical (for a given protein type, e.g. cytochrome c) in all living organisms; that is, they show no evidence of having evolved. He writes: 'Crystallographic studies have shown that the 3D structures of eukaryotic cytochromes c are scarcely distinguishable from each other, including those from higher plants to higher animals, even though they are presumed to be separated by many hundreds of millions of years of evolution.'[14]

Finally, to get back to the sickle-cell mutation, the SC trait is not a case where genetic information has been gained or augmented; nothing has been created. It is an example where a *deleterious* mutation, causing a *loss* of genetic functionality, has produced an unexpected side-effect which happens to be beneficial and selectable—but only under some circumstances and up to some limit (just as artificial breeding is effective only up to a certain point). What evolution requires are mutations that add to the information content of the genome, and SC anaemia simply doesn't do that.

There is one further lesson from the SC mutation; the malaria parasite has failed to evolve an effective 'weapon' against it despite billions of generations and huge parasite populations. So how stands the arms race concept now? Evolution's answer is that in other cases, such as drug resistance in malaria, drug resistance in bacteria and viruses, and insecticide resistance in insects, an arms race can be clearly demonstrated. So let's look at some examples.

### Drug resistance
In his book *The edge of evolution*, biochemist Michael Behe, Professor of Biological Science at Lehigh University, Pennsylvania, presents a detailed and fascinating account of the 'arms race' between malaria and the various drugs developed against it. He points out that although the malaria parasite has never found an answer to the SC mutation, it has mutated to produce resistance to a variety of anti-malarial drugs. For example, a drug developed in the 1930s called chloroquine proved extremely effective for over fifty years, but by the 1980s almost all strains of malaria were resistant to it. When doctors stopped using the drug, however, the chloroquine resistant strains died out and were replaced by non-resistant parasites. This shows that the resistant variety was not in itself a 'fitter' version of malaria—its 'fitness' dominated the scene only until the selective pressure of the artificial drug was removed. Again, we have an example of dynamic equilibrium within a population (of parasites in this case) where one variety gains a selective advantage only as long as a particular selective pressure is maintained. Behe also points out that another drug, atovaquone,

gave rise to resistance in laboratory cultures of malaria within weeks, and asks why it took decades for chloroquine resistance to develop. The answer he gives is persuasive: atovaquone resistance requires only a single point mutation in the parasite whereas chloroquine resistance requires two simultaneous mutations. The probability of two *particular* mutations occurring simultaneously is given by multiplying the probabilities of each separate mutation, and these probabilities are (as we have seen) very small indeed. Studies[15] show that resistance to atovaquone occurs spontaneously in about one in a trillion cells.[16] If resistance to chloroquine required two simultaneous point mutations, Behe calculates that this would account for the fact that the latter resistance took decades to develop while the former took only weeks. The point of the argument is that any beneficial changes requiring more than two accidentally cooperative mutations would occur far too rarely on historical time-scales to provide any 'arms race' type response—especially in 'higher' animals that lack the astronomical fecundity of bacteria and malaria parasites. By the time any such changes had spread through the organism's gene pool, the selective pressures could themselves have changed many times and in many ways, probably rendering the 'beneficial' mutations worthless. Behe extends his analysis to other cases of drug resistance and other rapidly reproducing organisms, such as *E. coli* and the AIDS virus (which mutates ten thousand times faster than the malaria parasite). He also considers several other cases which are said to exhibit beneficial mutations, including warfarin resistance in rats[17] and resistance to insecticide. But he reaches two important factual conclusions.

Firstly, all known 'beneficial' mutations involve loss of, or damage to, original gene function. They are changes that *fortuitously* protect the organism from attack by specific 'enemies' but which otherwise weaken it relative to the original ('wild type') organism. Thus regarding insecticide resistance, Swift comments: 'The mutation that confers resistance … is invariably inferior to the normal "wild type" macromolecule. That is, in the absence of the relevant insecticide, the resistant strain fares less well, is less fit, than the normal phenotype.'[18]

When Nazi forces invaded Russia during World War II, the Russians responded with a 'scorched earth policy', destroying roads, burning bridges and demolishing cities as they retreated. By eliminating habitations and infrastructures they slowed the invaders and denied them shelter and transportation routes during a savage winter. It proved to be an effective, even war-winning, strategy. In the same way, an organism under severe selective pressure may occasionally find protection in a damaged genome that frustrates the selective attack. But this is the very *opposite* of the technological *progress* attributed to the 'arms races' by which evolution seeks to explain increases in biological complexity.

Secondly, no known 'beneficial' mutation does anything but produce a new strain or variety within the same species, and the changes are trivial in the sense that no new biological structures are ever formed. For example, as Behe points out, such mutations have never been found to create new protein-to-protein binding sites—as would be necessary for the formation of novel molecular machinery within the cell. Let me expand this last point a little. The cell's molecular machines (like the ribosome we considered earlier) always require different proteins to act together in 'gangs' of six, seven or more different molecules. For this coordination to occur, the different proteins must bind together (must link arms, as it were) to form working structures. For a novel working structure to arise in a cell, therefore, new binding sites must be created on several different proteins, and these binding sites must match to allow the molecules to stick together. To make it easier, let's think how just two proteins that hitherto kept themselves at 'arms length' might be persuaded to link arms. A new binding site would have to be created on one protein by a cluster of *appropriate* random mutations on the *surface* of the folded protein. These must then be matched by corresponding mutations on the surface of an entirely different protein. Consider a lock containing hundreds of tumblers and a key that does not match. If I make random changes to the key profile it will never fit the lock, nor does it help to make random changes to the lock's tumbler system at the same time. Only if coordinated changes are made to lock and key can the system be made to work. Similarly, random mutations to one or more protein molecules, each containing hundreds of amino-acids, will never set up matching binding sites that did not exist before—allowing new protein structures to be assembled and new molecular machinery to be built. Even if you subscribe to the belief that in biology anything and everything will happen if you wait long enough, you must agree two things. One: cell lines don't live long enough for this to happen by random mutations; two: no new protein-to-protein binding sites (allowing different proteins to gang-up) have ever been observed to arise by random mutations, even after untold millions of generations of the most rapidly mutating organisms known to man. As far as factual science is concerned, mutations do not produce new structures within cells and thus do not increase biological complexity. Even when 'beneficial' in some respects, they have no creative power whatever.

## Mutations and the hypothesis of God

Finally, what does the hypothesis of God have to say about genetic mutations? At first sight the answer might seem to be 'nothing' but that would be hasty. Although you won't find the word 'mutation' in the Bible you will find two central concepts that underline the reality of change in the constitution of the biological world. These concepts are, respectively, the perfect nature of original creation and the Fall of man. Let me explain.

The Genesis 1 account of creation and the 'terraforming' of planet earth is marked by a repeated refrain. Following each act of creation we read: 'And God saw that it was good.' Thus in verse 4, 'And God saw the light, that it was good' while in verses 10, 12, 18, 21 and 25 the things pronounced 'good' are clearly implied. Finally, in verse 31, we are told: 'Then God saw everything that He had made, and indeed it was very good.' This high level of repetition indicates that the 'goodness' of creation, as it came from the hand of God, is a key element in biblical thinking. Of course, depending on the context, 'good' can mean many things but it is difficult to see how in Genesis 1 it could mean anything but 'perfect' or 'without defect'. For one thing, it is

God's own verdict on the created order and for another, there is no reason why an omnipotent God should create an imperfect world.

Interestingly, this is an argument often advanced by atheists. Why, they ask, should a beneficent God create a biosphere such as we observe today—one that is 'red in tooth and claw' and where the undoubted beauty of nature is marred by cruelty, suffering and death? And if God used Darwinian evolution to create the world of living things, as theistic evolutionists maintain, why ever would an allegedly caring creator employ such an amoral and remorseless process to do so? When I debated creation and evolution with the popular British TV botanist David Bellamy at Durham University in 1980, I remember that this was his chief and repeated objection to the concept of creation. 'If God created the world, why did he make such a mess of it?'

Well, the Bible proposes that when God created the cosmos it *was* in pristine condition—'everything that He had made ... was very good'. The imperfection we observe today came later, as we shall see. In the as-created world, for example, all animals and man himself were vegetarian. 'And God said, "See, I have given you every herb ... and every tree whose fruit yields seed; to you it shall be for food. Also, to every beast of the earth, to every bird of the air, and to everything that creeps on the earth, in which there is life, I have given every green herb for food."'[19] (The 'fish of the sea' are mentioned earlier and are by implication included in this scenario.) Further biblical evidence for a perfect creation is provided by the very fact that the Fall of man brought an end to this idyllic state of affairs (there had to be something to fall *from*); that is, there came a time when, as St Paul writes in Romans 8: 'the creation was *subjected* to futility' (emphasis added).[20] It didn't start out that way.

Furthermore, the Bible looks forward to a time when the creation will be restored to its original perfection. Paul continues: 'the creation itself also will be delivered from the bondage of corruption into the glorious liberty of the children of God. For we know that the whole creation groans and labours with birth pangs together until now ...

even we ourselves groan within ourselves, eagerly waiting for the adoption, the redemption of our [physical] body.'[21] These verses contain eschatological teaching that we can't go into here, but it is crystal clear what Paul is telling us. An originally 'good' material creation became corrupted—a place of suffering and pain—but it will one day be restored to its original perfection. In that day, says Isaiah, 'The wolf also shall dwell with the lamb, the leopard shall lie down with the young goat, the calf and the young lion and the fatling together; and a little child shall lead them. The cow and the bear shall graze; their young ones shall lie down together; and the lion shall eat straw like the ox. The nursing child shall play by the cobra's hole, and the weaned child shall put his hand in the viper's den. They shall not hurt nor destroy in all My holy mountain, for the earth shall be full of the knowledge of the LORD as the waters cover the sea.'[22]

## The Fall of man

It is a curious fact that the Fall of man is hardly ever mentioned by either side in the whole debate about the existence of God. Curious, because it is surely the elephant in the room. We shall discuss its spiritual implications in a later chapter but (as I hope we are already beginning to see) it has a direct bearing on the function and behaviour of the *physical* world—including, believe it or not, genetic mutations.

The story of the Fall is told in Genesis chapter three. Many, even professing Christians, dismiss it as mythological but I can see no reason to treat it as anything but a simple historical narrative. Adam and Eve were given complete freedom in the garden of Eden except for a single prohibition—they were not to eat the fruit of a particular tree. The prohibition was a simple test of obedience and they failed it. Admittedly, Eve was deceived by Satan but Adam knew better.[23] You don't believe in the devil? Perhaps the following verse might help:

Some say the devil has never been,
And some say the devil has gone,
But simple folk would like to know
Who carries the business on.

In any case, the blame falls squarely on Adam. His disobedience was not the momentary lapse of a hungry man but a deliberate attempt to seize a new status—that of equality with God. For Satan had said of the forbidden fruit, '…in the day you eat of it your eyes will be opened, and you will be like God…'[24]

Swift punishment followed. God said to Adam, 'Because you have heeded the voice of your wife, and have eaten from the tree of which I commanded you, saying, "You shall not eat of it":Cursed is the ground for your sake; in toil you shall eat of it all the days of your life. Both thorns and thistles it shall bring forth for you, and you shall eat the herb of the field. In the sweat of your face you shall eat bread till you return to the ground, for out of it you were taken; for dust you are, and to dust you shall return.'[25]

Clearly, this is the point at which the 'creation' was subjected to 'corruption'—the Greek word Paul uses in Romans 8 signifies something inappropriate, perverse, depraved or frail. Man now struggled to raise healthy food-crops. The ground became encumbered with hitherto unknown or unobtrusive plant varieties, which bore thorns and poisonous barbs instead of edible fruit. Man himself became mortal. I accept that the details are sketchy but the message is clear enough—when Adam was judged for rebelling against his Maker, the physical world over which he had been given dominion[26] underwent a profound change for the worse. And what more effective agency could there be for such a transformation than the onset of widespread genetic mutations? Certainly, on the basis of these Bible references, the hypothesis of God would lead us to expect what we actually see— the modern-day biosphere is riddled with mechanisms that produce deleterious changes in life forms as diverse as plants and primates.

On this view, mutations do not cause evolution from simple to complex organisms, but rather cause genetic 'devolution'. The biosphere has devolved from the originally created 'kinds', each having an ideal genome, to their modern descendants possessing depleted and labile genomes.[27] In the process, many new varieties have arisen *within* the

Genesis 'kinds', one obvious example being the descent of mankind's many races from one original pair—whose gene pool would have been rich enough to contain all the diverse genetic traits associated with modern man. This perspective is, of course, entirely consistent with the rise of new varieties and new species within limits—that is, with micro-evolution—and with the prevalence of harmful mutations and even 'beneficial' mutations where the benefit is a side-effect of a loss of genetic information. It is just what we would expect on the biblical hypothesis of God.

# Chapter sixteen ...

... in which we ask a new question, 'What is man?' We focus on the fact that man is the only species that possesses mind—the capacity for thought and self-knowledge. Atheism must interpret mind as the inconsequential by-product of electrical activity in the brain, but we'll see how this leads to an epistemological abyss—the conclusion that all thought is meaningless.

We examine the burgeoning field of evolutionary psychology which traces all human behaviour to genetic predestination and eliminates moral responsibility. It's not a pretty sight. Are our brains no more than computers made of meat?

Fortunately, we conclude that mind is more than meat; that it 'rides' on the physical organ we call the brain in much the same way that the genetic code 'rides' on the chemical structure of DNA. This is exactly what we would expect on the hypothesis of God—for God has a mind without a body and man is made in his image.

## New words?

*Dualism*: The idea that mind and matter (specifically the brain) are distinct and separate realities.

*Epistemological*: Relating to knowledge or thought.

*Monism*: The idea that mind is nothing more than the brain at work.

*p-n junction*: A kind of on-off switch that is basic to the operation of a computer chip.

*PET imaging*: Positron Emission Tomography imaging. A medical scanning technique that produces 3D pictures of functional processes in the body.

*Reductionism*: The view that everything can be explained in terms of naturalistic cause and effect.

*Vitalism*: The idea that living things are imbued with a non-material 'life-force'.

# 16. The second shoe

When I consider Your heavens, the work of Your fingers,
The moon and the stars, which You have ordained,
What is man that You are mindful of him,
And the son of man that You visit him?
For You have made him a little lower than the angels,
And You have crowned him with glory and honour.

(Psalm 8:3–5)

It's a hoary story but I'll tell it just the same. Dave returns each night to his bachelor pad, sits on his bed to take off his shoes, and throws them on the floor. In the apartment below, Michael (who needs his rest) cowers beneath the bed-clothes waiting for the 'thump, thump' from above—knowing that only then will he be able to fall asleep. Eventually he can take no more and storms upstairs to demand that the shoe-throwing ritual should cease. Dave apologetically agrees to the ultimatum. However, the next night he removes his left shoe and throws it down as before, but then, suddenly remembering his promise, he lays his right shoe quietly on the floor and goes to bed. An hour later he is woken by a frantic knocking on the door. Michael stands there, a nervous wreck, imploring him to throw the other shoe (OK, but it's funny when you first hear it).

As far as this book is concerned, the first shoe was the question, 'Who made God?' and up till now we have concentrated wholly on that subject and matters arising from it. But at least some readers may have been biting their nails waiting for the second shoe—the closely related question, 'What is man?' After all, one reason we are interested in the existence of God is because it profoundly affects the way we see *ourselves*. If man is ultimately the outcome of chance chemistry and random mutations, that is one thing. If he is an intelligent and moral being, made in the image of a transcendent God, that is something altogether different. The two questions, 'Who made God?' and 'What is man?' belong together like a well-fitting pair of shoes.

The shoes are far from new. The questions they represent have been asked from time immemorial. Psalm 8, cited above and written some 3000 years ago, adopts the hypothesis of God, beginning: 'O LORD, our Lord, how excellent is Your name in all the earth, who have set Your glory above the heavens!' But the psalmist's contemplation of God's glory leads him immediately to consider the place of man in the scheme of things—what is man, that such an exalted being as God should be 'mindful' of him? Good question, and one that demands an answer. So what alternatives are open to us? We have, I think, three broad options, namely, to believe: (1) that man is an accident of nature, the product of naturalistic evolution (I'll call this 'evolutionism' for short); (2) that man is the product of an evolutionary process put in place and/or guided by God (theistic evolution); and (3) that man is the product of special non-evolutionary creation (creationism). We're going to consider all these options, together with some of the variations that arise within them. However, it will serve our purpose best to focus on two particular topics—'man and his mind' and 'man and his Maker'. I shall cover the first in this chapter and the second in the next and final chapter of this book.

## Man and his mind

All living things respond to stimuli; this is a basic sign of life. Higher animals also display 'intelligence' which, broadly defined, reveals itself in such things as complex behaviour, the ability to learn, and capabilities for observation, emotion, communication and action. But as far as we know, only man possesses 'mind'—the capacity for self-knowledge and abstract thought. We'll never know, of course, but it's a fair bet that even the most highly trained chimpanzee never muttered to itself, 'I think; therefore I am.' As evolutionist Theodosius Dobzhansky wrote, 'The pressing problems [for evolutionary theory] today centre on the mechanisms of evolution and the biological uniqueness of man.'[1] Although he wrote this in 1958 it remains true, and nothing about man is more unique than his mental powers—abilities that represent an enormous gulf between *Homo sapiens* and every other species.

Needless to say, the debate about the nature of mind has gone on for millennia. Ancient literature is unashamedly 'dualistic', maintaining that mind and matter are two quite different things. Both Old and New Testaments, for example, treat mind, thought and all that goes with them as attributes possessed by God—a spiritual being who has no material existence. Here is a random example: 'For I know the thoughts that I think toward you, says the LORD, thoughts of peace and not of evil, to give you a future and a hope.'[2] Since the mind of God exists without any material substrate so, logically, does the mind of man. The Bible recognizes, of course, that in the case of man, thought resides in the head—a physical domain that we now identify with the brain. For example, Daniel says, 'I saw a dream which made me afraid, and the thoughts on my bed and the visions of my head troubled me.'[3] But nevertheless, if man is made in the image of God, his mind is derivative from God's non-material mind and dualism is preserved.

Greek philosophers such as Plato and Aristotle also taught (different) forms of dualism, as did Thomas Aquinas, while Descartes (also a dualist) started the snowball of modern debate that continues to roll and grow—creating a gargantuan literature which I will not attempt to explore here. Put simply, the chief antagonists are dualism in the blue corner and 'monism' (as a materialistic psychological theory) in the red corner. Monism denies that there is any real distinction between mind and matter and claims that mind is simply the brain at work.

If philosophical terms gives you a headache, try thinking of the brain as a factory. Its incoming raw materials are nerve impulses bringing information from the five senses of sight, hearing, touch, taste and smell. The brain-factory receives and processes the raw materials and outputs products—further nerve impulses which tell the body to react in appropriate ways. Thus, for example, a starburst of light causes your eyes to send a nerve impulse to your brain, which processes the signal and issues instructions to your eyelids to shut and your facial muscles to 'screw up' your eyes against the glare. Again, when you hear someone tell a joke, the signals from your ears are processed by your brain, which issues instructions to a whole collection of muscles that make you laugh (or not, as the case may be).

So where does 'mind' come into all this? If you are a monist, the conscious appreciation of such events is nothing but the hum and rattle of the factory's machinery—an inevitable but inconsequential by-product of brain activity. If, on the other hand, you are a dualist, the mind is the factory manager who may or may not consciously intervene in the factory's processes but is always in a position to do so. Furthermore, when the day is over, the manager can leave the factory and go home, but the machinery falls silent. The hum and rattle have nowhere to go.

Evolutionism (as distinct from theistic evolution) is monistic. It can offer only one explanation for the phenomenon of mind, namely that it is a by-product of electrical activity in the brain, which itself is an organ evolved by the Darwinian mechanisms of random mutation and natural selection. In his famous 1903 essay entitled *A free man's worship*, atheist philosopher Bertrand Russell reveals that monism is the *raison d'être* behind his nihilistic view of man. He writes:

> ... even more purposeless, more void of meaning, is the world which Science presents for our belief. Amid such a world, if anywhere, our ideals henceforward must find a home. That Man is the product of causes which had no prevision of the end they were achieving; that his origin, his growth, *his hopes and fears, his loves and his beliefs, are*

*but the outcome of accidental collocations of atoms;* ... all these things, if
not quite beyond dispute, are yet so nearly certain, that no philosophy
which rejects them can hope to stand. Only ... on the firm foundation
of unyielding despair, can the soul's habitation henceforth be safely
built (emphasis added).[4]

Russell reduces our hopes, fears, loves and beliefs—all our mental
experiences, in fact—to accidental atomic interactions. No wonder his
philosophy is one of 'unyielding despair'. The core problem with all
monistic explanations is, of course, that mind becomes meaningless.
To modernize Russell's terminology, our thoughts are preordained
by self-maintaining electro-chemical processes, which are themselves
dictated by our genes. Reasoning has no validity and all our theories
and explanations—no matter how energetically promoted or zealously
defended—have no more substance than the bubbles in a glass of
champagne. Avowed rationalist though he was, J. B. S. Haldane
confessed the monist's dilemma when he wrote: 'If my mental processes
are determined wholly by the motions of atoms in my brain, I have
no reason to suppose that my beliefs are true. They may be sound
chemically, but that does not make them sound logically. And hence
I have no reason for supposing my brain to be composed of atoms.'[5]

Victor Stenger falls into the trap.[6] Since mind is produced by purely
physical processes, he maintains, all religious beliefs, experiences and
impressions are illusory—like the 'highs' and 'out-of-mind' experiences
induced by certain drugs. Such arguments remind me of the animated
cartoon in which the Pink Panther accidentally sucks himself into the
vacuum cleaner he is holding and is swallowed up, followed by the
vacuum cleaner itself. This, of course, causes both panther and cleaner
to disappear. If Stenger is right, all his theories and arguments (along
with yours and mine) vanish without trace into the vacuum cleaner
of reductionism. Entertaining, perhaps, but not particularly helpful.

## Evolutionary psychology
A concrete example of monism is provided by evolutionary psychology,
which teaches that our brains are genetically preconditioned to produce

certain forms of behaviour. The anti-social person and the criminal are no longer responsible for their actions but are the victims of their genetic inheritance. Indeed, *whatever* our lifestyle, character and inclinations, we cannot help ourselves because we are simply living out our genetic predestination.

Reviewing a book 'explaining' rape as a Darwinian survival mechanism, evolutionary biologist Jerry Coyne comments as follows: 'Unfortunately, evolutionary psychologists routinely confuse theory and speculation. Unlike bones, behaviour does not fossilize, and understanding its evolution often involves concocting stories that sound plausible but are hard to test. Depression, for example, is seen as a trait favored by natural selection to enable us to solve our problems by withdrawing, reflecting, and hence enhancing our future reproduction. Plausible? Maybe. Scientifically testable? Absolutely not. If evolutionary biology is a soft science, then evolutionary psychology is its flabby underbelly.'

He continues: 'The public can be forgiven for thinking that evolutionary biology is equivalent to evolutionary psychology. Books by Daniel Dennett, E. O. Wilson, and Steven Pinker have sold briskly, and evolutionary psychology dominates the media coverage of the science of evolution ... In view of the scientific shakiness of much of the work, its popularity must rest partly on some desire for a comprehensive "scientific" explanation of human behaviour. Evolutionary psychology satisfies the post-ideological hunger for a totalistic explanation of human life, for a theory of inevitability that will remove many of the ambiguities and the uncertainties of emotional and moral life. Freud is no longer the preferred behavioural paradigm. Now Darwin is ascendant. Blame your genes, not your mother.'[7]

According to monism, our self-consciousness is like the shadow of a horse that moves along with the animal (representing the brain) but has no substance of its own. By contrast, dualism sees consciousness as the rider of the horse. Like the shadow, the rider must move with the horse, but unlike the shadow the horseman is both real and in control.

In dualism, consciousness 'rides' on the physical brain in much the same way as genetic information 'rides' on molecules of DNA. As we saw in chapter 12, the coded information that constitutes life cannot exist without a medium or substrate—the chemical structure of DNA. But the chemical structure no more constitutes the information than the paper and ink of this book constitute its argument. By analogy, human consciousness and mind 'ride' upon the physical organ of the brain. But they are not shadows—they have a reality of their own. What is more, it is a supervising reality.

The analogy is not perfect, however. According to the biblical hypothesis of God, there is more to human consciousness and mind than that which vanishes when we become unconscious or die. Most people who are anaesthetized for surgery have no recollection of what happened in the operating theatre (fortunately), but the *capacity* for conscious thought is not lost. This is equally true when death finally eliminates all brain activity. According to the Bible, the human mind lives on, together with its capacity to think and experience (this 'undying' entity is often loosely called the soul or the spirit of the individual). Referring to death, St Paul declares, 'To be absent from the body [is] to be present with the Lord,'[8] while the psalmist rejoices in the belief that 'In Your presence is fullness of joy; at Your right hand are pleasures for evermore.'[9] As the first Christian martyr Stephen died he saw 'the heavens opened and the Son of Man standing at the right hand of God'.[10] The whole purpose of Jesus Christ's coming into the world was, he said, to 'give eternal life to as many as [the Father had] given Him'.[11]

In short, the biblical hypothesis leads us to expect two things. Firstly, our minds have a meaningful existence of their own. Our thoughts, plans, feelings and desires have a real existence apart from the electrical activity of the brain by which they are maintained—just as the genetic code has a real existence apart from the DNA molecules on which it is stored. And just as the genetic code controls our physical life, so the human mind (not the physical brain) controls our psychological life. In other words, dualism is true and monism is false. This is something we all instinctively feel and which is a logical necessity if we are to avoid an epistemological abyss—the monistic conclusion that all thought is meaningless.

Secondly, the hypothesis of God predicts that man's mind (or soul or spirit) lives on after the death of the physical brain. Like the mind of God, the human mind can exist without a material substrate, even though it inhabits such a substrate (the brain) throughout our physical lifetime. This again accords with mankind's persistent and almost universal belief (atheists and monists excepted, of course) that life continues after death.

### Computers made of meat?

Another modern form of monism is the idea that the human brain is nothing but 'a computer made of meat' (in the words of artificial intelligence guru Marvin Minsky). Just as a computer can perform complex calculations at amazing speed, and thereby beat assorted grandmasters at chess, so the brain can be regarded as so much neural circuitry. Philosopher John Searle claims: 'we can find out how the mind really works by discovering what programs are implemented in the brain ... We just happen, by a kind of evolutionary accident, to be implemented in neurons [as distinct from microchips] but any sufficiently complex hardware would do as well as what we have in our skulls.'[12] The implication is, of course, that as computers grow more powerful they will eventually attain consciousness—the ability to think for themselves.

But Mario Beauregard and Denyse O'Leary[13] warn us against such over-optimism by reminding us of Douglas Adams' novel, *The hitch-hiker's guide to the galaxy.*[14] The second greatest computer of all time was instructed to answer the ultimate question of life, the universe and everything. After working on the problem for 7.5 million years, it finally announced the answer as 'forty-two'. The computer added: 'The problem ... is that you've never actually known what the question is.' Slapstick, of course, but the humour discloses an important truth, namely, that computers do nothing but compute. They obey implicitly the algorithms (instructions) input by human programmers and if you're not careful it's a classic case of 'garbage in, garbage out'. The idea that computers may some day acquire 'consciousness' and so dispense with their human masters is a pious speculation based on circular reasoning that is so artless as to be almost spherical. Thus:

1. The human brain is simply a complex computer (the monistic assumption).

2. The human brain exhibits consciousness.

3. Therefore complex computers can achieve consciousness.

4. This shows that the human brain is nothing more than a complex computer.

The belief that computers can ultimately achieve consciousness is just a new version of an old device, namely, the *deus ex machina*. According to the *Britannica Concise Encyclopaedia*, the term refers to a 'stage device in Greek and Roman drama in which a god appeared in the sky by means of a crane (Greek, *mechane*) to resolve the plot of a play ... The term now denotes something that appears suddenly and unexpectedly and provides an artificial solution to an apparently insoluble difficulty.' It couldn't be put better. Computer consciousness is the god which (many hope) will suddenly emerge from a tangle of p-n junctions in some futuristic computer chip—resolving at a stroke the embarrassment caused to monists by human self-consciousness. Never mind that way back in 1695, Gottfried Leibniz in his *Système nouveau de la nature* considered and rejected the whole idea of such an opportunistic solution to mind-brain duality. Monistic hope apparently springs eternal.

## How thinking changes the brain
The final nail in the coffin of monism is the long-assumed but recently proven fact that thinking (mind) can change the activity and performance of the brain. Clearly, this can never be the case if

thought is simply an inconsequential by-product of brain activity. In a column in *The Times* titled, 'If you pay more, you enjoy more', biochemist Terence Kealey describes[15] work by Baba Shiv, a professor of marketing at Stanford Business School. Dr Shiv gave the same wine to a group of people on two different occasions, but the first time he said it cost $45 a bottle and the second time $5. Unsurprisingly, the group declared that the 'more expensive' wine tasted better. However, he also used 'functional' MRI brain scans to examine the pleasure centres of his subjects' brains and found that these centres 'lit up' more strongly when they thought they were drinking expensive wine. The volunteers' false beliefs really did affect their brain activity—not the other way around.

A second example is a recent study[16] at the Garvan Institute in Sydney. Over a period of eight weeks, recreational athletes were given either growth hormones or inactive placebos—without knowing which they were taking. 'At the end of the study, volunteers who took placebos could sprint faster, jump higher and lift heavier weights' than they could before—and the volunteers who *thought* they were taking performance-enhancing drugs but were actually taking placebos, outperformed everyone else in their group.

Of course, the improved performance of the placebo group could be due simply to the care and attention they were receiving as participants in the trial. But even this is significant. We all know that encouragement stimulates improvements in performance, whatever the field of endeavour. But why should it do so? It can only be that the mind, motivated by *non-physical* encouragement, induces *physical* changes in the brain that result in greater effort being made. But, of course, the strongest evidence is the placebo effect itself. The trial showed that believing that you are receiving a performance-enhancing drug improves performance even when the belief is wrong. This can mean only one thing—the mind (belief) can change the brain (the ultimate physical source of improved performance).

The placebo effect has, of course, been known for a very long time. In a lengthy internet note issued to accompany the fourth edition of the book *Biological psychology*,[17] the *Biopsychology Newsletter*[18] comments as follows (page numbers refer to the book):

> Some of the proposed mechanisms [for the placebo effect] are these: (1) As the text notes (pp. 241–242), it was found in the 1970s that placebo reduction of pain is mediated in part by endogenous opioids, demonstrated by the fact that the effect could be reduced by the opioid-blocker naloxone. This suggested to some that the placebo effect is "real" because it is mediated by a known physiological mechanism ... (2) It was also found in the 1970s that immunosuppressive effects can be conditioned to originally ineffective stimuli (p.500). (3) The placebo might reduce stress, allowing the body to regain a natural, optimal level of functioning. Each of these mechanisms would be expected to be systemic, affecting the whole body ... Such results support the interpretation that the expectancies of people cause placebo effects. The role of the basal amygdala in interpretation of stimuli and expectancies is discussed on pp. 483–485, and further work is to be expected on how expectations translate into bodily responses.

The note further explains that the physical reality of these effects are confirmed by PET imaging scans: 'Brain imaging showed that both opioid analgesia and placebo analgesia activated the rostral anterior cingulate cortex and a region in the pons ... Those subjects who showed a greater placebo effect also showed greater activation of the anterior cingulate cortex. Thus this study helps to understand a mechanism involved in the placebo analgesic effect.'

You don't need to understand all of this to get the message—non-physical mental *expectations* translate into bodily responses via real physical changes in the brain. If non-physical mind can affect the physical brain in this way, then mind can hardly be the mere by-product of brain activity, as monism (however packaged) ultimately requires.

## Theistic evolution and the human brain

Evolutionism is monistic; creationism is dualistic; so where does theistic evolution fit in? It isn't easy to say, because it comes in several varieties. The simple statement that God 'used' the process of evolution to create the biological world, with man at its apex, actually hides some deep inconsistencies. This will emerge as we consider three versions of theistic evolution (TE for short).

Firstly, there is what I will call 'emergent evolution'—the idea that the laws of nature are such that the emergence of intelligent life was pre-programmed or fore-ordained. The mechanisms by which life arose and diversified, and by which man himself eventually came into being, are exactly as proposed by evolutionism, but cannot be 'reduced' to mere physics and chemistry. That is, evolution is accepted but 'reductionism' rejected. This view sees evolution as a teleological process (a process with an end in view), purposed by God when he originated the laws of nature. Some philosophers see 'emergence' as old-fashioned vitalism in disguise. Others, however, accept that whereas vitalism invokes a mysterious non-physical 'life-force', emergence simply attributes 'purpose' to natural processes. Yet here lies the fatal weakness of emergence as a theory of life—it endows the laws of nature with a mystical quality *that can only be discerned by the alleged consequences*. Its reasoning is wholly tautological, assuming purpose in natural law in order to explain apparent purpose in the results of natural law.

Next there is what I will call standard TE. This is identical to evolutionism except in two respects. Firstly, it implicitly assumes a form of emergence—if God always intended to create man, and did so by a naturalistic evolutionary process, he must also take credit for that process, naturalistic though it is. However, standard TE relies on evolution only for the creation of man's physical form. So, secondly, it attributes the unique nature of man to a special intervention by God. In other words, true man only came into being when God injected a soul or spirit into selected members of a pre-human race. This is the view propounded by C. S. Lewis and embraced, for example, by Francis Collins,[19] who quotes Lewis at length. Lewis declares:

> For long centuries, God perfected the animal form which was to become the vehicle of humanity and the image of Himself. He gave it hands whose thumb could be applied to each of the fingers, and jaws and teeth and throat capable of articulation, and a brain sufficiently complex to execute all of the material motions whereby rational thought is incarnated. The creature may have existed in this state for ages before it became man; it may even have been clever enough to make things which a modern archaeologist would accept as proof of its humanity. But it was only an animal because all its physical and psychical processes were directed to purely material and natural ends. Then, in the fullness of time, God caused to descend upon this organism ... a new kind of consciousness which could say 'I' and 'me' which could look upon itself as an object which knew God...[20]

The attraction of standard TE is, of course, that although it appeals to a creative miracle, the miracle in question is a *spiritual* miracle and not a physical one. It causes no rent in the seamless robe of naturalism. We may wonder how Lewis reconciled this approach with his clear stand on the reality of physical miracles in his book *Miracles*.[21] Perhaps he was simply accepting all he had been told about the evolution and saw no need to invoke a physical miracle to explain man's creation. But there can be no doubt that many who follow him today do take refuge in the 'spiritual miracle' get-out to avoid any implication of a physical miracle (interestingly, Collins makes an exception for the resurrection of Jesus Christ[22]).

But does the spiritual-miracle gambit actually work? The answer must surely be 'no'. For whatever powers of self-consciousness, self-knowledge and awareness of God were imparted by this spiritual miracle, they must have required *physical* changes in the brains concerned. New neural pathways and networks must have been suddenly created to 'carry' and accommodate this new awareness. Otherwise, there would be no act of creation and we would be back where we started—with self-consciousness as the meaningless by-product of a monistic growth in brain complexity.

Finally, there is the relatively new variety of TE proposed by ID leader and biochemist Michael Behe in his book *The edge of evolution*.[23] Behe accepts the Darwinian ideas of common descent and evolution by mutation and natural selection, but sets out to prove that cumulative mutations 'larger' than those involving two or three point mutations cannot have occurred randomly—they must have been the result of periodic interventions by a designer with an exquisitely light touch. Here, then, is a genuinely 'guided' evolution, although in true ID fashion Behe declines to identify the designer. The main problem I have with this concept is that it involves the *occasional* interference of the designer in an otherwise naturalistic process of evolution—an outstanding example of the doctrine of *deus ex machina* discussed earlier in this chapter. It shares with standard TE the hope that we can have the Darwinian cake and eat it—by superposing a deity who hovers in the background and, while not in complete control of physical events, can nudge them in the right direction when he chooses. I find this both biblically and philosophically unacceptable. Far from offering the best of both worlds it actually offers the worst.

# CHAPTER SEVENTEEN ...

... in which a doll's pram provides the unlikely vehicle for an exploration of man and morality. Like mind, morality and conscience are unique to man and, despite heroic efforts, atheism's attempts to explain them self-destruct in contradictions.

Consistent atheism must deny the very existence of morality and reduce all human behaviour, of whatever kind, to the machinations of selfish genes. Yet atheists continually lay claim to the moral high-ground not realizing that the moral landscape of atheism is as flat as a pancake. Thus Richard Dawkins claims that people can and should be *taught* to overcome their innate selfishness and behave altruistically. But this is impossible if morality is an illusion, as his world view logically implies.

Turning to the hypothesis of God, we first find a source for morality and then consider its implications—with special emphasis on the effects for human morality of original sin and the Fall of Adam. We'll see the futility of attempting to reform man's fundamental nature by merely commending good behaviour. Our redemption lies not in evolutionary self-improvement, or even in moral teaching, but in rebirth through God's grace and the atoning work of Jesus Christ.

### New words?

*Altruism*: Regard for others as a principle of action.

# 17. Man and his Maker

The means by which we live have outdistanced the ends for which we live. Our scientific power has outrun our spiritual power. We have guided missiles and misguided men.

From a speech by Martin Luther King Jr

For all have sinned and fall short of the glory of God, being justified freely by His grace through the redemption that is in Christ Jesus.

(Romans 3:23–24)

H uman beings are not only endowed with mind but also with morality. As we saw in chapter 9, we have consciences that monitor and judge our thoughts and actions. In short, man appears to be the only creature that can distinguish between 'right' and 'wrong'. In this chapter I shall use the term 'morality' to cover all moral attitudes and actions, whether they are judged 'good', 'bad' or 'neutral'. Just *how* we judge anything will, of course, depend entirely on the way it compares with some standard. For the theist, that standard is the law of God. For the consistent atheist, it can only be evolution—moral quality must be assessed in terms of evolutionary benefit or failure. But either way, morality really exists. Let me tell you a true story.

A family were standing in the large kitchen of their home talking to friends while their three-year-old daughter pushed her doll's pram to and fro with some vigour. In doing so, she ran the pram into her father's leg, inflicting (as I remember) a degree of pain. The child's older sister immediately issued a stern rebuke: 'Alison, say sorry to daddy!' The younger child continued her perambulations without response but we could see her mind was working overtime. 'Say sorry to daddy!', came the repeated command. No reply. A further interval elapsed and the older sister's voice rang out again: 'Say sorry!' There was a prolonged pause and then the worried frown on the toddler's face was suddenly replaced by a seraphic smile: 'Me can't talk,' she said.

The adults dissolved in laughter but I have never forgotten the incident because its implications are really quite profound, illuminating the whole question of human morality. Clearly, Alison knew she had done 'wrong' in hurting her father. Her stubborn refusal to admit guilt is evidence enough of that. If she had no sense of right and wrong she would have experienced no moral dilemma.

We could, of course, explain the episode away. It wasn't that the child had some innate moral awareness, we might say, but that her sense of guilt was a conditioned reflex. She recognized her sister's tone of voice and knew from past experience that it meant trouble. No doubt, children do have conditioned reflexes, but the appropriate reflex in my story would have been one of two things—either a simple denial of responsibility ('it wasn't me, it was my doll') or a quick apology (knowing that an apology defuses such situations). It was the devious guilt-reaction that revealed the toddler's moral awareness—her silent inward struggle spoke volumes. She knew she was guilty and should apologize, but exercised considerable ingenuity to bypass conscience and evade moral responsibility. And you can't evade what you don't have.

Such behaviour is typically and *uniquely* human. We can only experience such problems if we have a genuine moral sense in the first place. If, at that moment, the family's pet dog had walked into the kitchen leaving muddy paw-prints, it too might have been scolded.

It might have cringed and put its tail between its legs, recognizing disapproval in its master's voice. But this would be a genuine conditioned reflex, a response to an *external* signal. There would be no corresponding *inner* awareness of wrongdoing—otherwise, next time, it would have wiped its feet on the doormat.

## The moral argument for God

At the time of writing I had recently read *The language of God*[1] by geneticist Francis Collins. He abandoned his former atheism after reading C. S. Lewis' *Mere Christianity* and being won over by the moral argument for the existence of God. This argument points out that morality is a form of law and, as we saw in chapter 9, moral law necessitates a lawgiver. Collins is one among many who have started from morality and arrived at God. In the present book, of course, we are following the opposite path, beginning with the hypothesis of God and deducing human morality as a necessary consequence.

In doing so, we are following a route mapped out by St Augustine and Thomas Aquinas. Alister McGrath writes[2]: 'Aquinas's arguments have Christian assumptions—for example, that there is a God, and that this God has created the world. The arguments then proceed to demonstrate that these beliefs are consistent with the way the world actually is. For example, Aquinas asks where human values such as truth, goodness and nobility come from. What causes them? ... The origin of these ideas, Aquinas suggests, is God which is the ultimate cause.' If God exists as a moral being who has made man in his own image, then man must also be a moral being. Does this match our observations? Yes? Then the hypothesis is verified to that degree.

Whether we walk the path from morality to God or from God to morality, the path is there to be walked. However, the 'God downwards' approach has a distinct advantage. If we reason only from the nature of man to God we are in danger of fashioning a 'God' in the image of man. God is located as a moral entity but he may be that and nothing more—which offers a severely restricted perception of the divine nature. Even worse, because man's practice of morality is so numbingly inconsistent, we are likely to conclude that God himself is morally inconsistent—as Richard Dawkins does in his infamous tirades against the Deity.

Man's moral practice is bizarre by any measure. A tribe that applies strict laws against murder, adultery and theft may think nothing of making war on a neighbouring tribe—killing, raping and spoiling its enemies. It happens all the time—witness Stalin's purges, the Chinese 'cultural revolution', the killing fields of Cambodia and seemingly endless tribal conflicts in Africa. Strange as it may seem, this is all predictable on the hypothesis of God, as we shall see in a moment. Antithetically, the atheist seeks to interpret mankind's moral maze in evolutionary terms as the struggle for existence[3] but runs into all kinds of contradiction in the process, as we shall also see.

But what is commonly overlooked in the slanging match that ensues is that none of this affects the *fact* of human moral awareness. The debate between theists and atheists is often marked, on both sides, by a failure to distinguish between two quite different things, namely, the *practice* of morality and the *existence* of morality. The former is confusing to say the least, but the latter is unavoidable. There can be no more conclusive proof of this than the way that atheists, while attributing morality to amoral 'selfish genes', continually attempt to seize the moral high ground! For example, Richard Dawkins writes:

> My own feeling is that a human society based simply on the gene's law of universal ruthless selfishness would be a very nasty society in which to live. But unfortunately, however much we may deplore something, it does not stop it being true ... Be warned that if you wish, as I do, to build a society in which individuals cooperate generously and unselfishly towards a common good, you can expect little help from biological nature. Let us try to teach generosity and altruism, because we are born selfish.[4]

What Dawkins doesn't seem to realize is that if his atheism were true, there would be no moral high ground to occupy. I once visited

Minnesota in the depths of winter and, somewhat jet-lagged, was being driven home from the airport by my host. We passed a large snow-covered field and I remarked that it looked remarkably flat. 'That's because it's a lake', he replied laconically. Likewise, atheism ought to be a featureless plain, boasting not so much as a moral molehill, let alone the mountain from which the new Olympians hurl down their moral thunderbolts upon theists, religion and lesser gods. If our world is the product of amoral forces, and if man is simply cosmic flotsam scattered on the shores of time, then morality (including Dawkins' longed-for generosity and altruism) simply does not exist. Nothing can be 'good' and nothing 'evil'. 'Right' and 'wrong' are concepts devoid of meaning, and anyone who passes moral judgement dwells not on moral high ground but in cloud cuckoo land. To their credit, older atheists like Nietzsche, Russell, Sartre and Camus recognized this and saw that it led logically to nihilism or, at best, to absurdity. The 'new atheists' (who want us to call them 'brights') seem oblivious to the obvious.

To summarize, therefore, morality (whether good or bad) exists, and does so uniquely among humans. Whatever moral judgements we make does not alter the fact that there is a moral domain which manifests itself in both individual and social conscience. As we have seen,[5] this follows naturally and explicitly from the hypothesis of God, but cannot logically be ascribed to a wholly amoral process such as evolution or the supposed 'selfishness' of human genes.

### Is morality an evolutionary strategy?

In spite of this, of course, atheists argue that morality is an evolutionary phenomenon that arose because it has survival value. But quite apart from the difficulty of fashioning the silk purse of morality from the sow's ear of evolution, this is contrary to all the evidence. Man's actual moral behaviour, both good and bad, commonly bucks the evolutionary imperative, which is to maximize the number of one's offspring. Australian philosopher David Stove has argued this at length in his book *Darwinian fairytales*,[6] citing celibacy, contraception, abortion, altruism, heroism, parental care for offspring and many other common human practices—along with the sanctions against murder and marital unfaithfulness practised by most human societies.

Dawkins does, however, acknowledge certain important truths in the passage cited above, namely, that man is innately selfish and *needs* to rise above his inner nastiness and learn to live a kind and altruistic life. Whether intentionally or not, his statement is seminal, because it raises several key questions regarding the nature of man. Let me list them:

1. How did man's selfishness arise?

2. How does human altruism arise?

3. How may altruism triumph over selfishness?

Let's try to find some answers.

Dawkins believes that man's innate selfishness is readily explained by the Darwinian narrative—this, after all, is the thesis of his book *The selfish gene.*[7] Yet this belief is based on the bizarre assumption that genes somehow possess moral qualities and objectives. In reality, of course, the term 'selfish gene' is no more than a shorthand for Darwinian 'survival of the fittest'. But even so, how can an amoral process lead to *moral* consequences (like human selfishness)? The only *consistent* account of human nature provided by atheistic evolution is that there is no such thing as moral behaviour—all kinds of behaviour, good and bad, are simply survival mechanisms in disguise.

The problem becomes more acute when we ask specifically where generosity and altruism come from. Are they somehow magicked by Sooty out of nowhere? Or are they also, like the nastiness they must overcome, the result of evolution due to some selective advantage they afford? But if the latter, how can diametrically opposed moral traits—selfishness and unselfishness—arise and co-exist by courtesy of the same evolutionary process? If altruism among men imparts 'fitness' through selective advantage, why has selfishness not been eliminated by natural selection as being a poor evolutionary strategy? It would be different if there were two separate races of men, a selfish race and an altruistic race. Darwinism could explain *that* in terms of different selective pressures acting on segregated populations. But what wondrous selective pressures can there be that—within the same population and even the same individual—select for and against altruistic behaviour at the same time? It's the brownsnout spookfish all over again.[8]

Finally, as I pointed out at the beginning of the chapter, we can only distinguish good morality from bad morality by appealing to some independent standard. The atheist has only evolutionary advantage as his standard, and Dawkins insists in his seminal passage that evolution overwhelmingly favours selfishness. Yet if the evolutionary imperative is our only standard, it follows that selfishness is overwhelmingly 'good'. How, then, can Dawkins conclude that selfishness is 'bad' and altruism 'good'? He is clearly appealing to some standard of morality other than evolutionary success. Hahn and Wiker spend some time analysing the matter and conclude that Dawkins' standard 'is actually a pastiche of Christianity as filtered through 19th century liberalism ... and its radical extension, via Darwinism, into the farther reaches of 21st century liberalism'.[9] Bereft of moral clothes, evolution's emperor simply borrows them from someone else.

### Free will and the Fall of man

A far more logical explanation of morality is offered by the biblical hypothesis of God. It is one on which creationists and most theistic evolutionists agree. This also sees two natures in man—one selfish and one altruistic. Man's altruistic nature is a reality because he was created in the image of God and from the outset reflected God's moral character. But Adam was no automaton—he was created a free agent that he might render *willing* obedience to his Maker. By choosing to rebel[10] he employed his 'free will' to estrange himself from God and became a 'sinner', that is, one who falls short of God's righteous requirements.[11] This biblical definition of sin goes much deeper than the popular idea that only specially bad people are 'sinners', and catches in its net even the most respectable among us. As Isaiah declares, compared with the glory of God, 'We are all like an unclean thing, and all our righteousnesses [best deeds] are like filthy rags.'[12]

In the Fall of Adam, our race not only lost its original moral innocence but also its free will. This is often overlooked but is an essential aspect of the biblical scenario. Man is still free to act as he wills, but his will is now enslaved by his fallen nature. In short, man is the servant of his own sin. Jesus declares, 'Most assuredly, I say to you, whoever commits sin is a slave of sin,'[13] while St Paul reminds the Christians at Rome: 'For when you were slaves of sin, you were free in regard to righteousness. What fruit did you have then in the things of which you are now ashamed? For the end of those things is death.'[14] Nevertheless, in spite of universal human sinfulness, the image of God in man persists. It has been marred but not eliminated. Hence kindness and altruism sit side by side with sin and selfishness in the 'deceitful' heart of man[15]—explaining both the moral contradictions of human nature and the constant conflict they beget.

According to this teaching, then, the problem of selfishness and sin lies not in our biological nature as atheism requires, but in our fallen nature. So, which explanation accords best with observation? Surely, the biblical one. Quite apart from resolving the evolutionary dilemma in which the self-same selective pressures give rise to opposite moral traits, the biblical insight accounts for the battle between moral and immoral tendencies that we all experience. As St Paul writes, 'The flesh [fallen human nature] lusts against the spirit, and the spirit against the flesh; and these are contrary to one another, so that you do not do the things that you wish.'[16] Furthermore, the biblical scenario accounts for the 'me can't talk' syndrome—the phenomena of conscience and guilt. As far as we can tell, these are uniquely human experiences, yet if they had an evolutionary origin they should be found in other species too.

### Can altruism overcome selfishness?

The last of the three questions raised by Dawkins' statement is this: How may altruism triumph over selfishness? He answers as follows:

'if you wish, as I do, to build a society in which individuals cooperate generously and unselfishly towards a common good ... *Let us try to teach generosity and altruism*, because we are born selfish' (emphasis added). But how realistic is his hope that *teaching* generosity and altruism will have the desired effect? What evidence does science, history or experience provide to encourage such a belief? Very little, I suspect. And if, as evolutionary psychology maintains, our brains (and the behaviour they promote) are the products solely of our genes, what capacity do they have to absorb and act upon teaching that is diametrically opposed to our genetic disposition? And if our brains *can* be altered by mere teaching, is this not another case of 'mind over matter' and a further nail in the coffin of monistic theories of psychology? For all its apparent promise, Richard Dawkins' altruistic atheism turns out to be a can of worms.

The hypothesis of God proposes an entirely different scenario—one that is both pessimistic and optimistic. According to the Bible, man will never succeed in building 'a society in which individuals cooperate generously and unselfishly towards a common good'. Jeremiah states the case pithily: 'Can the Ethiopian change his skin or the leopard its spots? Then may you also do good who are accustomed to do evil.'[17] Our sinful nature is as much part of us as the colour of our skin (whatever it might be). A Rudyard Kipling leopard could no doubt do a deal and swap his spots for tiger's stripes, but in real life we humans are incorrigible. Our society may flourish politically, economically, educationally and technologically but, left to itself, such success is invariably accompanied by moral declension rather than betterment. Witness the near-collapse of the capitalist financial system in 2008, which most commentators blame on the greed and selfishness of banks and their directors, and neglect on the part of governments and regulators. It's not 'immoral systems' that are at fault but, rather, immoral people who build and operate such systems. And let's face it, if you or I had the power to take their place, we would do no better. Personal morality is a common casualty of affluence (if you don't believe me, read a newspaper).

That does not mean that societies can never be rejuvenated morally, but when this happens it is invariably the result of religious, not educational, influences. A remarkable article in *The Times* newspaper on 27 December 2008, written by journalist and sceptic Matthew Parris, illustrates the point. It was entitled, 'As an atheist, I truly believe Africa needs God'. The subtitle ran, 'Missionaries, not aid money, are the solution to Africa's biggest problem—the crushing passivity of the people's mindset'.

The article is an honest admission by someone brought up in sub-Saharan Africa that the biblical Christian gospel delivers men and women from tribalism and passivity, makes them walk tall, and empowers them to fashion their own personal and national destinies. Parris writes: 'Africans who had been converted and were strong believers ... were always different. Far from having cowed or confined its converts, their faith appeared to have liberated and relaxed them.' At the age of twenty-four he and four student friends travelled by land across the continent—through Algiers, Niger, Nigeria, Cameroon, Central African Republic, Congo, Rwanda, Tanzania and Kenya. Seeking places to camp at night they had to acknowledge that 'when [they] entered a territory worked by missionaries ... something changed in the faces of the people'—and they felt safe in a way they did not feel elsewhere. Such impressions, he continued, were strongly reinforced during a recent visit to Malawi.

The history of the Christian church provides countless examples of the way the Bible can transform society—locally, nationally and even internationally.[18] However, such transformations are neither total nor enduring. According to the Bible, the world will only be restored to an idyllic state by the return of Jesus Christ and 'the coming of the day of God'. At that time, writes St Peter, 'the heavens will be dissolved ... and the elements will melt with fervent heat. Nevertheless, we, according to His promise, look for new heavens and a new earth in which righteousness dwells.'[19] If you are inclined to scoff at such ideas that's fine—because it actually confirms biblical predictions! Earlier Peter declares: 'scoffers will come in the last days ... saying, "Where is the promise of His coming? ... all things continue as they were from the beginning of creation".'[20]

Until that time, claims the hypothesis of God, the biblical gospel ('good news') will continue to change human society by changing individual *members* of society.

## Is God moral?

Before we explore the final ramifications of the biblical view of morality and sin, however, I need to meet an objection that atheists raise against my thesis. The God of the Bible, they maintain, is himself immoral, so how can he be the source of 'good' morality? Richard Dawkins puts it thus: 'The God of the Old Testament is arguably the most unpleasant character in all of fiction. Jealous and proud of it; a petty, unjust, unforgiving control-freak; a vindictive, bloodthirsty ethnic-cleanser; a misogynistic homophobic racist, infanticidal, genocidal, filicidal, pestilential, megalomaniacal sado-masochistic, capriciously malevolent bully.'[21]

As often happens, Dawkins' logic disappears beneath the waves of his grandiloquence. If the Old Testament is fiction, as he seems to be saying, his accusations against a non-fictional God are groundless. But if he wants the charges to stick, he must admit the Old Testament as a reliable witness. Let's throw him a lifebelt and suppose that what he really meant to say is as follows: 'If the Old Testament is true, as you Jews and Christians maintain, then you have some explaining to do—because God is seen therein to act in an immoral manner.'

As any knowledgeable person will testify (let alone the archaeologists, historians and textual scholars who work in the field) the Old Testament is not fiction. It is a collection of well-authenticated ancient documents of various genres, including significant amounts of verifiable history. The onus is on Dawkins to prove his unlikely thesis that the authors made it all up in order to create moral dilemmas for themselves. I suggest that these dilemmas are, in fact, proof positive that in the Old Testament we are dealing with facts not fiction. They may sometimes be uncomfortable facts or even incomprehensible facts, but as long as they are facts we have to face them.

Drained of its vitriol, Dawkins' statement reduces to a question: How can we reconcile certain actions attributed to God in the Old Testament with the overall teaching of the Bible (in both Testaments) that 'The LORD is righteous in all His ways, gracious in all His works'?[22] The actions in question relate chiefly to the conquest of Canaan by the Israelites under Joshua, who was commanded by God to obliterate the Canaanite peoples. Yes, in this context the terms 'infanticidal' and 'genocidal' (though hardly the others) can logically be applied to God. But atheists seem to overlook an even greater 'crime', namely, the near-total destruction of the human race by the Flood in the days of Noah. That surely was the ultimate genocidal act on the part of God, but Dawkins ignores it[23] (presumably believing that it never happened). He therefore neglects to ask the obvious question: Why should God do such a thing? The answer is clearly supplied in Genesis 6:5–8:

> Then the LORD saw that the wickedness of man was great in the earth, and that every intent of the thoughts of his heart was only evil continually. And the LORD was sorry that He had made man on the earth, and He was grieved in His heart. So the LORD said, 'I will destroy man whom I have created from the face of the earth, both man and beast, creeping thing and birds of the air, for I am sorry that I have made them.' But Noah found grace in the eyes of the LORD.

Our problem so often is that our moral priorities differ from God's. We prioritize such things as the sanctity of human life, the minimization of human suffering, and the maximization of our own health, wealth and happiness. (These at least are our ideals; our behaviour constantly ignores them.) God is also concerned for these things, as the Bible amply testifies, but his top priority is that men should be 'righteous'— because unless they are, they remain estranged from him, the source of all life and goodness. Men should therefore conform to his moral laws—laws that are not only written in the Scriptures but also upon every man's heart and conscience.[24] When man becomes inveterate in his unrighteousness, as in the days of Noah or among the ancient tribes of Canaan (whose religious practices included child sacrifice) why should we think it strange if God's patience runs out and he eliminates the cultures in question? In modern society we are quick enough to demand justice and retribution upon the child-abuser, the rapist and the murderer—as your newspaper will probably demonstrate any time this week. Why should not God also visit justice on human societies that break his laws and spurn his call to repent of their sins?

The wonder is that he does this far less often than he might, but this is patience not neglect on his part. The Bible teaches that there will be a final day of reckoning between man and his Maker. As St Paul warns: 'And do you think ... that you will escape the judgment of God? Or do you despise the riches of His goodness, forbearance, and longsuffering, not knowing that the goodness of God leads you to repentance [i.e. gives you space to repent]? But in accordance with your hardness and your impenitent heart you are treasuring up for yourself wrath in the day of wrath and revelation of the righteous judgment of God, who "will render to each one according to his deeds".'[25] Paul included himself when he said, 'For we must all appear before the judgement seat of Christ, that each one may receive the things done in the body [i.e. during our lifetime], according to what he has done, whether good or bad.'[26]

So is there any way to 'escape the judgement of God'? No, there is no escaping the event. According to the Bible we shall all be there—you, I, Paul, Richard Dawkins and the rest of humanity from every era and society. But while we cannot escape the event, there is a way to escape condemnation at the bar of God. Remember how the quote about the Flood ended? 'But Noah found grace in the eyes of the LORD.'[27] 'Grace', as that word is used in the Bible, means free and unmerited pardon—offered on the grounds that atonement for sin has been made by a substitute, Jesus Christ, whose saving work has an efficacy unlimited by time or history. He is, says St John, 'the [sacrificial] Lamb slain from the foundation of the world'.[28]

## Reformation or rebirth?

The new atheists have a commendable desire to reform human nature.
'We are born selfish,' declares Richard Dawkins, but we can be taught
to behave unselfishly. The Bible, on the other hand, demonstrates that
such a strategy simply does not work. Dawkins misses the central
message of the Old Testament—men cannot be reformed simply by
giving them moral laws and instructions to obey. The covenant that
God established with Israel at Mount Sinai (the 'old covenant', also
called 'the law') epitomized the principle of loving our neighbour as
we love ourselves. This is the entire thrust of the last six of the Ten
Commandments handed down to Moses on the Mount (the first four
exhort us to love God). Israel was thus the perfect (and intentional)
test-bed for the idea that you can make people good by teaching them
to be good. It didn't work then and it doesn't work now. Much of the
Old Testament was written to demonstrate this fact. The test failed
miserably and the New Testament concludes: '…whatever the law
says, it says to those who are under the law, that every mouth may be
stopped, and all the world may become guilty before God. Therefore
by the deeds of the law no flesh will be justified in [God's] sight, for
by the law is the knowledge of sin.'[29] St Paul, who wrote these words,
was speaking out of personal experience. As a Pharisee he had striven
with all his might to obey the moral rules he had been taught under
the old covenant, but it didn't work because mere teaching couldn't
change his selfish heart.[30] That is why Dawkins' quest is hopeless and
why the Bible presents us with a new covenant—predicted in the Old
Testament by Jeremiah[31] and cited in the New Testament as follows:

> Behold, the days are coming, says the LORD, when I will make a new
> covenant with the house of Israel and with the house of Judah—not
> according to the covenant that I made with their fathers in the day
> when I took them by the hand to lead them out of the land of Egypt;
> because they did not continue in My covenant, and I disregarded them,
> says the LORD. For this is the covenant that I will make with the house
> of Israel after those days … I will put My laws in their mind and write
> them on their hearts; and I will be their God, and they shall be My
> people. None of them shall teach his neighbour, and none his brother,

saying, 'Know the LORD,' for all shall know Me, from the least of them to the greatest of them. For I will be merciful to their unrighteousness, and their sins and their lawless deeds I will remember no more.[32] [The New Testament applies this covenant to Jews and non-Jews alike.]

The hypothesis of God predicts that man's sinful heart can never be changed by mere instruction, no matter how good and noble that teaching may be. It can only be changed by a 'new birth' in which the Spirit of God himself takes up residence in a person's heart and mind—'writing' there the moral law and empowering the recipient to love and obey God. This work of new birth is accompanied by the forgiveness of man's 'sins and lawless deeds' on the grounds of Jesus Christ's atoning death and justifying resurrection.[33]

Does it work? Yes, indeed, as the author of this book can testify, along with countless others who have 'found grace in the eyes of the Lord' and salvation in Christ—who, says St Paul again, 'loved me and gave Himself for me'.[34] For all such people the hypothesis of God is amply proven to be true. I therefore end this book at the beginning of another story. Read more about it in 'the Gospel according to St John'.

# Appendix: God, Black Holes and Stephen Hawking

This appendix provides an update on a number of issues covered in Chapters 5–10 of the main text concerning the origins of the universe and the laws of nature. Since *Who made God?* (hereafter *WMG*) was first published in 2009 two significant books by atheists have appeared—*The Grand Design* by Stephen Hawking and Leonard Mlodinow (Bantam Press, 2010) and *A Universe from Nothing* by Lawrence Krauss (Atria Books, 2013). There has also been a courteous exchange of views with Victor Stenger, whose book *God, the Failed Hypothesis* (Prometheus Books, 2007) is subjected to a detailed critique in *WMG* but who has since died. Most of this appendix consists of a review of *The Grand Design* because Krauss' later book adds little that is contentious to the Hawking and Mlodinow volume. However, for completeness, I do include shorter comments on *A Universe from Nothing* and my exchange with Victor Stenger.

## 1. The Grand Design

Cosmologist Stephen Hawking is famous for his work on black holes but in his latest book he falls into a conceptual black hole of his own making. Stephen Hawking was formerly Lucasian Professor of Mathematics at Cambridge University and is currently Director of

Research at the Centre for Theoretical Cosmology. He is a renowned scientist and a victim of motor neuron disease, a familiar figure on British TV, seated in his motorised wheel-chair and speaking with a synthesized voice. In all, he is a remarkable man—a scientist to be honoured and respected and the subject of the acclaimed 2014 biopic movie 'The theory of everything'. But that doesn't mean he is right when he talks about God.

Hawking sold over nine million copies of his 1988 book *A Brief History of Time*. Now, twenty-two years later, he has co-authored *The Grand Design* which immediately hit the No.1 spot in the *New York Times* best-seller list. It is in fact a rather short book which speculates about creation using arguments that are by no means new. It also contains not a single literature reference, a remarkable omission in a science-based book since it makes it impossible to check the accuracy of material quoted from other sources. In fact the sequel is so inferior to the prequel in intellectual quality that a reviewer in *The Times Saturday Review* (London, 11 September 2010) wrote: 'It reads like a stretched magazine article … there is too much padding and too much recycling of long-stale material … I doubt whether *The Grand Design* would have been published if Hawking's name were not on the cover'.

So why is the new book a runaway best-seller? Because it claims that science makes God redundant. The media were quick to seize on its purple passages—which declare that there was no need for a Creator to 'light the blue touch-paper' and initiate a 'big-bang' origin of the universe. Why is no Creator needed? Because, says Hawking, the laws of science created the universe out of nothing, all on their own. Put another way, of course, this implies that the laws of nature *are* God. But this opens conceptual black holes from which there is no escape. So let's take a closer look at the claims advanced in *The Grand Design*.

## Black holes

Stephen Hawking didn't discover black holes but he has contributed notably to our understanding of them. A black hole is formed when a massive star burns out and collapses under the force of its own gravity. As the star shrinks, its internal gravitational field gets stronger and stronger until eventually even light can no longer escape from the collapsing star—which simply winks out leaving behind a literal 'black hole'. Black holes seem to lie at the centre of many galaxies including our own.

The gravitational attraction of a black hole is so huge that anything close by gets sucked into it and simply disappears. No one knows what happens inside a black hole because the laws of physics no longer apply there. However, Hawking showed theoretically that although light can't escape from it, a black hole should radiate energy. Vigorous attempts are currently being made by NASA and others to detect this 'Hawking radiation' experimentally. This is important, since it is the ability to test theories by experiment that distinguishes real science from speculation masquerading as science. Sadly, although Hawking's new book pays lip-service to this distinction, he ends up presenting completely un-testable speculations about multiple universes and self-creating laws of physics. Thus *The Grand Design* is sucked into logical and conceptual 'black holes' of its own making. Let's look at some of them.

## Philosophy is dead?

The introduction asserts that 'Philosophy is dead' and that science alone can provide '*New answers to the ultimate questions of life*' (the book's hubristic sub-title). But the authors then produce their own brand of humanistic philosophy, christen it 'science' and base their book upon it. They write; 'this book is rooted in the concept of scientific determinism which implies ... that there are no miracles, or exceptions to the laws of nature'. But 'scientific determinism' is simply the *philosophical assumption* that the laws of nature control all events (I argue precisely the opposite in chapter 11 of *WMG*). Thus, having cleared the field of rivals like philosophy and theology by a stroke of the pen, they quietly abandon the time-honoured view of science as a discipline limited to theories that can be tested by experiment, in favour of a new definition that embraces unverifiable speculation. By redefining science in this way, *The Grand Design* can claim that 'science' renders God redundant. But this is nonsense; they have simply replaced God by atheistic philosophical assumptions. This is a subtle ploy and will no doubt convince some readers. The fact is, however, that the authors base their conclusions on speculative mathematical constructions (like parallel universes and self-creating laws) that by their very nature can never be verified scientifically.

Pursuing their philosophical crusade, they maintain in chapter 3 that 'reality' is a construct of our minds—implying that there is no such thing as objective reality (Irish philosopher Bishop Berkeley had the same idea in 1710 but he wasn't widely believed). They conclude that 'there is no picture-[independent] or theory-independent concept of reality' and propose what they call 'model dependent realism' as a 'frame-work with which to interpret modern science'. Clearly, 'an interpretive framework' for science cannot *be* science but belongs in a different category altogether, namely, philosophy.

Since, they say, the mental models we construct 'are the only reality we can know ... It follows then that a well-constructed model creates a reality of its own'. The problem with this, of course, is that it undermines the very concept of reality. Hawking's 'reality' excludes God while my 'reality' majors upon God. These two 'realities' are mutually exclusive but both (according to Hawking) are equally 'real'. This is postmodernism by the back door and it is wholly inimical to science, which depends on there being a genuine, objective and unique reality to investigate.

## Determinism

In embracing scientific determinism the authors go yet further out on a philosophical limb. They declare; 'Though we feel we can choose what we do, our understanding of the molecular basis of biology shows that biological processes are governed by the laws of physics and chemistry and therefore are as determined as the orbits of the planets'. So, according to Hawking and Mlodinow, human beings are automatons and everything we do or think is predetermined. The reality is, of course, that biological processes are overwhelmingly 'governed' not by 'the laws of physics and chemistry' but by structured information—stored on DNA and expressed through the genetic code. It is *information* which controls the physics and chemistry of the living cell, not the other way round. Furthermore, if our minds are simply by-products of molecular processes in the brain, then all our thoughts are meaningless including the authors' own theories. Thinking atheists such as Bertrand Russell and J. B. S. Haldane long ago recognised and admitted this dilemma explicitly (*WMG* chapter 16) but Hawking and Mlodinow seem oblivious to it.

## Mighty M-theory

Chapter 4 is devoted to explaining the 'many histories' formulation of quantum mechanics proposed by Richard Feynman. This is well done except that by ignoring other formulations of quantum theory the authors give the false impression that Feynman's is the only valid approach. This is tendentious because they *need* Feynman's idea as a springboard for their own multiverse hypothesis. To admit that Feynman's 'many histories' approach is just one of several equally valid formulations of quantum mechanics would weaken their argument considerably.

Chapter 5 surveys the development of physics during the past 200 years, including general relativity (which describes the large-scale behaviour of the universe) and quantum mechanics (which describes its microscopic behaviour). Although containing nothing remotely new, this is by far the best part of this book. The chapter concludes, however, with comments on 'M-theory' that ring alarm bells.

In the book's opening chapter, M-theory is no more than 'a candidate for the ultimate theory of everything, if indeed one exists', and is 'not a theory in the usual sense' but 'may offer answers to the question of creation'. Theoretical physicist Lee Smolin is doubtful: '... we still do not know what M-theory is, or whether there is any theory deserving of the name' (*The Trouble with Physics*, Allen Lane 2007, p.146). Indeed, the authors themselves admit that 'people are still trying to decipher the nature of M-theory, but that may not be possible'.

But suddenly at the end of Chapter 5, this intractable and contentious mathematical model (which may not exist) is somehow transformed into a theory so powerful that its laws are 'more fundamental' than the laws of nature and 'allow' for 'different universes with different apparent laws'. This is a huge leap of speculative faith. Hawking and Mlodinow declare: 'According to M-theory, ours is not the only universe. Instead, M-theory predicts that a great many universes were created out of nothing. Their creation does not require the intervention of some supernatural being or god. Rather, these multiple universes arise naturally from physical law. They are a prediction of science'.

So what is this magical M-theory? The authors are rather coy about it. 'M-theory', they say, 'Is not a theory in the usual sense. It is a whole family of different theories, each of which is a good description of observations only in some range of physical situations'. The fact is that M-theory is an un-testable mathematical construction which many scientists believe bears no relationship to physical reality. But that doesn't deter our authors because they don't believe in 'objective reality' anyway. What we think is 'real', they say, is simply a model assembled in our brains from raw data input by our senses. But, confusingly, the authors then claim that the best models are those that reflect the way things really do happen in the real world—appealing to the very objective reality they say does not exist!

## Witches brew

The final three chapters rapidly descend into a witches brew of speculation and misinformation, confusingly blended with normal science. It certainly gave this reviewer a mental hangover—and I am no stranger to the territory. It is difficult to discern where science ends and speculation begins, but the key reasoning seem to be as follows.

1. The 'big bang' model predicts that the universe began its existence as such a tiny object that quantum theory must be applied to its origin. But hold on a moment! Quantum theory has only been validated under normal conditions of space, time, pressure, temperature and so on. We cannot know whether it applies to the supposed conditions at the origin of the universe, when space was intensely warped, time was at best fuzzy, and the pressure and temperature both approached infinity. What we do know is that massive objects do not exhibit quantum behaviour. No one can be sure that a new-born universe would obey quantum theory as we know it.

2. 'In the early universe all four dimension [of space-time] behave like space' allowing us to 'get rid of the problem of time having a beginning'. But if time and space were equivalent, and time did not begin, how could space begin? The authors' fundamental thesis is that

the universe *did* have a beginning, being created 'from nothing'. But to say that anything 'begins' necessitates the prior existence of time since where there is no time the word 'beginning' has no meaning. In fact the authors are here making a clumsy appeal to the 'no-boundary' model described by Hawking in *A Brief History of Time*—but they are seriously economical with the truth. The earlier book makes it abundantly clear that the model is valid *only in imaginary* time, not in real time (see *WMG* Ch. 8. Imaginary time is nothing more than a mathematical device employed to simplify the mathematics). But here in *The Grand Design* this caveat vanishes and imaginary time is misrepresented as real time. The narrative then descends into farce. They claim that 'the realisation that time behaves like space ... means that the beginning of the universe was governed by the laws of science and doesn't need to be set in motion by some god'. So apparently the universe *did* 'begin' after all, but not in time. Confused? Me too.

3. Picturing the early universe as a quantum particle (something they themselves describe as 'tricky') the authors consider how it might evolve from state (or 'point') A to state (or 'point') B by misapplying Feynman's sum-over-histories method thus: '[Since we are considering the beginning of the universe] there is no point A, so we add up all the histories that satisfy the no-boundary condition and end at the universe we observe today. In this view the universe appears spontaneously, starting off in every possible way. Most of these correspond to other universes.' This is logical gobbledygook. If the end point is 'the universe we observe today' then all the 'other universes' must have collapsed into the one real universe we know about. Yet they later use this argument to justify the *current* existence of a multiverse. Furthermore, by saying that point A does not exist they *assume* that the universe springs into existence somewhere between nothing (point A) and the present universe (point B). This tells us nothing about how or why the universe began; simply that it did begin. We knew that already.

4. Finally, on the book's penultimate page, the authors do offer an explanation of spontaneous creation. The conservation of energy means that a universe can only be created from nothing if its net energy is zero—with negative gravitational energy balancing out the positive energy of matter and radiation. This necessitates that a law

of gravity must exist. Because a law of gravity exists, they say, it 'must and will' of itself create universes out of nothing (no reasoning given). So gravity is God? Unfortunately the authors have no time to tell us who created gravity (earlier they rule out God because no one could explain who created him). Nor can they tell us *why* matter and gravity should pop out of nothing, except to argue that 'nothing' undergoes quantum fluctuations. However, this requires that (like gravity) the laws of quantum mechanics pre-existed the universe and that 'nothing' possesses the properties of normal space, which is part of the created order and cannot be its antecedent. We shall pursue this issue of the definition of 'nothing' and the origin of the laws of nature in my remarks below on Lawrence Krauss' book *A Universe from Nothing*.

A grand design? Only in the sense that this book is grandly designed to bamboozle the unwary and cloak atheistic philosophy in the garb of science. Fortunately, the clothes don't fit.

## 2. A Universe from Nothing

*The Grand Design* assures us that 'multiple universes arise naturally from physical law', being created from nothing by the operation of laws of nature such as quantum mechanics and gravitation (no God required). But, as Alice might say, this gets 'curiouser and curiouser', for what do we mean by 'nothing' and by 'the laws of nature'? These are issues that are elaborated in Lawrence Krauss' book *A Universe from Nothing*.

Let us first consider the laws of nature. These are the rules that describe the way nature behaves. They are thus *descriptions* of the way the cosmos works and can have no existence apart from the cosmos. They are an integral part of the created order. How, then, could they have created the universe in the first place? I call the reasoning being employed here 'the Cheshire cat argument' after the iconic cat in Lewis Carroll's *Alice's Adventures in Wonderland* which vanished leaving only its smile behind. Those who claim that the laws of nature created nature are observing the universe (the cat) with its face wreathed in smiles (the laws of nature) and then subtracting the cat leaving only the smiles (the laws) behind to arrive at a starting point for their cosmologies. That's fine in children's fiction but hardly admissible in either science or logic.

However, for the sake of argument, let us suppose that the laws of nature did somehow pre-exist the universe and were thus available to create it. Two problems arise. Firstly, who or what created the laws of nature? Krauss addresses this problem in his final chapter, offering the suggestion that universes can arise spontaneously *without* the help of specific laws of physics because the latter are or were 'random'. As a physicist I have no idea what he means by this and can offer no comment except that even 'random' entities must *exist* if they are to produce effects. But might the laws of nature (or some overarching precursor of these laws as we know them) constitute eternal truths having an eternal existence and thus no need to be created? If so we must ask in what form and medium did they exist? Where, exactly, were they located? A helpful analogy is the purchase of a house 'off-plan'. This is when someone buys (or commits to buy) a house that doesn't yet exist, relying solely on the architect's plans. Although the house is not yet built, the plans and drawings specify exactly what will eventually be created. However, the plans must exist in some form or medium—on paper or a computer disc for example. But what if there are no such things as paper or computers, or any other storage medium where the plans can reside? This surely is the situation for laws that pre-exist the origin of the material universe—there would be no *material* medium or space in which to inscribe them, so where would they reside? There is, of course, one (and I think only one) answer; they could exist in conceptual space, in the mind of the architect! This makes a lot of sense because the laws of nature as we know them are fundamentally mathematical in character, and by its very nature mathematics requires a mind to conceive its concepts and perform its processes. One objection to this argument is that the laws of nature don't have to reside anywhere—they can just be true in the same way that 2+2=4 is true whether or not it is written down or thought about. But this objection fails because to call something 'true' requires us to define a realm (or logical space) called 'truth' and distinguish it from the alternative realm of 'falsehood'. This separation is itself a logical process that can only be carried out by a mind.

## The nature of nothing

Lawrence Krauss highlights this issue in his title *A Universe from Nothing*. It is a subject I had already discussed in Chapter 10 of WMG where I define two kinds of 'nothing'. These are firstly 'void 1', a total *physical* vacuum in which a volume of space contains no physical particles capable of removal; and secondly 'void zero' which contains neither space nor time, matter nor energy. Void zero is the only kind of 'nothing' that could have existed before the creation of the physical universe since space, time, matter and energy are all components of such a universe. I equated void zero to that spiritual (non-physical) domain which the Bible calls 'eternity'.

When Krauss, Stenger, Hawking and other cosmologists talk about 'nothing' they are referring unequivocally to my 'void 1'. Their 'nothing' occupies space. It also occupies time because they appeal to spontaneous *processes* occurring therein such as the creation and annihilation of virtual particles. According to the latest ideas it also contains a veritable ocean of Higgs bosons, the recently discovered particles that are supposed to impart mass to other more familiar particles. Most important of all, their 'nothing' is a realm in which the laws of nature (or at least some of them) must function to produce 'creation from nothing' (remember Hawking's explicit claim that 'because there is a law like gravity the universe can and will create itself from nothing'). Put simply, Krauss' 'nothing' is in fact a very substantial 'something'. It is simply a feature of the physical universe and therefore cannot have preceded and caused the creation of that universe.

### 3. Discussion with Victor Stenger

This discussion, in which Stenger challenged several of the statements made about his own book in *WMG*, will not be reproduced here because it involves a number of disparate issues, none of which was developed in detail. However, the whole discussion, including my replies to his points, can be found by following this link; http://whomadegod. org/2011/06/victor-stenger-replies-to-who-made-god/ in the blog section of the whomadegod.org website.

## 4. Conclusion

Neither *The Grand Design* nor *A Universe from Nothing* actually says anything that has not been said and refuted before. The laws of nature are what constitute science and make it possible, but neither science nor these atheist authors can tell us where those laws came from. Nor can science explain why human beings can *understand* and use the laws of nature, which are often elegant and always mathematical.

But by contrast the Bible gives us some straightforward answers. We can understand (in measure) how the cosmos works because the laws that control its working are themselves the product of an intelligent mind—the creator we call God. And because, as human beings, we are 'made in the image of God' it follows that we can have insight into the mind of God. As Johannes Kepler is said to have exclaimed on discovering the laws of planetary motion, 'O God, I am thinking your thoughts after you!'

# References and notes

## Introduction

1. Robert Jastrow, *God and the astronomers* (W. W. Norton, New York, 1992), p.107. Cited by Francis Collins in *The language of God* (Simon and Schuster, London, 2007), p.66.

## Chapter 1

1. *The Times* (London), Body and soul supplement, p.7 (2 Feb. 2008).
2. Richard Dawkins, *The God delusion* (Transworld Publishers, London; 2006).
3. *The Shorter Oxford English Dictionary.*
4. *Stanford Encyclopaedia of Philosophy* (http://plato.stanford.edu).
5. *Stanford Encyclopaedia of Philosophy.*
6. Scott Adams, *God's debris* (Andrews McMeel Publishing, Kansas City, 2001), p.49.
7. Dawkins, *The God delusion,* chapter 4.
8. Richard Dawkins, *Climbing mount improbable* (Penguin Books, 1997).
9. Note that an ordered state of matter such as a crystal does not arise *spontaneously* but requires e.g. the removal of heat energy or solvent.
10. See e.g. Martin Rees, *Just six numbers* (Perseus, Basic Books; Weidenfeld & Nicolson, UK, 2000).
11. Dawkins, *The God delusion,* pp. 138, 171, 176.

## Chapter 2

1. See Brian Greene, *The fabric of the cosmos* (Alfred Knopf, New York, 2004), ch. 4, for a more detailed discussion of entanglements.

2. Laplace, P-S; Introduction to the *Essai*: 'We may regard the present state of the universe as the effect of its past and the cause of its future. An intellect which at a certain moment would know all forces that set nature in motion, and all positions of all items of which nature is composed, if this intellect were also vast enough to submit these data to analysis, it would embrace in a single formula the movements of the greatest bodies of the universe and those of the tiniest atom; for such an intellect nothing would be uncertain and the future just like the past would be present before its eyes.'

3. Albert Einstein, cited by Emeritus Professor of Philosophy Ray Bradley, http://www.eequalsmcsquared.auckland.ac.nz/sites/emc2/tl/philosophy/dice.cfm

4. Louis de Broglie, cited by Ray Bradley (as above).

5. Though sometimes attributed to Sir Arthur Eddington without citation, this seems to be derived from a statement by J. B. S. Haldane, in *Possible Worlds and Other Papers* (1927), p.286.

## Chapter 3

1. For a detailed but 'popular' treatment of string theory see Brian Greene, *The fabric of the cosmos* (Alfred A. Knopf, 2004), Part IV.

2. http://www.ast.leeds.ac.uk/haverah/cosrays.shtml.

3. Lee Smolin, *The trouble with physics; the rise of string theory, the fall of a science* (Allen Lane, Penguin, 2006).

## Chapter 4

1. Matthew 7:24–27.

2. Anthony Flew and Roy Varghese, *There is a God* (Harper One, 2007), pp. xiv; xviii–xxiv.

3. Victor J. Stenger, *God, the failed hypothesis* (New York, Prometheus Books, 2007), p.125.

4. As above.

5. Lewis Carroll, *Alice through the looking glass*, ch. 6.

6. Richard Dawkins, *The God delusion* (Black Swan, 2006), p.82.

7. As above, pp. 82–83.

8. Stephen J. Gould, *Rocks of ages*, cited in *The God delusion*, p.78.

## Chapter 5

1.  Stenger, *God, the failed hypothesis*.
2.  As above, p.28.
3.  Albert Einstein, according to the testimony of Prince Hubertus of Lowenstein; as quoted by Ronald W. Clark, *Einstein: The Life and Times* (World Publishing Company, New York, 1971), p. 425.
4.  Martin Rees, interviewed in *The Sunday Times* (London), 18 Dec. 2005.
5.  Stenger, *God, the failed hypothesis*, p.13.
6.  As above, p.16.
7.  As above, p.29.
8.  Johannes Kepler, *Gesammelte Werke*, ed. Max Caspar (Munich: C. H. Beck, 1937–83), vol.6, p.223.
9.  John 4:24.
10. Galatians 5:22–23.
11. Stenger, *God, the failed hypothesis*, p.28.
12. Romans 5:5, AV.
13. Stenger, *God, the failed hypothesis*, pp. 51–52.
14. Edgar Andrews, *From nothing to nature* (Evangelical Press, Darlington, 1978), p.51.
15. Didier De Fontaine, 'Flat worlds: today and in antiquity'. *Memorie della Società Astronomica Italiana, special issue* (2002) 1 (3): 257–62.
16. Anaximander; Fairbanks (editor and translator); Arthur, 'Fragments and Commentary', *The Hanover Historical Texts Project*, http://history.hanover.edu/texts/presoc/anaximan.htm (Plut., *Strom.* 2 ; *Dox.* 579).
17. Aristotle, *De caelo*, 297b31-298a10.
18. The venerable Bede, *De temporum ratione*, 32.
19. Francis Collins, *The language of God* (Simon & Schuster, London, 2007), p.192.
20. Fred Hoyle, *The Intelligent Universe* (Michael Joseph, London, 1983), pp.18–19.

## Chapter 6

1.  A. A. Milne, *Winnie the Pooh* (Methuen, London, 1926).
2.  Attributed to Clarence Darrow ('Mark Twain') but there appears to be no written source; other versions of the comment exist.
3.  Acts 17:24–28.
4.  Collins, *The language of God*.
5.  Isaiah 46:10.

6. Ephesians 1:11.
7. http://www.deism.com/deism_defined.htm
8. As above.
9. Isaiah 40:25–26.
10. Isaiah 45:22.
11. Genesis 1:1.
12. Genesis 2:16; 5:24.
13. Exodus 3:14, AV.
14. Exodus 19 - 20.
15. Hebrews 1:1–3.

## *Chapter 7*

1. Arno Penzias was vice-president and Chief Scientist at Bell Laboratories, the Research and Development unit of Lucent Technologies. In 1978 he shared the Nobel Prize in Physics for his research into the origin of the universe. Dr Penzias helped isolate the primordial celestial radio signal which helped validate the theory of the big bang. Earlier, Penzias was part of the group that developed the USA's first communications satellites Telstar and Echo.
2. For some reason, at the time of writing, Google only yielded 337 results.
3. Popper, K. R., and Eccles, J. C., *The Self and Its Brain* (Springer, Berlin, Heidelberg, 1977).
4. Eccles, J. C. (1994). *How the Self Controls its Brain* (Berlin: Springer-Verlag).
5. Stenger, *God, the failed hypothesis*, p.133.
6. As above, p.133.
7. Sidney Williams and Falconer Madan: *Handbook of the Literature of the Rev. C. L. Dodgson*, as quoted in Martin Gardner: *The Annotated Snark* (Penguin Books, 1974).
8. Stephen W. Hawking, *A brief history of time* (Bantam Press, 1988), pp. 140–141.
9. As above, p.175.
10. Hoyle's paper was published in the *Journal of the Royal Astronomical Society* in 1948. His *Nature of the Universe* (Blackwell, 1950) introduced the theory to a wider audience.
11. Their results were published in *The Astrophysical Journal*, vol. 142 (1965), p.1149.
12. Edgar Andrews, *From nothing to nature* (Evangelical Press, 1978), ch. 9.

## Chapter 8

1. H. G. Wells, *The chronic argonauts* (1888; Kessinger Publishing 2004).
2. H. G. Wells, *The time machine* (1895; New American Library, 2002).
3. Stephen Hawking, *A brief history of time* (Bantam Press, 1988).
4. Paul Davies, *How to build a time machine* (Penguin Books, 2002).
5. Omar Khayyám, in Francis Turner Palgrave, *The golden treasury* (OUP, 1861).
6. Bible references; Romans 1:20; Ephesians 1:4; 2 Timothy 1:9.
7. Psalm 90:2–4.
8. Brian Greene, *The fabric of the cosmos* (Alfred A. Knopf, New York, 2004), pp. 132–139.
9. Frederic Amiel, *Journal*, 16 Nov. 1864.
10. Edgar Allan Poe, *Eureka* (Kessinger Publishing 2007).
11. H. G. Wells, *The time machine* (1895).
12. Sir Arthur Eddington, *The nature of the physical world* (1928).
13. E. T. Jaynes, http://bayes.wustl.edu/etj/articles/ccarnot.pdf
14. Yunus A. Cengel and Michael A. Boles, Thermodynamics: an engineering approach (6th Edition; McGraw-Hill, 2008), ch. 6, 'The second law of thermodynamics', p.283.
15. Greene, *The fabric of the cosmos*, p.175.
16. As above, p.319.
17. Psalm 102:25–27; emphasis added.
18. 2 Peter 3:8–10.
19. See Jay M. Pasachoff and Alex Filippenko, *The Cosmos: Astronomy in the new Millennium* (Brooks/Cole, the Wadsworth Group, 2001).
20. For those who really want to know, imaginary time is real time multiplied by the square root of -1 (minus one), which is denoted by the symbol $i$. The quantity $i$ cannot be a *real* number because if you square any real number, either positive or negative, you always get a positive number, never a negative one. That is why the square root of a negative number is called an 'imaginary' number.
21. Hawking, *A brief history of time*, p.135.
22. As above, pp. 138–139.

## Chapter 9

1. *Fisheries Oceanography*, Vol. 13, Issue 4, pp. 283–286. Published Online: 20 Jun 2004. Journal compilation © 2008 Blackwell Publishing.
2. Maine, Henry Sumner. *Ancient Law: Its connection with the early history of society,*

*and its relation to modern ideas* (London, John Murray; 1861), ch. 5. Although a century and a half old, this book is still regarded as a classic and is required reading at some universities.

3. The words 'the whole family' can be translated more literally as 'all fatherhood' (Greek *patria*).
4. Ephesians 3:14–15.
5. Genesis 1:27.
6. Literally, 'of God'; the words 'the son' are omitted throughout the genealogy but are obviously implied.
7. Acts 17:28–29.
8. Daniel 4:34–35.
9. Philip Eveson, *The book of origins* (Evangelical Press, 2001), p.67.
10. Genesis 2:16–17.
11. Genesis 3:8.
12. Romans 2:14–15.

## Chapter 10

1. Philosophers often use 'natural law' in a legal or ethical context and distinguish it from the laws of nature, but here I will use the two terms interchangeably.
2. Martin Rees, *Just six numbers* (Perseus, Basic Books, 2000), p.175.
3. Brian Greene, *The fabric of the cosmos* (Alfred Knopf, 2004), p.219.
4. Paul Davies, *About time* (Penguin, 1995), pp.208–218.
5. Greene, *The fabric of the cosmos*, p.222.
6. http://www.nsf.gov/attachments/104515/public/Farwell_Welcome_Remarks_ at_PRConference092605.doc
7. Romans 1:19–20.
8. Ecclesiastes 3:11.
9. http://www.anobii.com/books/01c125a821ec26c873
10. Stenger, *God, the failed hypothesis*, pp. 129–132.
11. As above, p.131.
12. James Gleick, *Chaos; the making of a new science* (Vintage, Random House, 1988).
13. Stenger, *God, the failed hypothesis*, p.130.
14. John Baez, http://math.ucr.edu/home/baez/noether.html

## Chapter 11

1. We are indebted to Scott Hahn and Benjamin Wilker for drawing this Dawkinsian

purple passage to wider attention in their book *Answering the new atheism; dismantling Dawkins' case against God* (Emmaus Road Publishing, Ohio, 2008), pp. 10–13.

2. Richard Dawkins, *The blind watchmaker; why the evidence of evolution reveals a universe without design* (New York, Norton, 1996), p.159. See also *The God delusion* (Bantam Press edition, 2007), p.419.

3. Dawkins, *The blind watchmaker*, pp. 159–160.

4. Stenger, *God, the failed hypothesis*, p.125.

5. Brian Greene. See chapter 7 of *The fabric of the cosmos*, for an extended discussion of quantum decoherence.

6. Benedict De Spinoza. This is the first main point that Spinoza makes in chapter 6 ('Of miracles') in his *Theologico-political treatise* [on line at http://www.yesselman.com/ttpelws1.htm].

7. Quoted in John Cottingham (editor), *Descartes* (Cambridge University Press, 1992), p.268.

8. Cornelius G. Hunter, *Science's blind spot; the unseen religion of scientific naturalism* (Brazos Press, Michigan, 2007), p.19.

9. Hunter, *Science's blind spot*, p.23.

10. John Polkinghorne, 'God's action in the world', 1990, J. K. Russell Fellowship Lecture.

11. John Polkinghorne, *Belief in God in the age of science* (Yale University Press, New Haven and London, 1998).

12. C. S. Lewis, *Miracles; a preliminary study* (1947; Fontana, May 1988 edition), ch. 4.

13. Romans 8:28.

14. Daniel 4:35.

15. Genesis 50:20.

16. Psalm 65:9–11.

17. Exodus 14:21.

18. Hebrews 2:3–4.

19. Acts 2:24.

20. Acts 4:8–10.

21. C. S. Lewis, *Miracles*, p.137.

22. Colossians 1:16–17.

23. Acts 17:24.

24. Malachi 3:6.

25. Hunter, *Science's blind spot* (whole book).

## Chapter 12

1. J. B. S. Haldane, published posthumously in S. W. Fox (ed.), *The origins of prebiological systems and of their molecular matrices*, Proceedings of a Conference at Wakulla Springs, Florida, 27–30 October 1963 (Academic Press, New York, 1965, p.12).

2. Word order is important in English but not necessarily in other languages. For example, in Latin the use of word order to assign meaning is replaced by suffixes to indicate the role of the word in the sentence (subject, object etc.). However, 'word order' is paramount in genetic language.

3. Werner Gitt discusses the levels of information in detail in his book, *In the beginning was information* (Master Books, Green Forest, AR, 2006).

4. Strictly speaking the number is 22 not 20; the number 20 refers to the amino-acids that are coded for in genes, whereas the other two are formed later.

5. If you have worked out that a triplet code of four symbols provides 4 x 4 x 4 = 64 possible triplets (codons)—whereas only 20 are needed to specify the amino-acids actually used to build proteins—you are right. Most of these amino-acids are specified (coded for) by more than one codon.

6. Michael Behe, *The edge of evolution* (Free Press, Simon & Schuster, New York, 2007), pp. 191–192.

7. Francis Collins, *The language of God* (Simon and Schuster UK, Pocket Books, London, 2007).

8. Acts 17:25, 28.

9. John 1:3–4.

10. John 5:26.

11. John 11:25. This passage does in fact reveal a close relationship between physical and spiritual life in New Testament thinking.

12. Job 33:4.

13. Psalm 36:9.

14. Job 12:9–10.

15. Genesis 1:11.

## Chapter 13

1. Francis Crick, *Life itself; its nature and origin* (Simon and Schuster, New York, 1981), p.88.

2. Paul Davies, *The origin of life* (Penguin, 2003, p.4).

3. *The Times* (London), 26 January 2008, p.32.

4. Dawkins, *The Blind Watchmaker* (Norton; New York, 1987), pp. 139, 145–46.

5. The lectures were collected in H.-G. Elias: *Trends in Macromolecular Science*, Midland Macromolecular Monographs, Vol. 1 (Gordon & Breach, New York-London, 1973). They were also published in *Angewandte Chemie*, Inter Ed. 1974; Vol. 13, No.2.

6. http://www.pubmedcentral.nih.gov/articlerender.fcgi?artid=34290

7. Stephen Sowerby, Corey Cohn, Wolfgang Heckl and Nils Holm, *Proc. Natl. Acad. Sci. USA*, 2001; 98(3) pp. 820–822.

8. L. R. Croft, *How life began* (Evangelical Press, Darlington, 1988), ch. 4.

9. There are, in fact, chemical reactions that can 'isomerize' polymer molecules, but their effect is to produce a random chain containing both left-handed and right-handed isomers. There is no known reaction that can start with a mixed-isomer chain and make it completely one-handed.

10. Francis Crick and Leslie Orgel, *Icarus*, 19, 1973, p.341.

11. Leslie Orgel and Francis Crick, 'Anticipating an RNA world. Some past speculations on the origin of life: where are they today?' *Faseb J.* 7 (1): (January 1993) pp. 238–9. PMID 7678564. http://www.fasebj.org/cgi/reprint/7/1/238.pdf.

12. Davies, *The origin of life*, p.237.

13. http://www.exploringorigins.org/nucleicacids.html

14. Kathie L. Thomas-Keprta *et al.* 'Truncated hexa-octahedral magnetite crystals in ALH84001: Presumptive biosignatures', *Proc. Natl. Acad. Sci. USA*, 98(5), 2001: pp. 2164–2169.

15. There are exceptions to this general rule, but these do not include mixtures of different biopolymers, especially when the molecules are not simply mixed together but are organized into a structure.

16. Davies, *The origin of life*, pp. 237–238.

17. Genesis 1:2.

18. Jeremiah 10:12.

19. Ephesians 1:11.

20. Daniel 4:35.

21. Acts 17:25–26.

22. Isaiah 44:7.

23. Romans 13:1.

24. Edgar Andrews, *Free in Christ*: a Welwyn Bible Commentary on Galatians (Evangelical Press, Darlington, 1996), pp. 239–244.
25. 2 Samuel 23:5.
26. See for example Romans 4:23–25.

## Chapter 14

1. Rudyard Kipling, *Just so stories* (Puffin Books, London; 6th edition, 2008), p.62.
2. http://www.nature.com/news/2008/080107/full/news.2008.414.html#B1
3. Lewis Smith, *The Times*, 8 January 2009 (London).
4. L. C. Birch & P. R. Ehrlich, 'Evolutionary history and population biology', *Nature* 214, 349 - 352 (22 April 1967).
5. Dawkins, *The God delusion*, p.145.
6. As above, p.147.
7. Michael Behe, *The edge of evolution; the search for the limits of Darwinism* (Simon and Schuster, Inc., New York, 2008), p.41.
8. Dawkins, *The blind watchmaker*, p.178.
9. As above, p.181.
10. Although this is an over-simplification of the phenomenon of 'ring-species' (species which circle the globe with progressive phenotype changes) it does illustrate the point.
11. For further details see, e.g., http://sandwalk.blogspot.com/2007/02/genetics-of-eye-color.html
12. David Swift, *Evolution under the microscope* (Leighton Academic Press, Stirling, 2002), pp. 223–224.
13. See e.g. Motoo Kimura, *The neutral theory of molecular evolution* (Cambridge University Press; Reprint edition, 2008).

## Chapter 15

1. Michael J. Behe, *The edge of evolution*, pp. 74 and 67.
2. M. Ashburner and J. N. Thompson, 'The laboratory culture of Drosophila'. In: *The genetics and biology of Drosophila* (Academic Press, 1978), vol. 2A, pp. 1–81.
3. http://users.rcn.com/jkimball.ma.ultranet/BiologyPages/H/HomeoboxGenes.html
4. http://bsc5936-03.fa04.fsu.edu/MUTATIONsubmit.pdf
5. 'Fitness effects of advantageous mutations in evolving Escherichia coli populations',

*Proceedings of the National Academy of Sciences USA*, vol. 98 no. 3 (30 Jan. 2001), pp. 1113–1117.

6. *Art Show Magazine*, Issue 4, Jan-Mar 2008.

7. In December 1998, the complete 100Mb genome sequence of the nematode worm *Caenorhabditis elegans* was reported. This was the outcome of a long-standing international collaboration that began in 1980 between the Sanger Centre in Cambridge and the Genome Sequencing Center at Washington University, St Louis.

8. Francis Collins, *The language of God*, pp. 126–130.

9. I realize that this is not a fair comparison since rice genes differ significantly from human genes. However it helps to make the general point that genes are by no means the whole story.

10. *ScienceDaily*, 13 Oct. 2006.

11. *Nature*: Advance Online Publication doi:10.1038/nature06263

12. Frank J. Slack, *Genome Biology*, 2006, vol. 7, p.328.

13. This explanation is an oversimplification and has been disputed. See Jonathan Wells, *Icons of evolution* (Regnery Publishing Inc., Washington, DC, 2000), chapter 7, p.137 *et seq.*

14. David Swift, *Evolution under the microscope* (Leighton Academic Press, Stirling, UK, 2002), pp. 153–157. Quote from p.156.

15. N. J. White, *parasitologica*, 1999, vol. 41, pp. 301–308.

16. Behe, *The edge of evolution*, p.59.

17. As above, pp.76–77.

18. Swift, *Evolution under the microscope*, p. 237.

19. Genesis 1:29–30.

20. Romans 8:20.

21. Romans 8:21–23.

22. Isaiah 11:6–9.

23. 1 Timothy 2:14

24. Genesis 3:5.

25. Genesis 3:17–19.

26. Genesis 1:28.

27. An extended discussion of the Genesis 'kinds' can be found in *Issues in creation, 5. Genesis kinds* (WIPF & Stock, Eugene, Oregon, 2009).

## Chapter 16

1.  Theodosius Dobzhansky, *Science,* 9 May 1958: pp. 1091–1098.
2.  Jeremiah 29:11.
3.  Daniel 4:5.
4.  *The Collected Papers of Bertrand Russell,* Vol. 12: 'Contemplation and Action', 1902–14. (London, 1985; now published by Routledge.)
5.  J. B. S. Haldane (1892–1964), Professor of Biometry at University College, London, in *Possible Worlds* (1928), p.220.
6.  Stenger, *God, the failed hypothesis,* pp. 81–85.
7.  Jerry A. Coyne, *The New Republic,* 4 March 2000.
8.  2 Corinthians 5:8.
9.  Psalm 16:11.
10. Acts 7:56.
11. John 17:2. See also John 3:16.
12. John R. Searle, *Mind; a brief introduction* (Oxford University Press, 2004), pp. 69–70.
13. Mario Beauregard and Denyse O'Leary, *The spiritual brain* (Harper Collins, New York, 2007), pp. 19–20.
14. Douglas Adams, *The hitch-hikers guide to the galaxy* (Pan-Macmillan, 1979; Del Ray Books 2005 edition), p.181.
15. Terence Kealey, *The Times* (London), 25 February 2008, p.16.
16. Reported in *The Times* (London), 18 June 2008, p.24.
17. Mark R. Rosenzweig, S. Marc Breedlove and Neil V. Watson, *Biological psychology* (Sinauer Associates Inc., USA; 4th Revised edition, July 2004).
18. http://www.biopsychology.com/newsletters/vol5no1item8.html
19. Collins, *The language of God,* pp. 208–209.
20. C. S. Lewis, *The problem of pain* (Simon & Schuster, New York, 1966), p.50.
21. C. S. Lewis, *Miracles* (1947; Fontana Books, 12th impression, May 1988).
22. Collins, *The language of God,* p.221.
23. Michael Behe, *The edge of evolution.*

## Chapter 17

1.  Collins, *The language of God,* pp. 21–31.
2.  Alister McGrath, *The twilight of atheism* (Doubleday, New York, 2004), pp. 181–182.
3.  For a detailed account of the way evolution seeks (and fails) to account for man's

moral inconsistency, see Scott Hahn and Benjamin Wiker, *Answering the new atheism* (Emmaus Road Publishing, Steubenville, Ohio, 2008), chapters 5 & 6.

4. Richard Dawkins, *The selfish gene* (Oxford University Press, 1989) p.3.
5. See chapter 9 and Romans 2:14–16.
6. David Stove, *Darwinian fairytales* (Encounter Books, New York, 1995).
7. Dawkins, *The selfish gene* (whole book).
8. See chapter 14.
9. Scott Hahn and Benjamin Wiker, *Answering the new atheism*, p.132.
10. See discussion on the Fall of man and nature in chapter 15.
11. Romans 3:23.
12. Isaiah 64:6.
13. John 8:34.
14. Romans 6:20–21.
15. Jeremiah 17:9.
16. Galatians 5:17. Some English versions capitalize the word 'spirit' to make it refer to the Holy Spirit, which makes sense in the context. However, the original Greek mss had no lower-case letters, being written entirely in capital letters (uncials).
17. Jeremiah 13:23.
18. See for example Brian Edwards, *Revival* (Evangelical Press, Darlington, 1990).
19. 2 Peter 3:12–13.
20. 2 Peter 3:3–4.
21. Richard Dawkins, *The God delusion* (Black Swan edition, 2007), p.51.
22. Psalm 145:17.
23. The only mention of the Flood in Dawkins' *The God delusion* occurs in his brief discussion of 'flood geology'. I could find no mention of the moral implications of the Flood.
24. Romans 2:14–15.
25. Romans 2:3–6.
26. 2 Corinthians 5:10.
27. Genesis 6:8.
28. Revelation 13:8.
29. Romans 3:19–20.
30. Romans 7:1–24.
31. Jeremiah 31:31–34.
32. Hebrews 8:8–12.

33. Romans 4:22–25.
34. Galatians 2:20.

# Index